A FILIPINO RESISTANCE READING OF JOSHUA 1:1-9

INTERNATIONAL VOICES IN BIBLICAL STUDIES

Jione Havea
Jin Young Choi
Musa W. Dube
David Joy
Nasili Vaka'uta
Gerald O. West

Number 9

SBL PRESS

A FILIPINO RESISTANCE READING OF JOSHUA 1:1–9

by
Lily Fetalsana-Apura

 PRESS

Atlanta

Copyright © 2019 by Lily Fetalsana-Apura

All rights reserved. No part of this work may be reproduced or transmitted in any form or by any means, electronic or mechanical, including photocopying and recording, or by means of any information storage or retrieval system, except as may be expressly permitted by the 1976 Copyright Act or in writing from the publisher. Requests for permission should be addressed in writing to the Rights and Permissions Office, SBL Press, 825 Houston Mill Road, Atlanta, GA 30329 USA.

Library of Congress Control Number: 2019932273

Printed on acid-free paper.

*To Cecilia Forio Fetalsana my mother
an epitome of courage
and strength*

Contents

Abbreviations ix
Preface xi
Acknowledgements xv

1. Resistance Hermeneutics 1
    The Bible and Power   1
    The Bible and Resistance   3
    The Case of Joshua 1:1–9   5
    The Contextuality of Texts and Readers   12
    The Context of This Study   16

2. The Colonial Ancient Near East 23
    Rulers and Control   26
    Ancient Near Eastern Empires and Nations   29
    The World(view)s of the Ancient Near East   37

3. The Impact of the Ancient Near Eastern World(view)s on Israel 41
    The Land and Life of Ancient Israel   42
    The Impact of Imperialism on Israel and Its Literature   60

4. Resistance in the Early Prophets 65
    Purpose and Central Themes   71
    Ideology and Historiography   86

5. Early Prophets as Resistance Literature 89
    Power and Resistance   89
    Interpreting the Early Prophets Today   100

6. Joshua 1:1–9: Literary and Rhetorical Observations 109
    The Book of Joshua   109
    Textual Variants and Translation of Joshua 1:1–9   114
    Redaction, Literary, and Rhetorical Criticisms   118

7. Joshua 1:1–9: Colonial Readings 129

8. The Philippines Context 139
    Spanish and American Colonization/Christianization   139
    Resistant Movements   143
    Independent yet Colonialist   150
    Biblical Interpretation in the Philippines   154

9. Joshua 1:1–9: A Filipino Reading 163
    Reconstructing a People Shattered by Colonialism   163
    The Filipinos Are Not Israel   167

Bibliography 177
Index of Biblical Citations 207
Index of Subjects 211
Index of Modern Authors 219

ABBREVIATIONS

AB	Anchor Bible
BA	*Biblical Archeologist*
BAR	*Biblical Archeology Review*
CBQ	*Catholic Biblical Quarterly*
DH	Deuteronomistic History
EP	Early Prophets
HSM	Human Systems Management
HUCA	Hebrew Union College Annual
IEJ	*Israel Exploration Journal*
JBL	*Journal of Biblical Literature*
JETS	*Journal of Evangelical Theological Society*
JSOT	*Journal for the Study of the Old Testament*
JSOTS	Journal for the Study of the Old Testament Supplement
SBLMS	Society of Biblical Literature Monograph Series
RSR	Religious Studies Review
WBC	Word Bible Commentary

Preface

I was raised in a pietistic home by tenant farmers. My protestant parents (converts by American missionaries) rejected all forms of folk beliefs and practices common in our rural neighborhood and instilled a modern outlook in us along with a love of reading and learning. Open, honest, and respectful discussions about differing views were encouraged in our family. Early in life I realized that no subject or topic, including one's faith, is exempt from scrutiny.

Reading materials at home consisted of church literature, *Reader's Digest*, and books from the public library coming from the United States. My parents regaled us with stories of missionary exploits all over the world. American hymnbooks and the English Bible were my early introduction to literature. How I loved hymns. I remember singing through the hymnbooks to the last hymns titled "America, America" which, young as I was, I substituted "My Philippines, dear Philippines." Even now we still sing "summer and winter and springtime and harvest." But I only know two seasons: summer and rainy season. I have become proficient in English, as it is the language of learning, as well as in church.

All is well; nothing seemed amiss, until as a nineteen-year-old Bible seminary student I read *The Little Brown Brothers*. It opened my eyes to the atrocities of American occupation of the Philippines and the fact that my faith, a very important aspect of my being, has molded me in the thought and ways of the colonizer. The poverty of my cultural heritage is evident in a home devoid of traditions shared with other Filipinos, though many of these traditions have roots in the Spanish times: kissing of hands, community fiesta celebrations, beliefs about departed family and relatives, and *all saints* day practices, to name a few. I cannot even pray in my mother tongue!

That summer, I was sent for "gospel team" field exposure to the central highland of Negros Island, Canlaon, a beautiful city with cool climate and abundant crops, owing to the perennial lava flow and spewing of fertile ash by the volcano, and watered by cool waters from verdant forest around. It was also a battleground between communist rebels and the Philippine government forces. For the first time, I saw dead bodies of rebel fighters, and I understood the reason why. Few landowning families control land in Canlaon and in most parts of Negros Occidental. The local people rent even the lots where their homes are built. The majority of them are sugarcane plantation workers with no land of their own, even for a small vegetable garden, and were dependent on their pittance daily wage in the plantation. When the sugar stalks are grown, they have no work until harvest, and hunger was their constant lot. But in busy days even children work. While there, news of a man arrested for trespassing a well-fenced land was the talk of the town: he only wanted to pick up a fallen coconut fruit.

Being the youngest in a family with three elder brothers, I remember being aware of the oppressive stereotyped view of gender. "You are typically an Asian woman, who cannot sit down and allow men to do housework" (as a European seminar coparticipant commented). That remark made me painfully aware that being raised in a patriarchal household, church, and community made me servile. Even people who love us can be enslaving when they know no better. As a brother had predicted, being a woman, even if I studied in the seminary, I will end being a teacher (though not a kindergarten teacher).

All the reading that comes with teaching developed my interest in the Bible particularly the Hebrew Bible. In line with my interest in biblical interpretation and faith integration, I came to realize the disruption in Filipino psyche brought by Spanish and American colonization. Christianity facilitated that. Christianity in the Philippines carries the Western worldview. With deep regret I embraced that worldview and have become proficient in the language and faith symbols of our colonizers at the cost of my own.

I have also come to the awareness of the tendency and temptation to use the scriptures for class, national, ideological, religious, and personal interests. Realizing the consequences of scriptural interpretation and its impact on antisemitism, the crusades, colonization, among others, instilled in me the importance of rigorous study and the need to listen to "the other" especially to those at the periphery. The Bible has been cited to condone slavery and legitimize women's oppression. As a student of the Bible I believe it is my responsibility to allow the liberating, life-giving texts to speak especially to those who need it most—the weak and oppressed. Indeed, the struggling oppressed see things in better light. Their suffering and struggle is the illuminating lens that refines interpretation.

A hermeneutics that is anchored in Filipino culture and national aspirations would pave the way for change in the Philippines. And, because of my struggles as a woman, I count myself with those at the periphery, the weak and oppressed, the Filipino people in general, who face formidable obstacles to attain better life. It is in this context that the exhortation of Josh 1:1–9 to be strong and be of good courage is read and translated. Today, the day of the commemoration of the proclamation of the Malolos Republic of 1898, the first republic in Asia, Josh 1:1–9 exhorts the Filipino people (see pages 8–12 for an English translation and discussion of this translation):

> ¹ Pagkamatay ni Bonifacio, ang hinirang ng Panginoon na pagpangulo ng kilosan ng mga Anak ng Bayan, nangusap si Bathala sa mga lingkod na sumunod sa mga yapak nito. ² "Yumao na ang lingkod kong nanguna sa pakikibaka sa pagkamit sa inyong kalayaan. Ngayon, paghandain ninyo ang sambayanan sa pagkamit ng tinubuang lupa na ipinagkakaloob ko sa kanila, sa sambayanang Filipino. ³ Sang-ayon sa layunin ng Katipunan, ang lupang inyong kinatatayuan, simula pa sa inyong kaninununuan, ay mapapasainyo. Ito ang lupang inyong sinilangan. Ito ang tahanan ng inyong lahi. ⁴ Ang hanganan nito sa hilaga, timog, amihan, kanluran at silangan, ay ang dagat. Magiging matagumpay kayo sa anumang gagawin ninyo. ⁵ Walang makagagapi sa inyo habang kayo'y nabubuhay. Susubaybayan ko kayo kagaya ng pagsubaybay ko sa naunang pangulo ninyo. Hindi ko kayo pababayaan. ⁶ Magpakatatag kayo, tibayan ninyo and inyong loob. Maipamamana ninyo sa mga anak ng bayan ang kanilang tinubuang lupa na adhikain pa nang inyong mga ninuno. ⁷ Subalit dapat lamang kayong magpakatatag at magpakatapang sa pagsasabuhay ng diwa ng Katipunan at kautusan ng inyong Saligang Batas. Huwag ninyong suwayin ang mga ito upang kayoy matuntunan ng dunong at aral nito saan man ang inyong patunguhan. ⁸ Ang diwa ng Katipunan at aral ng Saligang Batas ang dapat bukambibig ninyo. Pagmunimunihan inyo ang mga ito araw at gabi, ng sa gayon ay maingat ninyong maisabuhay ang mga nakakapaloob dito. Sa gayon ay uunlad kayo at magiging matagumpay. ⁹ Sinasabi ko nga sa inyo, magpakatatag kayo. Tibayan ninyo ang inyong loob. Huwag kayong matakot o panghinaan ng loob. Ako si Bathala ay kasakasama ninyo saan man kayo patutungo.

Lily Fetalsana-Apura
June 12, 2018

Acknowledgements

I am deeply grateful to missionaries Dr. Steve Mosher (New Testament) and Dr. Tim Bose (Old Testament), for sowing the ideas that developed my interest in contextualization. They made me aware of colonial violence and the ways mission and Western spirituality abetted colonialism in the Philippines.

But how can a seed grow without the right environment? Rev. Dr. Noriel Cortez Capulong provided all these, and more, being a mentor, pastor, and *ninong* to me. With him and his wife Ate Becay at my side, I felt that I can overcome all odds, academic or otherwise. The Silliman University Divinity School community and the insights provided by its faculty in many ways shaped my thoughts. I acknowledge with gratitude Dr. Victor Aguilan, Dr. Muriel Orevillo-Montenegro, Dr. Joshephat Rweyemamu, and Dr. Dennis Solon.

I am grateful for the support of Silliman University's President Dr. Ben S. Malayang III, Vice President for Academic Affairs Dr. Betsy Joy B. Tan, and the Religion and Peace Studies Department. The support of ATESEA Theological Union (ATU) through Dr. Limuel Equiña, the Executive Director, deserve special mention. My research was enriched by the seminar opportunities here in the Philippines, in South Korea, Hong Kong, and Indonesia, as part of ATU's program. Special thanks, too, to the United Evangelical Mission, which sponsored my participation at the International Organization for the Study of the Old Testament 2013 Congress in Munich, Germany, and for defraying part of my research expenses.

To my colleagues and friends in the Religion and Peace Studies Department and the Divinity School, too many to name here, thank you for being a part of my academic journey. I also thank Rev. Dr. Ngoei Foong Nghian (Principal), Rev. Seok Chin Yap (Registrar), Dr. Michael C. Mukunthan (Librarian), Ian Ming Leong, Dawn Lee, and Gladys Grace Caole for their help during my four months research at Trinity Theological College (TTC), Singapore.

The manuscript reads better because of my editor Jione Havea's editing and SBL Press's Nicole Tilford's corrections. Dr. Nestor Bunda and my brother Rev. Renato Fetalsana also commented on my ideas, which greatly improved my work.

To Princeton, my husband, thank you for your unconditional support and confidence. You, Evriel Prince, and Horace took sacrifices to give me the space and time I needed to research and write.

A lifelong teacher, guide, provider, and friend, the reason for the passion behind this project, I thank God above all.

Lily Fetalsana-Apura
January 6, 2019

1.
RESISTANCE HERMENEUTICS

For many modern Jewish and Christian Zionists, Palestine is the "homeland of the Jews."[1] Palestine is claimed to be the land promised to Abraham, a promise said to be realized in the time of Joshua.[2] Reading Joshua as history privileges this claim. The Palestinians are driven out, dispossessed of their land as the state of Israel claims Palestine for Jews. From a conquered and persecuted people (at the beginning of the book of Exodus), the Jews have become powerful.[3] This outlook is based on and justified with the Bible, the authoritative text of Jews and Christians.

The Bible and Power

The Bible is now in the hands of dominant powers. This development is the opposite of the subjugated and persecuted situations of the communities that produced and transmitted the Bible. Such reversal has significant implications for the interpretation of the Bible.[4] In the hands of the powerful, the Bible was used to institutionalize the hegemonic culture. It was interpreted to justify dominance and expansion. In particular, the book of Joshua

---

[1] Arthur Hertzberg, "Zionism," in *Collier's Encyclopedia*, vol. 23 (New York: Collier, 1994), 784; Emily Taitz, *Introduction to the World's Major Religions Judaism* (Connecticut: Greenwood, 2006), 53.
[2] Naim Stifan Ateek, *Justice, and Only Justice: A Palestinian Theology of Liberation* (New York: Orbis, 1997), 103.
[3] Oliver McTernan identifies religious sentiments as the "focal point" of the conflict and failure to establish peace between Palestinian Arabs and Jews in Palestine. Particularly, as the overwhelming victory on the part of the Jews in the 1967 war was understood as God's intervention in the repossession of the ancestral biblical lands. Oliver McTernan, *Violence in God's Name* (Maryknoll, NY: Orbis Books, 2003), 108, 113–14.
[4] Foucault proposes that knowledge makes power insidious. See Michael Foucault, *Discipline and Punish: The Birth of the Prison*, trans. Alan Sheridan-Smith (London: Penguin, 1977). Edward Said elaborates the corrupting effect of power on knowledge. See Edward Said, *Orientalism: Western Conceptions of the Orient*, 3rd ed. (London: Penguin, 1991), 328.

was read as an imperial blueprint in favor of the ideology of the dominant groups. Such interpretations take the religiocultural and sociopolitical construction in the book of Joshua out of context.

The Bible documents the struggles of ancient Israel and the early Christian communities against oppressive systems.[5] The construction of a just and peaceful society was the context and purpose of the production of the Bible. The Hebrew Bible provided the ideological basis for Israel's struggle against imperial impositions. It is resistance literature. But most readings of the Hebrew Bible from the perspective of the dominant power obscured its context and purpose. Firmly rooted in Anglo-European imperial culture, "biblical knowledge" greatly influenced the interpretation and teaching of the Bible worldwide.[6]

There is thus a need to rescue the Bible from traditional and dominating interpretations. In Christianity, the Bible remains the primary witness to God's revelation in and through the accounts of Israel and the stories of Jesus. The Bible describes the alternative community under the rule of God. However, every word and deed written in the Bible should not function as a magisterial statement to which all must subscribe.

The Bible must be interpreted in its context. The appropriation of meaning must take into account changing contexts. A text of the weak surely means another thing when interpreted by the dominant power. The community life of ancient Israel and the early church serves as lessons for today's readers (see, e.g., Neh 9:16–19). But this does not mean that the social construction of ancient Israel should therefore be transposed to any context. A biblical text is a product of its context; its meaning is firmly anchored in the context of ancient Israel and the early church.

Nonetheless, the transformative function of the Bible as text remains unsurpassed. In this regard, hermeneutics plays an important role in the construction of meaning. Linking the words of the Bible with the world of the receivers, hermeneutics translates the tenets of the faith. The text and the reality of the receiver is linked by sound hermeneutics. Close attention

---

[5] For J. G. McConville, the Bible's "message (in the course of its growth and development) ran counter to the interests of great powers from Assyria to Rome." J. G. McConville, *God and Earthly Powers* (New York: T&T Clark, 2006), 1.

[6] In the words of Duiker and Spielvogel, "the Christian church played an increasingly important role in the emergence and growth of the new European civilization." William J. Duiker and Jackson J. Spielvogel, *World History*, 2nd ed. (New York: West & Wadsworth, 1998), 403. Whitelam says that the reading of the Hebrew Bible following "Israelite" perspective has privileged Zionist claims. See Keith W. Whitelam, *The Invention of Ancient Israel: The Silencing of Palestinian History* (London: Routledge, 1996), 46.

to the context of the text, the text itself, and the context of the hearer ensures a responsible interpretation of the biblical message.

The Bible and Resistance

Domination based on a territorial power center is past. Powerful forces control the world market, which in turn impacts the world's economy. The power of empire over distant nations is advanced by globalization. It accesses the world's resources and integrates local economies under its control. The dominance of the empire is established as it shapes reality according to its interests. Empire saps the earth of life, sows violence, and monopolizes power and wealth.

Hegemony, the nonviolent way of securing conformity, has to be established for domination to operate. As the ascendant ideology takes hold of people's thoughts, it is accepted in polity and economy. Presupposing an all-encompassing worldview, empire tolerates other sociopolitical arrangements in so far as these are cognizant of its power. Otherwise, it seeks ascendancy at the cost of local cultures and communities. Assimilation to the dominant culture serves the empire's purpose. To this end, the broadcast and print media under the control of empire trumpets the capitalist system's gospel of prosperity. But the power to allocate surplus is securely in the hands of capitalists that dominate the market.

Domination directly affects emotions, bodies, relationships, and societies. It undermines community wellbeing as it seeks profit at all costs. The advance of exploitative power has always been met with resistance. In situations of weakness, resistance is expressed in ways that may not invite further violence and economic sanctions. Resistance can be coded. The ways through which the weak mitigate harm and assail the powerful, though not openly confrontational, can be categorized as resistance.

In history, imperial drive for power and wealth are the cause of the subjugation and colonization of weaker peoples and nations. Death, destruction, disease, and misery accompanied imperialistic advance in Asia, Africa, and the Americas. In former colonies nowadays, Christianity is associated with Western hegemony and economic interests. It is closely identified with the capitalist system.

At the receiving end of imperialism are colonized and Christianized nations like the Philippines. Colonial domination has significantly defined Philippine history. It interrupted its development as nation and influenced its political structure and polity.[7] Filipinos are victims of the imperialistic drives by Christian nations such as Spain and the United States. Christianity

---

[7] Renato Constantino, *The Philippines: Past Revisited*, vol. 1 (Quezon City: Renato Constantino, 1975), 11.

was introduced in the Philippines under the banner of an oppressive cross and the sword. Interpreted by colonial masters, the Christian message was equated with Western civilization. Christianization was associated with colonization, political and economic oppression, and destruction of local cultures.[8]

Imperial institutions that thrived on subjugation have misrepresented the biblical notion of salvation to moralize and legitimize domination. Salvation was interpreted mainly in supernatural and personal senses. A spirituality that is otherworldly became the norm. Such spirituality is detached from the sociopolitical reality of local peoples. To a great extent, biblical interpretation and biblical resources that were conceived in Western contexts prevent people from critically analyzing and confronting dominant powers. Consequently, theologizing process in former colonies is highly reflective of the dominant knowledge and colonial culture.

As the Bible can be interpreted to perpetuate oppressive human structures, resistance hermeneutics can be a powerful tool to recover and rediscover the contextual meanings of biblical texts. It can empower resistance to the empire and lead towards the construction of alternatives. Taking the experience of ancient Israel as reference, resistance hermeneutics resists ways of coopting the text to advance the sociocultural and political interests of the powerful.[9] Grounded in the struggle of the oppressed, resistance hermeneutics opposes domination in any form. It asserts the Bible as a resistance tool. Employing contextual and social-scientific approaches, resistance hermeneutics has the capacity to examine the ideologies reflective of dominant contexts. Such a stance calls attention to lessons gleaned from Christianity's past association with imperial powers. It opens "biblical knowledge" to scrutiny. It paves the way for the construction of a genuinely contextual interpretation thereby liberating the biblical text from hegemonic Western reading. It retrieves the voices silenced by colonial impositions. The critique of dominant ideology, which has always been a feature of biblical discourse, is emphasized in resistance hermeneutics.

---

[8] See Frances Gardiner Davenport, ed. *European Treaties bearing on the History of the United States and Its Dependencies to 1648* (Washington, DC: Carnegie Institution of Washington, 1917), 75–78. Horacio de la Costa, *Readings in Philippine History* (Manila: Bookmark, 1992), 5; James Rusling, "Interview with President McKinley," in *The Philippine Reader*, ed. Daniel Schirmer and Stephen Rosskamm Shalom (Boston: South End Press, 1987); Perry M. Rodgers, ed., *Aspects of Western Civilization: Problems and Sources in History*, vol. 2, 3rd ed. (New Jersey: Prentice Hall, 1997), 164.

[9] See Oral Thomas, "A Resistant Biblical Hermeneutics within the Caribbean," *BT* 6 (2008): 330–42.

The biblical community must reclaim the Bible as a resistance text. Postmodern biblical interpretation stressing the ambivalence of texts cannot ignore the context of struggle for survival and the construction of alternative societies that gave rise to the production of the Bible. Hence, there is a need to also insist on the liberating purpose of the Bible.

The Case of Joshua 1:1–9

Joshua 1:1–9 is a case in point. The passage, a divine speech (except for v. 1), is cited in triumphalist, militarist, colonialist, racist, and xenophobic interpretations.[10] On the surface this text claims the land of Palestine and exhorts ancient Israel to occupy it. In Josh 1:1–9, God grants the land to the Israelites. Success is made dependent on strict observance of the law and execution of God's instructions. Joshua 1:1–9 appears as an authorizing text for the violent conquest stories that follow. Removed from its context, the passage may be understood as sanction for modern expansionist drives and the occupation of other lands by a people identifying with Joshua and the Israelites. As the introductory speech,[11] the interpretation of Josh 1:1–9 is significant for the understanding of the book of Joshua and the former or early prophets (EP).[12]

From the perspective of colonized peoples like the Filipinos, such an interpretation is problematic. That interpretation can be taken as sanction of the Spanish and American occupations and the resulting suffering, death, and destruction of precolonial Filipino societies. It further supports the present imperialist and colonial policies of the West and the ascendant empire

---

[10] Unqualified statements such as, "The glorious conquest of the past meant the possibility in the future of Yahweh's re-establishing Israel in her land," can be easily taken as support for Zionist ideology of "Jewish homeland in Palestine." See Joseph R. Sizoo, "The Book of Joshua," in *The Interpreter's Bible: Leviticus, Numbers, Deuteronomy, Joshua, Ruth, Samuel*, ed. George Arthur Buttrick (New York: Cokesbury, 1953), 553, 555.

[11] As the introductory part, not only of Joshua, but also of the prophetic section of the Hebrew Bible, Josh 1:1–9 serves as the key through which the meaning of the book and the EP can be understood. In the words of Brevard Childs, Josh 1 serves as "programmatic statement for the occupation of the land." Brevard Childs, *Introduction to the Old Testament as Scripture* (Philadelphia: Fortress, 1979), 244. See also Carolyn Pressler, *Joshua, Judges and Ruth* (Louisville: Westminster John Knox, 202), 9. Edesio Sanchez Cetina sees Josh 1:1–18, 22–24 as the "Theological Framework that directs the message of the whole book and of every section." See "Joshua," in *The International Bible Commentary*, ed. William R. Farmer (Quezon City: Claretian, 2001), 528.

[12] Henceforth "Early Prophets" (EP) will be used to refer to these books.

that extract surplus wealth from vulnerable communities all over the world propagating a consumerist culture based on capitalist drive for profit.

The prevailing theories of authorship dates the book of Joshua in the reign of Josiah (640–609 BCE). It was revised and edited during the exilic (550 BCE) and postexilic periods.[13] Joshua was written and transmitted in the context of Judah's helplessness as a small nation at the mercy of ancient empires. Hence the words, "Be strong, be courageous" ... "do not be frightened or dismayed" (1:6, 7, 9). Upon closer exegetical examination the text appears to tell about a theoretical occupation of Canaan as past history.[14] The idealized construction of the history of Israel as a united powerful people in Joshua projects unity under a prophetic leadership based on the observance of the law. The law was the rallying ground of the oppressed, colonized people of Judah at the time of Josiah. Joshua as a part of the prophetic books affirms the observance of the torah as a condition for Israel's success.

It must be noted that Israel's religion and ethnic composition was not as pure as one may imagine it to be. The body of rituals and cultic laws found in Leviticus and Deuteronomy was not yet the law presupposed in Joshua.[15] The book of Joshua narrates a covenant making ceremony where Joshua the leader confronted the people to choose whom they would serve.

---

[13] Frank Moore Cross, "The Themes of the Book of Kings and the Structure of Deuteronomistic History," in *Canaanite Myth and Hebrew Epic* (Cambridge: Harvard University Press, 1973), 174–89.

[14] Hittites (v. 4) is a geographical terminology used by the Assyrians and the Babylonians to refer to the region of Syria and Palestine. M. C. Astour argues that "no ethnic Hittite ever settled in Palestine." M. C. Astour, "Hittites," in *The Interpreter's Dictionary of Bible*, ed. Keith Crim (Nashville: Abingdon, 1976), 411–12.

[15] Oesterley and Robinson observe two types of religion prevailing in Israel before the appearance of the eight century prophets. There existed a "purer, more primitive tradition, with its stress on ethics and its comparative indifference to ritual and especially to sacrifice" practiced by the desert dwellers in the east of the Jordan and the southernmost part of Judah on one hand and the royal sponsored sacrificial rituals presided by the priesthood in the temples (south and north). W. O. E Oesterly and Theodore H. Robinson, *Hebrew Religion Its Origin and Development* (London: SPCK, 1952), 220–21. Von Rad clarifies what the law was for the prophets (eighth century) in the positive statements of what the Lord required, as stated by the prophet Micah, "You have been told, O man, what is good, and what the Lord requires of you; only to do right and to love goodness, and walk humbly with your God" (NAB). Gerhard Von Rad, *Old Testament Theology* (New York: Harper & Row, 1965), 2:186. Pedersen says it was "un-Israelitish to rise above others in power and wealth." Johs Pedersen, *Israel Its Life and Culture*, vols. 3 and 4 (London: Oxford University, 1953), 584.

The people chose Yahweh over the gods of the Canaanites. The covenant was confirmed. The same renewal happened in the reformation led by Josiah aimed at arresting the prevalent syncretism among the people.

Religious imperialism was not the purpose for the writing of the book of Joshua. Nor was Joshua meant to document history. The composition of Joshua and the former prophets was spurred by the need to construct a strong society against being assimilated by oppressive empires. Joshua is thus a clear illustration of the importance of attentiveness to the context of the text, the text itself, and contextual interpretation.

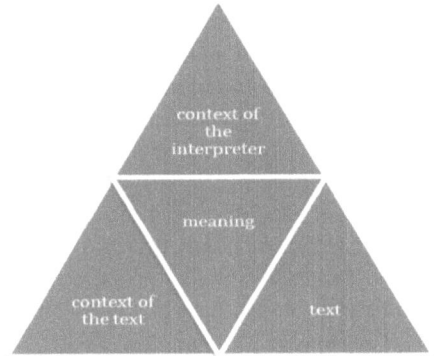

The context of the text, the text, and contextual interpretation are frameworks that cannot be disregarded in the hermeneutics of resistance.

Most of the biblical resources are however produced in the West. The Bible is read and studied mainly in the English language. As Western thought is imbedded in biblical resources it is also used in interpretation. Theological libraries are filled with Euro-American biblical resources that reflect Western modernist context. Moreover, local theologies largely echo Western knowledge as seminaries have roots in the West and members of its faculty were trained and educated in Western epistemology. In a postcolonial nation such as the Philippines, Western interpretation is viewed as the more objective and more reliable basis in constructing biblical meaning. Contextual hermeneutics has not flourished because of colonial mentality and influence.

For those reasons, Josh 1:1–9 will be examined in the postcolonial context of the Philippines. The Philippine context will be studied and analyzed as an important part of the hermeneutical process. The aim of this exercise is to discover and recover the contextual meaning of the text and translate its meaning into the Philippine context and sociohistorical codes. Moreover, biblical commentaries produced in the West will be critically analyzed for western cultural and imperial biases.

This study builds on the proposition that Josh 1:1–9 was composed and redacted during imperial domination of Assyria, Babylon, and Persia. Historical-critical studies will be employed to affirm this proposition. It was composed in the context of colonialism. It introduces the prophetic books that speak against established powers. In the course of history, however, it came to be interpreted as an imperial and colonial sanction for the domination of other nations by the Christian West. Western, colonial, male, white, and privileged assumptions lie behind dominant readings of Josh 1:1–9, but the text itself, being a resistance text claims a God-given right of a community to its land. It is a social and political construction of Israelite society according to its communal values, against the dominant ideology and rule.

The features that characterize resistance texts will be identified. The study will point to discernible resistance meaning and function of the chosen text. As part of the prophetic literature the observed resistance motif in this passage will be linked with Hebrew Bible prophetic themes. Further, the study will trace the development of the understanding of Joshua as a sanction of colonial expansion, based on accessible sources.

Joshua is resistance literature. Hence, the interpretation of Joshua as a sanction for triumphalist expansion will be resisted. Conversely, the meaning of the passage will be constructed using cultural and historical symbols that are meaningful to Filipinos. The translated passage (in the preface and discussed in the next section) demonstrate that meaning is translatable to other cultures and contexts.

Translating Joshua 1:1–9 in the Philippine Context

According to Josh 1:1–9, God sanctions the people's fight for homeland, for their way of life, and for freedom against the tyranny of powerful nations. By its claim of being a gift from God, Israel claimed divine sanction. It did so to resist imperial drive. Joshua 1:1–9 employs historical symbols and cultural codes that arouse nationalistic spirit and emphasize Israel's identity as a people. It calls all Israelites and its leaders to rally around their sociopolitical construction and make a strong and courageous stand for the land, the law, and their faith. The text appeals to the divine warrior no less, to conscript the people against imperial occupation. The holy war concept was employed against hegemony. In defeat the claim of land as a rallying point of resistance was superseded by the emphasis on living as Yahweh's covenant people made operative in observing the law.

Translating Josh 1:1–9 in the Philippine context calls for the use of historical symbols and cultural codes that speak to Filipinos for strengthening identity and unity, as a way of resisting internationalization. Western dominance is facilitated by the promotion of a culture that promotes and patronizes the products of transnational corporations. Joshua 1:1-9 is Israel's resistance text that legitimates the peripheral nations' struggle for self-determination and well-being.

Tagalog, the language spoken in Manila and other surrounding provinces, was used by Bonifacio as the language of the movement for independence that he founded. Anyone not speaking or writing in Tagalog in Katipunan meetings and official communication was fined.[16] The apparent reason was, it is the language common to the immediate areas. The term Tagalog was used alternately with Filipino/Filipinas/Katagalugan in referring to the people and the land.[17] It was a departure from a common practice among Filipino elite. The use of Spanish was an indication of high social rank and education. Rizal wrote his famous novels *Noli Me Tangere* and *El Filibuterisimo* in Spanish. Bonifacio's book collection were all written in Spanish.[18] But the Katipunan used an indigenous language.

With its historical significance, Tagalog was adopted as the Philippine national language and came to be called Pilipino. The teaching and learning of Pilipino language is compulsory in Philippine schools from the elementary to the tertiary level. Pilipino while actually spoken only in some parts of Luzon, have common features with other major Filipino languages such as Visayan or Cebuano, Ilonggo, and Ilocano.[19] The use of Pilipino (language) therefore contributes to the development of Filipino (nationality) thought. Unlike English, the worldview presupposed by Pilipino is not dualistic. It does not distinguish between sexes in personal pronouns. Pilipino language is more concrete. Leonardo Mercado sums up the worldview that is presupposed by Pilipino language this way: "The Filipino's holistic view of himself, his concrete way of thinking, his non-dualistic world view indicates that he thinks differently from the Westerner."[20] Translation necessitates the articulation of the meanings in Pilipino language, in addition to the historical-cultural codes that orients meaning towards Philippine reality.

The translation of Josh 1:1-9 in the Philippine context demands the inclusion of historical and cultural codes that speak to Filipinos. Katipunan captures the militant demands of the struggle for liberation. Moses and

---

[16] Digna B. Apilado, "Andres Bonifacio as Nationalist and Revolutionary," in *Determining the Truth: The Story of Andres Bonifacio*, ed. Bernadita Reyes Churchill (Quezon City: Manila Studies Association, 1997), 86–87.
[17] Leonard Y. Andaya, "Ethnicity in the Philippine Revolution," in *The Philippine Revolution of 1896: Ordinary Lives in Extraordinary Times*, ed. Florentino Rodao and Felice Noelle Rodriguez (Quezon City: Ateneo de Manila University Press, 2001), 74.
[18] Apilado, "Andres Bonifacio as Nationalist and Revolutionary," 86–87.
[19] Leonardo N. Mercado, *Elements of Filipino Philosophy* (Tacloban City, Philippines: Divine Word University, 1976), 75.
[20] Mercado, *Elements of Filipino Philosophy*, 79.

Joshua are historical personalities that were particular to Israel. The law is a social and political construction that was specific to ancient Israel. Similarly, the equivalent of ancient Israel's law in the Philippine context is the fundamental law of the land—the textual achievement of the Filipino people that must embody the people-aspired polity and leadership, as well as the unwritten law of *kagandahang loob* (inner good) expressed in being *makabayan* (pro people), *makatao* (humaneness), and *makadiyos* (godliness). Bonifacio is a hero that undisputedly lived and died for the liberation of Filipinos. His name is untainted with personal interest and compromise with enemies of people native or foreign.

In light of the foregoing, the passage must be translated in the language, worldview, and values of the Filipinos. *Kalayaan* is a Filipino aspiration that captures the essence of having shared well-being. The Filipino name for the supreme God, *Bathala* affirms the presence and hand of God in the pre-Hispanic societies. Referring to God as Bathala is an affirmation of the Filipino worldview and culture, as well as the social and historical movements towards freedom and good life. Joshua 1:1–9 is nationalistic in tone. This must be taken into consideration in translation. Thus the use of the terms *Inang Bayan, tinubuang lupa*.

In light of the foregoing discussion, I offer the following translation and appropriation of Josh 1:1–9 in the Philippine context:

> 1 Pagkamatay ni Bonifacio, ang hinirang ng Panginoon na lingkod sa pagpangulo[21] ng kilosan ng mga Anak ng Bayan,[22] nangusap si Bathala sa

---

[21] Having or showing an unselfish desire for public good. See Leo James, "Makabayan," in *Tagalog—English Dictionary* (Quezon City: Capitol Publishing House, 1986), 182. Bonifacio died for the struggle for freedom and liberation against Spain.

[22] Padilla expounds on the word *bayan*, "The word 'bayan' also has very strong political and nationalist overtones. 'Bayan' (Inang Bayan, Puring Haring Bayan, Anak ng Bayan) populate the language used by the revolutionary forces during the Philippine Revolution of 1898 (against Spain). 'Bayan' is the sum-total of a community's lives, struggles, aspirations, energies to collectively work for their wellbeing (kaginhawahan at kasaganaan ng bayan). 'Bayan' is also the rootword for 'bayanihan'—a popular cultural practice which means cooperation or collective effort of neighbors/community to help each other achieve a common goal, for example, helping each other during harvest time, during times of celebration (wedding, etc.) or during natural calamities. Bayan in Pilipino mean both the people and place. The term literally means communal solidarity." See Estela P. Padilla, "Theologizing in the Philippines INSeCT REPORT," https://insecttheology.files.wordpress.com/2013/11/regional-reportphilippines-theologizingphilippines.pdf. Moses who as Num 12:3 mentions is the meekest man on earth, can be equated with the mentioned Filipino revolutionary leader.

mga lingkod[23] na sumunod sa mga yapak nito. 2 "Yumao na ang lingkod kong nanguna sa pakikibaka sa pagkamit sa inyong kalayaan.[24] Ngayon, paghandain ninyo ang sambayanan sa pagkamit ng tinubuang lupa[25] na ipinagkakaloob ko sa kanila, sa sambayanang Filipino.[26] 3 Sang-ayon sa layunin ng Katipunan, ang lupang inyong kinatatayuan, simula pa sa inyong kaninunununoan, ay mapapasainyo. Ito ang lupang inyong sinilangan. Ito ang tahanan ng inyong lahi. 4 Ang hanganan nito sa hilaga, timog, amihan, kanluran at silangan, ay ang dagat. Magiging matagumpay kayo sa anumang gagawin ninyo. 5 Walang makagagapi sa inyo habang kayoy nabubuhay. Susubaybayan ko kayo kagaya ng pagsubaybay ko sa naunang pangulo ninyo. Hindi ko kayo pababayaan. 6 Magpakatatag kayo, tibayan ninyo and inyong loob. Maipamamana ninyo sa mga anak ng bayan ang kanilang tinubuang lupa na adhikain pa nang inyong mga ninuno. 7 Subalit dapat lamang kayong magpakatatag at magpakatapang sa pagsasabuhay ng diwa ng Katipunan at kautusan ng inyong Saligang Batas. Huwag ninyong suwayin ang mga ito upang kayoy matuntunan ng dunong at aral nito saan man ang inyong patunguhan. 8 Ang diwa ng Katipunan at aral ng Saligang Batas ang dapat bukambibig ninyo. Pagmunimunihan inyo ang mga ito araw at gabi, ng sa gayon ay maingat ninyong maisabuhay ang mga nakakapaloob dito. Sa gayon ay uunlad kayo at magiging matagumpay. 9 Sinasabi ko nga sa inyo, magpakatatag kayo. Tibayan ninyo ang inyong loob. Huwag kayong matakot o panghinaan ng loob. Ako si Bathala ay kasakasama ninyo saan man kayo patutungo."

Into English, the translation and appropriation read:

1 After the death of Bonifacio, God anointed servant to lead the people's struggle, Bathala spoke to their successors saying, 2 "My servant who led the people's struggle for liberation is dead. Now, prepare the whole assembly to overcome the obstacle towards the possession of your God-

---

[23] Literally, servant.
[24] Digna Apilado says that the reformists were pushing for reforms towards assimilation but Andres Bonifacio founded a separatist organization aiming for *kalayaan*. "*Kalayaan* was … not merely a state of being free. *Kalayaan*/Freedom was also *Kalayaan*/Liberation, an act of will dictated by reason. It was an active process that begins by destroying the blinders that kept the people from knowing the real source of their suffering…. Thus a people's revolt (*paghihimagsik*) is fired by overwhelming emotions, but the desire to freedom (*kalayaan*) is dictated by reason (*katuiran*) and justice" (Apilado, "Andres Bonifacio as Nationalist and Revolutionary," 78–79).
[25] Bonifacio penned a poem entitled "Pag-ibig sa Tinubuang Bayan" (love for one's land of birth) where the Anak ng Bayan (children of the motherland; note that Filipino language do not distinguish between sons and daughters since both are equal in the mother's eyes) feels deep yearning for the motherland who is devotedly loved and honored.
[26] Dynamic equivalent of "sons of Israel."

given land, your ancestral land. 3 The land you are standing on, to you I am giving in accordance to the aspirations of the Katipunan. 4 It is bounded on all sides by the sea, this is the land of your birth, this is the home of your people. 5 No one will be able to stand against you all the days of your life. I will be with you as I was with your former leaders. I will not forsake you. 6 Be strong! Be courageous. You will make this people to inherit the land of their birth for which your ancestors before you have aspired. 7 Only be very strong and be courageous in living according to the spirit of the Katipunan and laws of your Constitution. Meditate on it day and night all your days, so that it will guide you and make you wise in all your endeavors. 8 The spirit of the Katipunan and your Constitution shall be the words of your mouth. Study and meditate on it day and night, so that you will be wise in all your actions and you will be prosperous and will succeed in all your endeavors. 9 Have I not commanded you, be strong and be courageous. Do not be afraid or be dismayed. I, Bathala will be with you wherever you may go."

The Contextuality of Texts and Readers

Given that the Bible is grounded in its context and readers in their contexts, reading must be contextual. Along this line, biblical interpretation necessarily starts with the recognition of the commitments and agenda of interpreters: feminist, liberationist, evangelical, postcolonial, to name some. The interpreters' contexts and preunderstandings need scrutiny. As sociology, anthropology, and psychology have established, the material environment profoundly shapes human beings and their ways of thinking. All learning, and therefore knowledge, is mediated. A reading of a text uses the symbols and thought categories that are familiar and meaningful to a person. These are products of one's culture and personal experiences.

As part of culture, language presumes a social structure. Language is reflective and derivative of its culture. Language, as a way of conveying meaning, is intertwined with its function in a given society.[27] And English, one of the universal languages, presupposes Western thought framework. The western worldview imbeds in the apprehension and communication of (biblical) meaning. I have to write in English, which is not my preferred language of communication, in order to be engaged, but not because I subscribe to Western thought frameworks or worldviews.

---

[27] Ngugi Wa Thiong'O explains the function of language as a culture carrier and the effects of colonial language imposition in education and communication. Ngugi Wa Thiong'O, *Decolonizing the Mind: The Politics of Language in African Literature* (Portsmouth, NH: Heinemann, 1986), 13–14, 16.

Translation is already a part of interpretation. Translation is constructed using cultural and sociohistorical codes meaningful to a group of people. It goes beyond mere restatement of textual meanings. Translation reconstructs the meaning of a text in the receptor's context. In a different context, a text that originally empowered the weak may appear to support established power. Hence, a text's meaning for the original community should not be lost. The interpreter must translate the meaning of a text for the original community by reconstructing it in context.[28] A translation must bridge the gap between the text and the reader. The readers' worldview and reality are encoded in translation. Translation reconstructs the text's meaning in the language and thought of the recipient community, so that the text speaks in a concrete sociocultural and political reality.

To make the Bible relevant to a different context, translation must take the language and worldview of the receptor community. In the Philippines this would entail translation to Filipino thought and language. This precludes hegemony and underscores the particularity of the translation. The text is rooted in its cultural and contextual particularity. This way the text is opened to local study and scrutiny. It is accessible to the lay people. A contextualized text articulates its ideology, political location, and commitment in view of the addressed reality—the Philippine context.

Any text, including the biblical text, is a product of a particular culture.[29] Israel's worldview is imbedded in the Hebrew Bible. Indeed, the Hebrew Bible was written for Israel's purpose. Hence, it must be read in its context and interpreted critically to another context. The English translation of texts transposes the meaning and purpose of Israel's text to Western context. But the English text carries the Anglo-European cultural, social, and political location and commitment.

Furthermore, contrary to Western modernist presumptions, critical methodologies do not rule out users' biases. The products of these approaches carry the interests of the culture and the person using it. Tim Gorringe, for example, observes that the various methods of studying the Bible in Europe are mostly framed within the "hermeneutics of privatism,"

---

[28] Virginia Fabella comments that contextualization is more comprehensive as it takes into account the people's culture and sociopolitical and economic realities. See Virginia Fabella, "Inculturating the Gospel: The Philippine Experience," www.theway.org.uk/Back/39Fabella, pp. 119–20.

[29] Eleazar Fernandez alleges that the Bible "re-inscribe imperial ways of thinking and structures of domination." Eleazar S. Fernandez, "(Home)land, Diaspora, Identity, and the Bible in Imperial Geopolitics: What Does the Asia-Pacific Region Have to Do with Israel-Palestine?" (paper for the Fourth International Conference in Bethlehem, August 8–12, 2011).

which is directed towards the enrichment of piety and avoidance of politics.[30]

Hence, the product of established methodologies vis-à-vis historico-textual criticisms originating in the West are to be interrogated.[31] The presumption of objectivity comes into question. Methodologies and those who use it carry the social and political context, if not the commitment of the West. For instance, Juan Luis Segundo citing James Cone points to the failure of the white dominated American Biblical scholarship in addressing the plight of the blacks in the United States.[32]

The fact that colonization (characterized by violence, oppression, imposition of religion, and destruction of indigenous cultures) has been understood as sanctioned by biblical teachings speaks volumes of the ways interpretation has served the imperialists' agenda.[33] The ugly heads of racism, religiocultural bigotry, exploitation, oppression, and intellectual conceit appear from the side of the West. The claim and presumption of universal truth in theology has driven the oppressive and imperialist agenda—the so-called "white man's burden."[34] Further, adherence to Western idealization of abstract truth has prevented the church from engagement with oppressive situations for fear of deviating from stated truths.[35] But abstractions do not have priority over historical reality.[36]

The starting point then for reading is to recognize the concrete reality (context) from which a text arose as well as the context of interpretation. These are the location of revelation. As Paul Tillich so profoundly reasons,

---

[30] Tim Gorringe, "Political Readings of Scripture," in *The Cambridge Companion to Biblical Interpretation* (Cambridge: Cambridge University Press, 1998), 67–68.

[31] H. S. Wilson, "A Tryst with Theology: Self Theologizing as a Perennial Discipleship Mandate" (a lecture delivered at the ATESEA Theological Union Methodology Seminar in Adventist Institute for Advanced Studies [AIAS] Silang Cavite, Philippines, June 13, 2013]).

[32] Juan Luis Segundo, *The Liberation of Theology* (Maryknoll, NY: Orbis, 1985), 28.

[33] See Yvonne Sherwood, "Francisco de Vitoria's More Excellent Way: How the Bible of Empire Discovered the Tricks of [the Argument from] Trade," *BibInt* 21 (2013): 215–75.

[34] The poem "The White Man's Burden," written in reference to the United States' occupation of the Philippine Islands by Rudyard Kipling in 1899, describes the burden of the white race in bringing about civilization and salvation to the colonized Filipinos described as "Your new-caught, sullen peoples, half-devil and half-child." See Rudyard Kipling, *Verse Inclusive Edition 1885–1918* (New York: Hodder & Stoughton, 1930), 371.

[35] Segundo, *Liberation of Theology*, 41.

[36] See Wilson, "Tryst with Theology."

the "ultimate concern" is the point of correlation.[37] Concrete life experiences present valid points that determine one's action. In interpretation, concrete reality must be given as much attention as the text.

The interpreter's social location, ideological commitments, and religious assumptions also influence reading. Responsible interpretations of the Bible come from interpreters who are aware of their biases. No interpreter can strip oneself of personal sociopolitical conditioning and claim interest free reading.[38] Such issues must be addressed. Doing so comes from self-critical and humble interpreters grounded in their own community of accountability.

Historical-critical methods lean on the side of the past and deduct objective propositions from it. This approach presupposes the superiority of abstract concepts over material conditions. It paves the way for a triumphalist totalizing reading. With respect to the issue raised above, historical studies support the claim of the modern State of Israel on Palestine. It also privileges Western way of thinking.

To rectify the Western bias, the recipient context must be given full attention in the interpretive process. Doing so gives importance to the here and now. This opens the hermeneutical task towards a self-correcting process where the context of the text, the text itself, and the recipient's context, are in dialogue. The biblical critic must take contextual reality seriously. Meanings must be concretized to be relevant and practicable.

In this regard, biblical hermeneutics must take into account established hegemonic knowledge through which the West maintains dominance. As well as give space towards local conceptual construction.[39] The Hebrew Bible was scripture for a weak and small nation. This connects with the undeniable historical reality where the weak are at the mercy of the powerful. Such imbalance of power creates a situation of domination and calls for giv-

---

[37] In Paul Tillich's words, "*Our ultimate concern is that which determined our being or non-being. Only those statements are theological which deal with their object in so far as it can become a matter of being and not-being for us*" (italicized in the original). Paul Tillich, *Systematic Theology*, vol. 1. (Chicago: University of Chicago Press, 1951), 14.

[38] In Carol A. Newsom's words, "All cultural constructions, no matter how natural or commonsensical they present themselves, are understood as encoding the interests of some elements in the society." Carol Newsom, "Reflections on Ideological Criticism and Postcritical Perspectives," in *Method Matters*, ed. Joel LeMon and Kent Harold Richards (Atlanta: Society of Biblical Literature, 2009), 544.

[39] R. S. Sugirtharajah, *Postcolonial Criticism and Biblical Interpretation* (Oxford: University Press, 2002), 18.

16 | A Filipino Resistance Reading

ing priority to oppressed communities.[40] Engagement with concrete historical reality complements preoccupation with epistemology in postcolonial theory. Hermeneutics is not just a theoretical task; it is an engagement with reality. In view of the Philippine situation, it has to take a stand and be in solidarity with the oppressed.

The Context of This Study[41]

The justification of violence on account of religious expansion generally corroborated by mainline studies understands the annihilation of the Canaanites as an example of zeal for the Lord. Samples of such readings are discussed in chapter 7, leaving this section to introduce recent readings that provide the platform and context for my study.

S. R. Driver takes the context narrated in the book for granted.[42] He presumes a normative meaning that aligns with the aim of the writer to "illustrate and emphasize the zeal shown by Joshua in fulfilling the Mosaic ordinances, especially to extirpate the native population."[43] It is in the context of the overall theme of Joshua in emphasizing observance of the law, and "the strict segregation from the heathen whom Yahweh has driven out from them" that Julius Bewer ascertains the intent of the book of Joshua.[44] The superiority of Israel's religion over any other is reiterated by E. Powers[45] while Michael David Coogan claims that the underlying theme in the narrative is the conviction that "Yahweh had given Israel the land."[46] The repudiation of Canaanite religion is also emphasized by Th. C. Vriezen,[47] who also presumed the superiority of Hebrew religion. Very little is said of the struggle against domination and the pursuit of wellbeing by a people

---

[40] See Roland Boer, "Marx, Postcolonialism, and the Bible," in *Postcolonial Biblical Criticism* (New York: T&T Clark International, 2005), 166–80. See also E. San Juan Jr., *Beyond Postcolonial Theory* (New York: St. Martin's, 1999).

[41] This review is limited to the resources found in Silliman University Library, which represents a typical theological library from the developing world.

[42] S. R. Driver, *Introduction to the Old Testament as Scripture* (New York: Scribner's, 1913), 104.

[43] Driver, *Introduction to the Old Testament as Scripture*, 104.

[44] Julius A. Bewer, *The Literature of the Old Testament* (New York: Columbia University Press, 1962), 232.

[45] E. Powers, S.J., *A Catholic Commentary on Holy Scripture* (New York: Nelson, 1953), 280–81.

[46] Michael David Coogan, "Joshua," in *The New Jerome Bible Commentary*, ed. Raymond E. Brown (New Jersey: Prentice Hall, 1968), 111–12.

[47] Th. C. Vriezen, *The Religion of Ancient Israel* (Philadelphia: Westminster, 1963), 160.

who were former slaves. The context of the writing of Joshua when Israel was in danger of being totally assimilated and annexed into the dominant empire is glossed over. The emphasis on religious reasons and historical legitimation for the possession of land concealed resistance.

The understanding of the accounts in the book of Joshua as reflecting the actual history of Israel's taking over the land is the view of Lindsay B. Longcare,[48] C. F. Keil and F. Delitzsch,[49] Fleming James,[50] Georg Fohrer,[51] and John Hayes and Maxwell Miller.[52] Joseph R. Sizoo emphasizes separation and superiority, and notes the theological problem presented by the violence in the book. Yet it insists that such acts were "justified."[53] Roland De Vaux and Brevard Childs[54] proposed that the accounts were not history but theological constructs to emphasize separation from the Canaanites. For Childs, obedience is the central theme of the text, which supports an exclusivist religious bias.[55]

Robert G. Boling presents a comprehensive view of what biblical scholarship has reached concerning Joshua. Boling notes the Deuteronomist character of the book[56] and illustrates the positive contributions and limitations of historical-grammatical criticism. So much has been written (mostly by men) about the book of Joshua. Boling alluded to the presence of the empire in talking about the context of the divine warrior motif as a foil against institutionalized self-interest: "The biblical manner of making this situation vividly clear is by the use of language and pictures drawn primarily from the ancient world's highest achievement in government—the suzerain and the empire."[57] Boling's notes and comments dwell on the translation, redaction issues, and meaning in its narrated context. He argues that the religion of Moses "brought to Canaan the long, needed and seldom repeated libera-

---

[48] Frederick Carl Eiselen, ed., *The Abingdon Bible Commentary* (New York: Cokesbury, 1929), 346.
[49] C. F. Keil and F. Delitzsch, *Joshua, Judges, Ruth*, vol. 4 of *Biblical Commentary on the Old Testament* (Grand Rapids: Eerdmans, 1950), 15.
[50] Fleming James, *Personalities of the Old Testament* (London: Scribner's, 1951), 49–50.
[51] Georg Fohrer, *Introduction to the Old Testament as Scripture*, trans. David E. Green (London: SPCK, 1968), 197.
[52] John H. Hayes and J. Maxwell Miller eds., *Israelite and Judean History* (Philadelphia: Westminster, 1977), 279–84.
[53] Sizoo, "Book of Joshua Exposition," 550–53.
[54] Roland De Vaux, *The Early History of Israel* (Philadelphia: Westminster, 1978), 594.
[55] Childs, *Introduction to the Old Testament as Scripture*, 244, 250.
[56] Robert G. Boling, *Joshua: A New Translation with Notes and Commentary*, AB 6 (New York: Doubleday, 1982), 41–51, 66.
[57] Boling, *Joshua*, 36.

tion movement."[58] However, he makes no attempt at interpreting the meaning of Josh 1:1–9 for today's reality.

Anderson directs the understanding of the passage towards sociohistorical construction though still presuming the thirteenth century historical context.[59] Hence, the conquest wars were understood in the context of the "wars of Yahweh" through which the former slaves were delivered. The context of oppression and violence serve as the context in Capulong's exposition of the wars of conquest. In view of the pervasiveness of oppression, violence is seen as an option to effect change.[60]

More recent books by Keller and Flanders et al. still interpret Joshua in terms of "religio-military" imagery.[61] However, Flanders critiques the morality of such a limited understanding of God yet states: "This mandate for conquest and victory stands as one of the most heroic and valid statements of divine decree in all of the Old Testament Scriptures."[62] The stress of Joshua's leadership in taking the promised land is, for Pressler, the theme of Josh 1:1–9.[63] This is also the reading of Coote,[64] which aligns with historical legitimation of the occupation of lands for religious purposes.

In the works cited above, biblical scholars reconstruct the history behind the text, and the redaction history of the text (Kaiser, Eissfeldt, Fohrer, Bewer).[65] On the one hand, historical reconstruction gives primacy to the past and legitimizes current historical movements. On the other hand, stud-

---

[58] Boling, *Joshua*, 130.

[59] Bernhard W. Anderson, *Understanding the Old Testament* (Quezon City: Claretians, 1986), 122, 140–42. See also Frank S. Frick, *A Journey through the Hebrew Scriptures* (New York: Harcourt Brace College, 1999), 259–75. Most Old Testament introductory textbooks written in the West rely on historical reconstruction as the platform of interpretation.

[60] Noriel C. Capulong, *Reading and Hearing the Old Testament in Philippine Context* (Quezon City: New Day, 2003), 1:101–2. This is also the view of Anthony Ceresko, *Introduction to the Old Testament: A Liberation Perspective* (Quezon City: Claretians, 1992), 91–97. From this perspective violence is understood as defensive act by oppressed peoples.

[61] Henry Jackson Flanders, Robert W. Crapps, and David A. Smith, *People of the Covenant: An Introduction to the Hebrew Bible*. 4th ed. (New York: Oxford University Press, 1996), 231; W. Phillip Keller, *Joshua: Man of Fearless Faith* (Waco, TX: Word, 1983), 58–61.

[62] Keller, *Joshua*, 58.

[63] Pressler, *Joshua, Judges, and Ruth*, 9–14.

[64] Robert B. Coote, "The Book of Joshua: Introduction, Commentary, and Reflections," in *The New Interpreter's Bible* (Nashville: Abingdon, 1998), 2:584–87.

[65] Otto Kaiser, *Introduction to the Old Testament* (Minneapolis: Augsburg, 1975), 134–39.

ies of compositional history give priority to earlier traditions. For instance, John Hamlin notes the layers of redactions and the appropriation of meanings through the redaction process in the present text, inviting fresh interpretations in the process.[66] The works of Morton Smith and Robert Coote, connecting the Bible with the ideology of the powerful in Israel, fail to uncover the ideology of the powerless.[67] Yet, the imperialistic drive of King Josiah (620 BCE) has been prominently tied up with the interpretation of Joshua.

Danna Nolan Fewell notes the fluidity of the boundary between outsiders and insiders but fails to read the exhortation to be strong in the observance of the law as an assertion of a subjugated people and thus reads a "rhetoric of exclusion."[68] In Joshua, identity is neither exclusive nor ethnocentric, and the text can best be appreciated if situated in the context of sociocultural annihilation. It is important to stress the intent of resistance as it undermines triumphalism and religious conceit. The context of resistance for the sake of survival is an important consideration for the meaning of the text. In the same mold, Arnold Rhodes does not situate the text as resistance hence his problematic reading of the conquest of the land.[69] He rationalizes the account as a narrative reflective of ancient people's legitimation of land possession. In his reading the account is invented history reflective of ancient Near East conquest narrative styles. Interpreted apart from Israel's subjugated condition the text appears to privilege ancient Israel. While such approach minimizes the problem of violence, it robs the text of relevance for today.

While adhering to historical reconstruction, Robert Houston Smith emphasizes the active involvement of God in history in the book of Joshua. Smith notes the progressive view of Israel in rejecting oppression, asserting equality of human persons, and constructing an alternative social structure that is inclusive and democratic.[70] Joshua is read as theological literature,

---

[66] E. John Hamlin, *Inheriting the Land: A Commentary on the Book of Joshua* (Grand Rapids: Eerdmans, 1983), xxii–xxiii.

[67] Robert B. Coote and Mary P. Coote, *Power, Politics, and the Making of the Bible: An Introduction* (Minneapolis: Fortress, 1990); and Morton Smith, *Palestinian Parties and Politics That Shaped the Old Testament* (New York: Columbia University Press, 1971).

[68] Danna Nolan Fewell, "Joshua," in *Women's Bible Commentary*, ed. Carol A. Newsome and Sharon H. Ringren (Minneapolis: Westminster John Knox, 1998), 69–72, 70. Fewell says in part, "Goaded by divinely ordained intolerance, Israelites are pitted against Canaanites in the struggle for differentiation" (69).

[69] Arnold B. Rhodes, *The Mighty Acts of God* (Louisville: Geneva Press, 2000), 90.

[70] Robert Houston Smith, "The Book of Joshua," in *Interpreter's One-Volume Commentary* (Nashville: Abingdon, 1971), 123–24.

with social scientific information that bears on the context of oppression and powerlessness within which the text was understood.[71]

Dora Mbuwayesango of Zimbabwe starts with the context of Africa. She notes how the Christian British and Boer settlers gave them Bibles and took their lands. But her interpretation of Joshua relies on historical reconstruction. Reading Joshua from the perspective of power as Israel's construction of its "political, religious, and economic" identity based on the land, Joshua is read as "divine entitlement" that can only be read with "revulsion ... for its narratives."[72]

Walter Brueggemann articulated the aspect of the Hebrew Bible as the product of human decision-making resulting from marginality. A mixed rabble who had no linguistic, racial, ethnic, or territorial identity except for exclusive allegiance to its God, asserted its own claims.[73] From his standpoint the Hebrew Bible narratives function as resistance ideology. The Hebrew Bible asserts that the Israelites who inhabit the land have rights over the land claiming that God has given it to them. Through the stories, Israel presents an alternative to the imperial construction of reality. In conjunction with Brueggemann's proposition, Norman Gottwald, applying socioliterary criticism, notes the intentional ambiguity of the narratives in dealing with identity boundaries.[74] In relation to violence he points to the prominence of both extermination and inability of the Israelites to drive out non-Israelite inhabitants of the land (Josh 13:1, 2, 4–5, 13; 15:63; 16:10; 17:12).[75] But Gottwald observes the determination of a people in composing a literary support to their socio-political construction labeled "Israel."[76] In another article Gottwald explains the conquest as a metaphor needed to rally the peasantry against the tyrannical conditions that confronts them.[77] It is in the anti-imperialist purpose of Israel and not in the historicity of the accounts that Gottwald interprets these narratives. Gottwald's approach

---

[71] Jerome F. D. Creach, *Joshua*. Interpretation: A Bible Commentary for Teaching and Preaching (Louisville: John Knox, 1989), 6–7, 14–16.

[72] Dora Mbuwayesango, *Global Bible Commentary* (Nashville: Abingdon, 2004), 64ff, 68–69.

[73] Walter Brueggemann, *The Creative Word* (Philadelphia: Fortress, 1982), 28–29. See also Brueggemann, "Faith in the Empire," in *In the Shadow of the Empire*, ed. Richard Horsely (Louisville: Westminster John Knox, 2008), 25–40.

[74] Michael David Coogan corroborates Gottwald's suggestion that Joshua is meant to be understood as "literary creation" (Coogan, "Joshua," 111).

[75] Norman K. Gottwald, *The Hebrew Bible: A Socio-literary Introduction* (Philadelphia: Fortress, 1985), 260.

[76] Gottwald, *Hebrew Bible*, 288.

[77] Richard Horsley, "Early Israel as an Anti-Imperial Community," in Horsley, *In the Shadow of the Empire*, 17.

moved beyond historical reconstruction to focus on the context and the text itself. In employing social and literary approaches, he provided a link to contextual interpretation.

The works of interpreters go beyond mere replication or restatement of the message for the original community. They necessitate the deconstruction of the carrier culture and invites reconstructing the meaning of the text in the context and the language of a particular community. In this way, biblical interpretation becomes life affirming rather than a tool for colonial dominance.

Postcolonial studies give a glimpse of how anti-empire studies may contribute to biblical hermeneutics. McConville opens the possibility for a symbolic understanding of the accounts in Joshua. He proposes that in the Joshua narratives, Yahweh counters Assyria's claim over the land and the people of Israel. It is upon Yahweh's will that land may be appropriated and war may be waged, for it is Yahweh who holds the future.[78] He asserts that the image of battles brings back the primordial battle against chaos. Hence, a new people who successfully resisted the empire is created. In his view, monotheism rather than engendering superiority serves as a source of harmony. Order is the essence of creation where peace and harmony are inherent. McConville asserts that Yahwism was advocated in political weakness and "never sanctions domination."[79] This theme is elaborated in the book *In the Shadow of the Empire* edited by Richard Horsley, which reclaims the Bible as a resistance text.

To remedy biblical colonial captivity, this book traces the origins and development of hegemonic masculine and imperial structure to the ancient Near East. It outlines the way Israel resisted domination based on its literature particularly the "Early Prophets" (or Former Prophets, Deuteronomistic History) and Josh 1:1–9.[80] Experiencing the onslaught of dominant powers, Israel, based on the exodus and covenant traditions, constructed a belief system and sociopolitical structure that opposes and undermines human-centered power. It assails its violence and exposes the greed for power and wealth behind it. This book outlines the ways in which early prophetic books engage ancient imperial powers.

Along this line Josh 1:1–9 will be interpreted in the Philippine context. The interpretation presented in this book takes into serious consideration Filipino life in the land and sociocultural symbols and constructs the meanings of the passage in a way that speaks to Filipinos. The resistance function of the passage for ancient Israel is decoded then recoded in the Filipino translation. Hence, the passage is read as exhortation to resist dominating

---

[78] McConville, *God and Earthly Powers*, 26.
[79] McConville, *God and Earthly Powers*, 26.
[80] The term *Early Prophets* directs interpretation in line with the prophetic books.

powers. It further exposes Western imperial discourse that has been imbedded in Western produced biblical literature. Doing so, it demonstrates how contextual interpretation paves the way for the deconstruction of imperial knowledge in biblical resources.

Contextual interpretation is rooted in land and culture. In contextualization (or inculturation)—the process by which the biblical message is situated in a particular culture and sociopolitical reality—homogenization is preluded.[81] Contextualization gives space for the critique of the hegemonic culture, leading to deconstruction and resistance. Contextualization creates the space for pluralism.

Undeniably, Christianization of the Philippines and of other nations and land was accompanied by oppression and cultural imposition. There is thus a need to liberate biblical hermeneutics from Western dominance. Recognizing Western knowledge in texts is a start, but the goal is genuine sociocultural translation of the biblical message so that its empowering and liberating spirits are realized. As an example, see my translation of Josh 1:1–9 in the preface.

The dominance of the West has been established in part by the tacit acceptance of its epistemology. Hence biblical hermeneutics must pave the way for its critique, on the one hand, and, on the other, the affirmation of life-enhancing cultural norms in indigenous cultures.

Ancient Israel recognized and resisted imperial structures. The present hermeneutical community must be cognizant of the empire. Putting hermeneutics in the service of societies at the periphery will correct its past complicity with dominating powers.

As the center of gravity of Christianity is shifting to the global south, the production of biblical knowledge must follow. Hermeneutics must contribute towards the dismantling of Western hegemony over the global south. It will accordingly contribute to the redress of local cultures and knowledge slandered by colonial propaganda.

---

[81] Fabella, "Inculturating the Gospel."

2.

THE COLONIAL ANCIENT NEAR EAST

Biblical literature need to be situated in the context of the imperial ancient Near East. The colonial experience is crucial to everything that happened in Israel and Judah.[1] The Hebrew Bible is about a people's struggle and resistance, not the documenting of a people's faith for documentation's sake.[2]

The eminent anthropologist Clifford Geertz insists on the importance of viewing religion in relation to the system of meanings and the social and psychological structures of which it is a part. The proper understanding of religion involves "an analysis of the system of meanings embodied in the religious symbols, and how this relates to social-structural and psychological processes."[3]

The "systems of meaning" embodied in Israel's symbols primarily addressed imperial dominance and its effects on a community. Israel's religion is not just about the narrow class, political, and religious interest within Israel. The actual experience and trauma of wars, of slavery, and subjugation and the threat of cultural annihilation by the death-dealing empires

---

[1] Berquist clarifies that the meaning of the term *Yehud*: "The Persian name for the province or area that included Jerusalem and its environs. The use of the term differentiates Jerusalem and 'Judah' during the postexilic period from the independent Judah of the monarchy as well as from Judah in other periods. Also, 'Yehud' restricts the analysis to the Period of Persian rule (539–333 BCE)." Jon L. Berquist, *Judaism in Persia's Shadow* (Minneapolis: Fortress, 1995), 1, 10, 23.

[2] As Daniel Smith-Christopher states, "The wider anthropological work of Frederick Barth and Nelson Graburn on strategies of boundary maintenance mechanisms allows us to see that the social forms that a minority, exiled, or refugee community creates can be the result not of a desperate attempt to cling to pointless and antiquated traditions from a previous era or homeland, but rather a creative construction of a 'culture of resistance' that preserves group solidarity and cultural identity." Daniel Smith-Christopher, "The Politics of Ezra Sociological Indicators of Postexilic Judean Society," in *Community, Identity, and Ideology: Social Science Approaches to the Hebrew Bible*, ed. Charles E. Carter and Carol L. Meyers (Winona Lake: Eisenbrauns, 1996), 546.

[3] Clifford Geertz, *The Interpretation of Cultures* (New York: Basic Books, 1973), 125. See also Paula McNutt, *The Forging of Israel: Iron Technology, Symbolism, and Tradition in Ancient Society*, JSOTSup 108 (Sheffield: Sheffield Academic, 1990), 266.

were the catalysts in the production of a worldview and identity that resists imperial powers.[4]

Biblical scholars recognize that Israel is a part and product of the ancient Near East. But historical reconstructions of ancient Israel presumed a history that is driven by ideas peculiar to Israel.[5] In this regard, the cultural and imperial milieu in the midst of which Israel emerged has received little attention. Israel's sociocultural construction must be linked with the external factors within which it is situated.

Preoccupation with objective truth has been interposed in the understanding of the Bible,[6] and this has paved the way for triumphalist faith and theologies.[7] The Hebrew Bible is Israel's literature for Israel's purpose. It is spatially and temporally located. The nature and message of Israel's scripture is contextual.

Biological and human sciences have drawn attention to how material and actual situations affect the lives and thoughts of peoples.[8] Further, advances in anthropological, cultural, and sociopolitical sciences have elucidated important aspects in the development of society.[9] Such information calls attention to the sociocultural factors that gave rise to societies. These studies at the same time bridge the gap between ancient societies (including Israel) and the present.

The Hebrew Bible and the early prophets (henceforth EP), of which Joshua is a part,[10] must be interpreted in conjunction with the thoughts and events of the ancient Near East that shaped it. What we have in the Hebrew Bible are not abstract ideas but a people's historically grounded faith.[11]

---

[4] T. R. Hobbs, *A Time for War: A Study of Warfare in the Old Testament* (Delaware: Michael Glazier, 1935, 1989), 181.

[5] Baruch Halpern, "Sociological Comparativism and the Theological Imagination: The Case of the Conquest," in "Sha'rei Talmon," *Studies in the Bible, Qumran, and the Ancient Near East Presented to Shermayahu Talmon*, ed. M. Fishbane and E. Tov (Winona Lake: Eisenbrauns, 1992), 54.

[6] Ferdinand E. Deist, *The Material Culture of the Bible: An Introduction* (Sheffield Academic, 2000), 100.

[7] Halpern, "Sociological Comparativism," 54.

[8] Karl Marx and Charles Darwin have argued that history and human evolution are significantly determined by environmental and sociopolitical factors.

[9] See Francis Fukuyama, "The State of Nature," in *The Origins of Political Order: From Pre-human Times to French Revolution* (New York: Straus & Geroux, 2011), 26–46.

[10] Some Hebrew Bible scholars use the term Deuteronomic for Deuteronomistic. See Moshe Weinfeld, *Deuteronomy and the Deuteronomic School* (Winona Lake: Eisenbrauns, 1992).

[11] As Christopher Hill says, "Ideas do not advance merely by its own logic…. Ideas were all important for the individual whom they impelled into action; but the histo-

Ideas do not come out of a vacuum. The context profoundly shapes individuals and societies.[12] Ideas and concepts are not products of mere abstraction but connect with the broader reality of the material and conceptual world that generated and transmitted them. This is particularly true of the land of Canaan, which is located in the crossroads of ancient civilizations.[13]

The Hebrew Bible calls the readers' attention to the lands of Mesopotamia, Syria, Canaan, and Egypt, all of which figure prominently in the EP. The EP name the dominant sociopolitical powers: Egypt, Assyria, Babylon, and Persia. The general term *other nations* are also referenced.[14] Ancient Israel cannot be isolated from the historic stream of which it is a part.[15]

Isolating Israel from its historic stream has engendered views that serve as springboard for the appropriation of the Hebrew Bible as a product of narrow interests within the society of ancient Israel. This perspective highlights internal power play within Israel alone. Such approach dismisses the importance of the broader context against which ancient Israel asserts its ideas. Further, it disregards the fact that the Hebrew Bible, and the EP in particular, is a people's literature. Indeed, the composition, collection, canonization, and transmission of the Hebrew Bible were done in the context of foreign domination. Historical studies have not given sufficient attention to the ramifications of imperialism in ancient Israel's history. The EP particu-

---

rian [or interpreter] must attach equal importance to the circumstances which gave these ideas their chance." Christopher Hill, *The Intellectual Origins of the English Revolution* (Oxford: Oxford University, 1965), 13; cited by Albert I. Baumgarten in *The Flourishing of Jewish Sects in the Maccabean Era: An Interpretation* (Leiden: Brill, 1997), 23.

[12] In Boyd and Richerson's opinion, "*every* bit of the behavior (or physiology or morphology, for that matter) of every single organism living on the face of the earth results from the interaction of genetic information stored in the developing organism and the properties of its environment." Robert Boyd and Peter J. Richerson, *The Origin and Evolution of Culture* (New York: Oxford University Press, 2005), 8. See also Rene Herrera et al., eds., *Genomes, Evolution, and Culture: Past Present, and Future of Humankind* (New Jersey: Jon Wiley, 2016).

[13] William Hallo, "Biblical History in Its Near Eastern Setting: The Contextual Approach," in *Scripture in Context Essays on the Comparative Method*, ed. Carl D. Evans, William W. Hallo, and John B. White (Pennsylvania: Pickwick, 1980), 12.

[14] The number of times the names Assyria and Babylon are mentioned in EP is an indication of preoccupation with Assyria and Babylon as empires. Babylon is mentioned 31x in 2 Kings alone, 9x in Isa 1–39, and 168x in Jeremiah. Assyria is mentioned 46x from 2 Kgs 15–23 alone, and 42x in Isa 1–39.

[15] Shemaryahu Talmon, "The 'Comparative Method' in *Biblical Interpretation—Principles and Problems*: *Congress Volume: Göttingen 1977*, VTSup 29 (Leiden: Brill, 1978), 326.

larly were composed and edited at the time when Israel was at the claws of ancient empires. Hence, its interpretation must take into consideration the pressures that affected the life and the thought of Israel as a people. It is important to repeat that the biblical writers were not writing for historical documentation per se but for the purpose of setting the foundation and direction for the continuing life of a nation according to its faith, against relentless imperial onslaught.

The reconstruction of the ancient imperial context therefore provides the direction towards understanding how ancient international politics affect everyday life and thinking in ancient Israel. These include the religiocultural and the sociopolitical and economic structures of the ancient Near East. Relevant analyses will help elucidate the impact of domination and subjugation on Israelite societies.

Rulers and Control

Social classes developed in ancient societies as those who possessed power and wealth were distinguished from those who lacked them.[16] The experience and enjoyment of economic surplus led rulers to seek to protect it. Hence the creation of bureaucracy and military forces developed from centralized social structure.[17]

Taste of power and surplus of wealth whet the appetite for more. The ancient civilizations in Egypt and Mesopotamia are products of the inordinate desire for wealth and power by the ruling elite.[18] Military build-up became a necessity to meet internal and external threats and as instruments of expansion. The weak and smaller communities had no choice but to submit or suffer annihilation.

In the time of imperialism, the wealth of surrounding communities came under the control of the powerful center. This has reverse effect, which is the impoverishment of the masses.[19] Farmers were reduced to serfdom as the state exacts goods from farmers in form of taxes for the

---

[16] Donald Kagan, *Problems in Ancient History: The Ancient Near East and Greece*. 2nd ed. (New York: Prentice Hall, 1975), 6–7.

[17] Ralph Turner, *The Great Cultural Traditions*, vol. 1 (New York: McGraw-Hill Book, 1941), 284–85.

[18] As Murnane says of the political development in Egypt, "As in Mesopotamia, kingship seems to have developed around the figures of war leaders, in different protostates in the Nile valley." See William Murnane, "The History of Ancient Egypt: An Overview," in *Civilization of the Ancient Near East*, ed. Jack M. Sasson (New York: Scribner's, 1995), 4:693.

[19] See Turner, *Great Cultural Traditions*, 302.

temple and the government. Some farmers lost their lands because of unpaid debts and accumulated loan interests. Further, they were required to render free labor as needed by the state. The law on private property in Mesopotamia protected the interests of the privileged classes.[20] Ancient Near East states were less a system of government than a mechanism of control over the masses by the few to appropriate for themselves economic surplus.[21]

The Elites and Peasants

In ancient imperial states, the aristocracies and the priestly classes were the pillars that defended royal prerogatives. The masses had no means to defend themselves. As empires expanded, the conditions favorable for economic and industrial growth allowed merchants to have a share in surplus wealth. The merchants were a part of the royal officials.[22] In the ancient Near East, aristocratic families were the arms of the state in collecting taxes from the peasants.[23]

Estates aggressively expanded, resulting in the loss of land among peasants who were reduced to slavery. This contributed to the weakening of Assyria, as former free farmers lost their lands.[24] The elites lived on exacted surplus from the peasants who constituted the majority of the population.

The Workers and Slaves

Most of the population in Mesopotamia and Egypt enjoyed a degree of freedom within the bounds of social and state obligations. Free laborers did not have property and were employed by the state as farmhands and laborers. Below them were the "subordinates" or "subalterns" who worked and lived in the lands belonging to the king. They could be called on to bear arms. Freed slaves also belonged to this lowly class along with the farm hands who were tied up with the royal and temple lands.[25]

With the exception of the king's officials and the artisans that catered to the needs of the bureaucratic class, the majority of Egypt's farming popula-

---

[20] Turner, *Great Cultural Traditions*, 294.
[21] Turner, *Great Cultural Traditions*, 310.
[22] Christopher Monroe, "Money and Trade," in *A Companion to Ancient Near East*, ed. Daniel Snell (Oxford: Blackwell, 2005), 163, 165.
[23] George M. Lamsa, *Old Testament Light: The Indispensible Guide to the Customs, Manners, and Idioms of Biblical Times* (Cambridge: Harper & Row, 1964), 373.
[24] Turner, *Great Cultural Traditions*, 295.
[25] Samuel Greengus, "Legal and Social Institutions of Ancient Mesopotamia," in Sasson, *Civilization of the Ancient Near East*, 1:477.

tion lived difficult lives, toiling the king's land like the slaves among them, except that they were free.[26] Agricultural workers were organized in the Egyptian Old Kingdom in units of five under a leader who had the power to discipline them. These units were combined in bigger gangs.[27] Egyptian documents record that Rameses presented 113,000 slaves to the temples at the course of his reign.[28] Slaves may have had the opportunity to free themselves.

The skilled workers under imperial Egypt were registered in guilds that were supervised by royal overseers. They, together with the chariot-makers, enjoyed better living conditions than the ordinary workers.[29] But like the rest of the workers, their conditions were dependent on the state officials.

Differentiated from the skilled workers, who largely catered to the needs of the elite, were the urban workers. The free artisans sold their labor as a group and received individual pay under their leader or overseer.[30] Mario Levirani explains that the life expectancy of peasants was twenty-five to thirty years due to malnutrition and low water quality. He credits the impressive infrastructures of the ancient Near East to "forceful sourcing of food and labour."[31]

The pyramids were built through compulsory state labor.[32] Herodotus estimates 100,000 laborers working on and off for twenty years were needed to complete such massive projects.[33] One can imagine that work accidents resulting in injuries and loss of lives were common occurrences.

Sargon I of Akkad (ca. 2500 BCE) first practiced large-scale slavery of subjugated peoples. As chattels, slaves had no right over their person and bodies. The earliest slaves may have been war captives. When Egypt engaged in imperial expansion, captives were taken and organized following the military structure. They were branded and employed as workers. Assyria would later transport conquered people and enslave them. As the

---

[26] See also Jacquetta Hawkes and Leonard Woolley, *Prehistory and Beginnings of Civilization* (New York: Harper & Row, 1963), 436, 468.

[27] Hawkes and Woolley, *Prehistory and Beginnings of Civilization*, 294.

[28] Will Durant, *Our Oriental Heritage: The Story of Civilization* (New York: Simon & Schuster, 1954), 159.

[29] Turner, *Great Cultural Traditions*, 296–97.

[30] Durant, *Our Oriental Heritage*, 159.

[31] Mario Levirani, *The Ancient Near East: History, Society and Economy*, trans. Soraia Tabatabai (London: Routledge, 1988), 24.

[32] Junius P. Rodriguez, "Pyramid Construction," in *O–Z and Primary Documents*, vol. 2 of *Encyclopedia of Slave Resistance and Rebellion*, ed. Junius P. Rodriguez (Westport, CT: Greenwood, 2007), 400.

[33] Rodriguez, "Pyramid Construction," 400.

demand for slaves increased, slaves were recruited or captured by raiding bands. Debtors and children born to slaves further added to the ranks of slaves who constitute a significant portion of the population of ancient imperial centers in Egypt and Babylon. Ancient Near East societies were mainly stratified in two classes, the governed and those who governed.

Underlying slavery as a state practice was the drive for profit at the least cost. As kingdoms prospered, commerce and industry developed and created wealth. The reverse effect was the maximization of human resources towards wealth production, through the mechanism of slavery and labor requisition.

Ideological propaganda clearly played an important role in legitimizing the exploitative social structure.[34] Where it failed, the military coerced submission. Lacking knowledge and organization skills, the peasants were left at the mercy of their overseers, the governing class, and on top of that, the imperial power.

Successful revolts in the history of the ancient Near East had been staged by subjugated states that had a standing army and could muster reasonable military force. Revolts were launched in alliance with other subjugated states such as the attempt of Israel and Aram against Assyria. To discourage rebellion, brutal and total destruction of rebellious nations countered such attempts.[35] Exile and resettlement policies were meant to facilitate assimilation and destroy the identity and aspirations of conquered nations.

Ancient Near Eastern Empires and Nations

The Egyptian Empire

South of Israel, sustained by the Nile river, was the Egyptian kingdom. Egyptian dynastic rule had continuously existed since 3200 BCE.[36] Egypt's great pyramids attest to the technology and human power of this ancient nation. Regarded as a god, and god's son, the pharaohs had absolute power over both land and people.

---

[34] See Peter Machinist, "Literature as Politics: The Tikulti-Ninurta Epic and the Bible," *CBQ* 38 (1978): 455–82. Mordecai Cogan states of Assyrian inscriptions, "Assyrian historical inscriptions are first and foremost ideological statements, aimed at promulgating Assyrian imperial ideology." See Mordecai Cogan, "Judah under Assyrian Hegemony: A Reexamination of Imperialism and Religion," *JBL* 112 (1993): 406.

[35] Marl Healy, *The Ancient Assyrians* (London: Osprey Publishing, 1991), 8. See also Paul Bentley Kern, *Ancient Siege Warfare* (Bloomington: Indiana University Press, 1999), 74–76.

[36] Charles Alexander Robinson Jr., *Ancient History: From Prehistoric to the Death of Justinian*, 2nd ed. (New York: MacMillan, 1951), 59.

30 | A Filipino Resistance Reading

Military imperialism was adopted as a policy in the struggle to expel the Hyksos in 1580 BCE, after a short-lived disruption of native Egyptian rule. Thus Ahmose I (1580-1557) ushered the period of the New Kingdom (1580-1085).[37] Phoenicia, Syria, and Palestine served as a buffer zone that secured Egypt. Palestine is closest to Egypt.[38] At the height of its power under Amenhotep III (1411-1375), Egypt's territory included Northern Syria and Palestine and to the fourth cataract in the south.[39] Turmoil followed during the reign of Akhnaton/Ikhnaton (1375-1358), who transferred the capital to Thebes. Akhnaton abandoned the imperial ambitions of the former rulers and introduced a new religion in Egypt. This caused political fallout among the military and religious leaders.

Ramses II (1292-1225) revived the former imperial policies. Colossal buildings and monuments were erected in his honor. By the time of Ramses III (1198-1167), Egypt had exhausted its military power and resources. They were unable to drive away the Philistines who settled in the southern coast of Palestine. After Ramses III's death, the Libyans became dominant in the Egyptian kingdom.[40] Egypt, the "enslaving nation" in the collective memory of Israel, once more extended power over Syria and Palestine under the leadership of Pharaoh Sheshonk (935-918) mentioned in 1 Kings 14:25-26.[41]

More than three hundred years later, in an attempt to revive the policies of war and trade of the Old Kingdom, Necho II's father Psammatichus I rebelled against Assyria. It was Necho II of Egypt (609-594) who cut short the life of Josiah, the king who was unequaled by any before and after him (2 Kgs 23:25). With the death of Josiah, Judah once again was under Egypt. While Assyria was fighting for its survival, Judah its former vassal state was caught between Egypt's encroachment and the certainty of Babylonian incursions in the south.

The Mesopotamian Nations

Ancient Mesopotamia extended from Syria, Turkey, and Iran to the north, to Iraq and Kuwait to the Persian Gulf. Much of the land was sandwiched by

---

[37] Robinson, *Ancient History*, 73.
[38] M. Rostovtzeff, *A History of the Ancient World*, trans. J. D. Duff, vol. 1 (Oxford: Clarendon, 1930), 75.
[39] Robinson, *Ancient History*, 74.
[40] Robinson, *Ancient History*, 82.
[41] Luigi Pareti, Paolo Brezzi, and Luciano Petech, eds., *The Ancient World 1200BC to AD 500*, vol. 2 of *History of Mankind*, trans. Guy E. F. and Sylvia Chilver (New York: Harper & Row, 1965), 12.

the rivers Euphrates and Tigris. Since the third millennium BCE, Mesopotamian early populations centers had centralized governments. The center of power shifted from time to time between Sumer in the south, to Akkad, Mitanni, Assyria, and Anatolia in the north. Dynasties such as those of Kish, Uruk, and Ur rose and fell. Centralized government emerged when city of Kish subjugated the formerly independent city-states (ca. 2,500).[42] The city of Lagash became one of the strongest states. By the time of Sargon I (ca. 2334–2274),[43] wars of aggression became the preferred strategy of protecting the interests of the state.[44]

Expansion facilitated exchange of goods and knowledge. Defeated rulers submitted and paid tribute. The threat posed by the violent mountain tribes against the established Akkadian and Sumerian plain communities further pushed towards coalition of these relatively advanced societies. As the most prosperous, the Sumerians were established as the dominant state. Towards the end of the third millennium BCE, the Elamites took the place of Sumerians. At its decline, Babylon became the center of power and held it throughout the first half of the second millennium BCE.[45] It was the Babylonians of the eighteenth century BCE that gave the present world the famous Hammurabi code. The Hittites in Anatolia had their turn of supremacy in the sixteenth century BCE. Babylonian power was restored in the time of King Nabopolassar, who was succeeded by his son Nebuchadnezzar.

The Arameans

At the time of the emergence of Israel, desert tribes from the Arabian desert south of Mesopotamia were on the move. These wandering bands were found throughout Mesopotamia and Syria by the middle of the fourteenth century BCE. These groups established the cities Kadesh, Damascus, and Aleppo.

The other coastal cities in Syria—Tyre, Sidon, and Byblos—also have connections with the people in Mesopotamia.[46] By their location these cities served as a melting pot of peoples coming from the sea and the lands to the

---

[42] Dominique Charpin, "The History of Ancient Mesopotamia," in *Sasson, Civilizations of the Ancient Near East*, 2:809.
[43] The dates of the reigns of the kings in Mesopotamia and Egypt coming from what Cryer calls high, middle, and low chronologies before the first millennium are at best an educated guess because of conflicting records. See Frederick H. Cryer "Chronology: Issues and Problems," in *Sasson, Civilizations of the Ancient Near East*, 2:659–62.
[44] Rostovtzeff, *History of the Ancient World*, 1:25–27.
[45] Rostovtzeff, *History of the Ancient World*, 1:27–29.
[46] Turner, *Great Cultural Traditions*, 238.

northeast and the south. The Phoenicians and the Habiru originated from southern Arabia.[47]

The Hittites and the Hurrians

Mentioned in Josh 1:4, what later became the Hittites were independent tribes who settled and ruled the indigenous peasant population in Anatolia.[48] King Labarna dominated rival chiefs. His son Hattusilis I led an army that conquered Syria and the nearby kingdoms at the end of the seventeenth century BCE. The succeeding King Mursilis I ended the Hammurabi dynasty in Babylon in 1585 BCE.[49] With a superior technology of smelting iron, the Hittites overran Egypt.

Settled in upper Euphrates close to Assyria, the Hurrians gained ascendancy in the first half of fifteenth century. To resist the Hurrians, the Hittites made a peace treaty with Egypt. The Hurrians eventually dominated the smaller states in Syria that were under the Hittites, but the dominance of the Hurrians did not last long.[50]

Between 1385–1345 BCE, a Hittite king named Suppiluliumas dominated Syria.[51] With Akhenaton in Egypt, the king extended his rule over the Mediterranean, Mesopotamia, and Anatolia. When this kingdom weakened and eventually disappeared, Phoenicia and the states south of Syria descended to chaos as kings fought for dominion and loot. Egypt, who was in a state of turmoil, was unable to maintain its power over Simyra, Byblos, Berytus, Tyre and Sidon, and Palestine.[52]

The Assyrians

At the end of the Hittite and Hurrian hegemonies, Assyria emerged as a strong state. Tiglath-pileser I subjugated Babylon in the eleventh century.[53] The new empire was on the rise. Conquest was a principal function of this

---

[47] Turner, *Great Cultural Traditions*, 239.
[48] The term *Amorites* is sometimes confused with other nations in Syria because Syria was the center of the Amorites civilization in fifth century BCE. Albert T. Clay says that the Semitic Babylonians came from Amurru. See Albert T. Clay, *The Origin of Biblical Tradition Hebrew Legends in Babylonia and Israel* (New Haven: Yale University, 1923), 30–31.
[49] Hawkes and Wooley, *Prehistory and the Beginnings of Civilization*, 387.
[50] Hawkes and Wooley, *Prehistory and the Beginnings of Civilization*, 389.
[51] Turner, *Great Cultural Traditions*, 234.
[52] Hawkes and Wooley, *Prehistory and the Beginnings of Civilization*, 393.
[53] Turner, *Great Cultural Traditions*, 240.

state.[54] Known for its military might, efficient communications, and transportation systems, Assyria brought distant lands under its control. Its military government collected booty and imposed tribute on surrounding nations. With sophisticated siege technology, it expanded Assyrian reach and instilled fear among nations.[55] By the eight century BCE, Assyria controlled Egypt, Anatolia, and Mesopotamia.

The Assyrian army is known for extreme cruelty and destructiveness and was feared by enemies and subjects alike.[56] Such a policy naturally bred hostility, which the Assyrians met with cruelty and aggression. Ashurbanipal boasts in his annals of beheading, flaying, and dismembering the captive king of Elam in a feast.[57]

Second Kings 17:5-6 mentions how Tiglath-pileser (744–727) dealt with the Aramean coalition in the west of which Israel was a part. When Judah withheld tribute and resisted Assyrian subjugation, the strategy of diplomacy, siege, then conquest, was employed against Jerusalem. Stubbornly rebellious states were annexed as provinces.[58] Resettlement was implemented against rebellious states to destroy the identity and political aspirations of conquered peoples. This entailed a wholesale deportation of indigenous population from Israel. People coming from other conquered nations were resettled in Samaria. Sargon II (722–706 BCE) recounts his conquest of Samaria in these words:

> I conquered them Samaria, taking 27,290 prisoners of war along with their chariots. I conscripted enough from prisoners to outfit two hundred groups of chariots. The rest were deported to Assyria…. I repopulated it

---

[54] John Zhu-En Wee, "Assyria," in *Encyclopedia of World History*, ed. Marsha E. Ackermann et. al., vol. 1 (New York: Facts on File, 2008), 32, 34–35. See also Anthony Esler, *The Western World: A Narrative History Prehistory to the Present* (Upper Saddle River, NJ: Prentice Hall, 1997), 13.
[55] David Aberback states, "Assyria, by the late eight century, had built the most powerful empire in history to date, over a hundred times larger than Judah, with the vast majority of the population under its rule. It had the strongest army ever to be assembled and pioneered revolutionary techniques of warfare, for example in the use of cavalry and the implement of siege—these would be used in the next two and a half millennia." See David Aberback, *Imperialism and Biblical Prophecy 750–500 BCE* (New York: Routledge, 1993), 2.
[56] Esler, *Western World*, 13–14.
[57] Hawkes and Wooley, *Prehistory and the Beginnings of Civilization*, 269.
[58] Liverani, *The Ancient Near East: History, Society and Economy*, trans. Soraia Tabatabai (New York: Routledge, 1988), 485–87. See also Herbert Donner, "The Separate States of Israel and Judah," in Hayes and Miller, *Israelite and Judean History*, 417.

with people from other counties I conquered. I appointed one of my officials over them, and made them Assyrian citizens.[59]

Assyria's god Ashur sanctioned the exaltation of the power center and of conquest.[60] The king was considered the human representative of God. Hence, the worship of Ashur served to rally its army towards imperial expansion. Assyrian relics depict a strongly masculine world, where discipline, brute force, and toughness are valued. These are exemplified by the Assyrian military monarchy.[61]

Assyria, supported by hundreds of thousands of fighters, reached the peak of its power in the first half of the seventh century.[62] A royal inscription proclaims that Sennacherib commanded 208,000 troops.[63] They made an example of showing the fate of those who refuse to submit peacefully. Ashurbanipal's annals narrate:

> In strife and conflict I besieged (and) conquered the city. I felled 3,000 of their fighting men with the sword. I carried off prisoners, ox (and) cattle from them. I burnt many captives from them. I captured many troops alive. I cut off of some of their arms (and) hands; I cut off of others their noses, ears, (and) extremities. I gouged out the eyes of many troops. I made one pile of the living and one pile of the heads. I hung their heads on trees and

---

[59] Victor H. Matthews and Don C. Benjamin, *The Old Testament Parallels: Laws and Stories from the Ancient Near East*, rev. and expanded (New York: Paulist, 2006), 129.

[60] Of Ashur, Tiglath-pileser I says, "Ashur and the great gods, who made my kingdom great, and who have bestowed might and power as a gift, commanded that I should extend the boundary of their land." Jack Fenigan, *Light from the Ancient Past: The Archeological Background of the Hebrew-Christian Religion*, vol. 1 (Princeton: Princeton University Press, 1976), 170.

[61] Duiker and Spielvogel, *World History*, 37. A. P. Thornton says of imperialism, "[it] is something for men only. It molds an entirely masculine world, whose keynote is stridency. In it the aggressive instinct holds, and must keep, pride of place.... Whenever it arises, the aggressive instinct is sooner recognized than explained." A. P. Thornton, *Doctrines of Imperialism* (London: Wiley, 1965), 3. Francis Fukuyama noting that human and chimpanzee genes are 99 percent similar observes the common aggression among male Chimpanzee and male dominated societies. Fukuyama, *Origins of Political Order*, 323.

[61] Duiker and Spielvogel, *World History*, 37.

[62] A. K. Grayson, "Assyrian Rule of Conquered Territories," in Sasson, *Civilizations of the Ancient Near East*, 2:960.

[63] Stephanie Dalley, "Ancient Mesopotamian Military Organization," in Sasson, *Civilizations of the Ancient Near East*, 1:418.

around the city. I burnt their adolescent boys (and) girls. I razed, destroyed, burnt, (and) consumed the city.[64]

Tiglath-pileser III tells of Menahem:

> ... [As for Menahem I ov]erwhelmed him [like a snow-storm] and he ... fled like a bird, alone, [and bowed to my fee(?)]. I returned him to his place [and imposed tribute upon him, to wit:] gold, silver, linen garments with multicolored trimmings ... great ... [I re]ceived from him. Israel [lit.:"Omri-Land" *Bît Humria*] ... all its inhabitants (and) their possessions I led to Assyria. They overthrew their king Pekah [*Pa-qa-ha*] and I placed Hoshea [*A-ú-si'*] as king over them. I received from them 10 talents of gold, 1,000 (?) talents of silver and their [tri]bute and brought them to Assyria.[65]

The prophet Nahum's description of Nineveh, the capital city of Assyria, captures its essence, "the bloody city, all full of lies and booty" (3:1). But its turn to receive aggression came. Towards the end of the seventh century BCE, Assyria failed to defend itself against the onslaught of the nations that had suffered at its hands.

Chaldea was the center of Babylon, the emerging empire. However, Egypt in the closing years of the seventh century was in a position to pose a challenge to the power of Babylon in Palestine and Syria. The diminutive kingdom of Judah was caught between colliding empires. The defeat of Pharaoh Necho II in 605 BCE in Carchemish brought the nations west of Mesopotamia, including Palestine, under the control of Babylon.

The Babylonians

The Neo-Babylonian Empire (605–562 BCE) is the most glorious period for Babylon as the capital of that empire. Archeological and historical records attest to the wealth and glory of Babylon. But the Bible has a very negative view of the city instrumental in the destruction of Jerusalem and the exile. It is in Shinar (the location of the Tower of Babel in Gen 11:2) that the temple vessels were placed in the temple of Nebuchadnezzar's god.

Early into the Babylonian rule, Jehoiakim (602 BCE), an Egyptian appointed king, rebelled. Judah's rebellious stance prompted Babylonian attacks that eventually reduced Jerusalem to ruins and sent its national and religious leadership into exile. Nebuchadnezzar (also called Nebuchadrezzar) was as cruel as Assyrian kings in the way he treated defeated nations.

---

[64] Grayson, "Assyrian Rule of Conquered Territories," 961.
[65] James B. Pritchard ed., *The Ancient Near East: An Anthology of Texts and Pictures* (Princeton: Princeton University Press, 1958), 194.

The Persians

Cyrus's leadership of the Persian and Medes coalition ended the Babylonian supremacy. It was the Persians who allowed the Jews to return and rebuild Jerusalem. Unlike previous empires, Persia did not impose homogenization. Cyrus's edict of restoration was in accordance with the Persian imperial policy that managed cultural differences towards Persian interest.[67]

Smaller Nation-States Surrounding Israel

Coming from the sea, perhaps as a result of the destruction of Mycenaean cities (1400-1200 BCE), the Philistines landed on the coast of Egypt. Dealing with the Hittites, Egypt was not able to prevent the Philistines from settling on the coast of Palestine. But settlers were also displacing the Hittites, even as the Medes and the Persians were settlers in northwestern Mesopotamia.[68]

The breakdown of Egypt's control in Syria-Palestine in the thirteenth to the ninth century paved the way for the emergence of nation-states like Israel, Ammon, Moab, and Edom. A point of contention between Israel and Ammon is the lot beyond the Jordan settled by Gileadites. Second Kings 24:2 excoriates the participation of Ammon in the plunder of Jerusalem (also in Zeph 2:8-9). Ammon was regarded as a relative by Israel together with Moab and Edom. The close affinity and conflict between Jacob (Israel), Esau (Edom), and Lot (Moab and Amon) are the subject of several passages (Gen 25, 32:1-21). The Moabite Stone mentions that Moab was oppressed by Omri but was able to retake Gad and put the Israelites to forced labor.[69] Ruth, the main character of the book so-named, was a Moabite.

Earning the strongest censure from Israel for attacking them in their most vulnerable state after leaving Egypt are the Amalekites. The Midianites, on the other hand, are depicted as traveling bands and desert dwellers. The book of Judges tells of the Midianites oppressing the Israelites. However, Jethro, who played an important role in introducing Yahwism to Israel, was a Midianite.

---

[66] *IBD* 3, s.v. "Nebuchadrezzar," 529-30.
[67] Michael Coogan, *The Old Testament: A Historical and Literary Introduction to the Hebrew Scriptures* (Oxford: University Press, 2006), 412.
[68] Coogan, *Old Testament*, 237.
[69] Matthews and Benjamin, *Old Testament Parallels*, 112.

The World(view)s of the Ancient Near East

Temples led by priests and priestesses were at the heart of established communities in Mesopotamia.[70] Prehistoric religion was concerned with deities, nature, and death. Fascinated with the benefits and destructive effects of nature, ancient religions delved into its mystery.[71] Those who appeared wise and knowledgeable about such mysteries became the first leaders. Their advices and services were sought.[72]

The ancients' understanding of reality was embodied in rituals. Ancient religious rituals served to reconcile communities with the realities of life. Life is celebrated in the commemorations of cyclical festivals, and death is accepted in the natural order of things.[73] In the naturally religious worldview of the ancient peoples, supernatural forces both good and evil are presumed.[74] Rituals relieve anxiety about the unknown and beyond what can be controlled.[75] Designed and led by religious and political leaders, the rituals enacted worldviews. Eventually these were established as social structures and norms.

The earliest human social groups were bound by kinship and were egalitarian.[76] Independent communities led by assembly of free people

---

[70] William H. McNeil, *The Rise of the West: A History of Human Community* (Chicago: University of Chicago Press, 1990), 33.
[71] Åke Hultkrantz, "Religion before History," in *Introduction to World Religions*, ed. Christopher Patridge (Minneapolis: Fortress, 2005), 39–40.
[72] Norman Yoffee, *Myths of the Archaic State: Evolution of the Earliest Cities, States and Civilization* (New York: Cambridge University Press, 2004), 41. Yoffee (following Kantorowicz) states that religious leaders as "officiants of rituals came to possess institutionalized 'body' in addition to their human one ... and thus became the chief symbols of the state's sovereignty." See also McNiel, *Rise of the West*, 34–35. McNiel proposes that the ancient priest leaders were the first to enjoy production surplus justified as requirements of deities.
[73] Henri Frankfort, *Kingship and the Gods: A Study of Ancient Near Eastern Religions as the Integration of Society and Nature* (Chicago: University of Chicago Press, 1978), 4–5; Fukuyama, *Origins of Political Order*, 38; Turner, *Great Cultural Traditions*, 306. See also Elizabeth C. Stone, "The Development of Cities in Ancient Mesopotamia," in Sasson, *Civilizations of the Ancient Near East*, 1:236.
[74] Fukuyama, *Origins of Political Order*, 36; Henry Lucas, *A Short History of Civilization* (New York: McGraw-Hill Book, 1953), 25. See also E. O. James, *Prehistoric Religion: A Study in Prehistoric Archeology* (London: Thames & Hudson, 1957), 232–34.
[75] Frankfort, *Kingship and the Gods*, 4–5. Anthropologists Roy Rappaport and Emile Durkheim before him have solidly demonstrated the positive function of rituals for human communities.
[76] Fukuyama, *Origins of Political Order*, 54ff.

flourished in the vast plains of Mesopotamia.[77] Early writings in ancient Mesopotamia point to temporary appointment of leaders in times of emergency.[78] However, the challenge of living with the harsh realities of droughts and at times extreme flooding gave additional push towards centralized organization.[79]

In a study of the archeological remains of temples and palaces, Elizabeth Stone observes that palaces or government buildings and temples tend to be built separately, suggesting a separation between the two institutions in earlier times. She also points to less stratified society in the mixed residences of rich and poor population.[80]

As communities grew, resource and border conflicts arise.[81] In Mesopotamia the growth of cities gave rise to kingship as distinct from temple leadership. Emerging as leaders in times of war, warrior leaders rose to power. They arrogated judicial and religious prerogatives.[82] Eventually they superseded the priests in power. Unequal progress also entailed that some communities grew in power to subjugate others.[83] City-states were formed from the former independent communities.[84]

With warrior kings assuming religious function, autocratic rule was established. Ideological supports for ascendant political and economic systems were produced.[85] The standing army under the command of the king was conscripted. They protected the governing class and carried out the king's expansion plans.[86] The production and preservation of literature were in the hands of the governing class, who through scribal schools spon-

---

[77] Thorkild Jacobsen, "Primitive Democracy in Ancient Mesopotamia," *Journal of Eastern Studies* 2 (1983): 159–72. Midlarsky notes that in places where land is not so valued, egalitarian societies continued to exist. Manus I. Midlarsky, *The Evolution of Inequality: War, State Survival, and Democracy in Comparative Perspective* (Stanford: Stanford University Press, 1999), 63.

[78] McNiel, *Rise of the West*, 4; Frankfort, *Kingship and the Gods*, 219.

[79] Marlies Heinz, "Sargon of Akkad: Rebel and Usurper in Kish," in *Presentation of Political Power: Case Histories from the Times of Change and Dissolving Order in the Ancient Near East*, ed. Marlies Heinz and Maria H. Feldman (Winona Lake: Eisenbrauns, 2007), 79.

[80] Stone, "Development of Cities in Ancient Mesopotamia," 248.

[81] Midlarsky observes the appearance of fortified cities in 2800 BCE connecting this with receding water level and the change in the course of the water channels. Midlarsky, *Evolution of Inequality*, 63.

[82] McNeil, *Rise of the West*, 4; Frankfort, *Kingship and the Gods*, 219.

[83] Frankfort, *Kingship and the Gods*, 215–17.

[84] Frankfort, *Kingship and the Gods*, 218.

[85] Frankfort, *Kingship and the Gods*, 229–30.

[86] McNeil, *Rise of the West*, 43.

sored literature production.[87] Literature in the ancient Near East was produced and preserved primarily for the rulers' purpose and benefit.[88]

In Egyptian lore, the Pharaoh was a central figure in Egyptian religion. Ancient Egyptians believed that the first pharaoh came from the gods.[89] In the Egyptian view, the land derives its being from the creator Ptah "the Risen Land," the fruitful earth that emerged from the primeval chaos.[90] Earliest Egyptian literature points to a time when Egypt was divided into two lands, ruled by the sons of Osiris, Horus and Seth. It became one as Horus, the legitimate heir, overcame "chaos"—Seth. In death, Osiris was embodied by Horus, his son and successor, and became a part of the "ultimate reality." His power and character continued to operate through the incumbent king for the well-being of Egypt.[91] The enactment of a generally accepted ideology facilitated the ascendancy of the Old Kingdom in Egypt.[92]

For the purpose of bolstering the legitimacy of Egyptian rulers, the great pyramids and colossal monuments of Egypt were built.[93] The Eloquent Peasant, a narrative which originated from the twelfth dynasty, also served to justify injustice. The Instructions to the King Merykare to the Tenth Dynasty projects justice to be the main concern of kings.[94] At his ascension, Amenemhet I commissioned the Prophecy of Neferti, which presents him as a savior. Likewise, the story of the Lord of the Two Lands portrays universal approval for the reigning ruler in Egypt.[95] The Story of Sinuhe justifies the harsh measures taken in defense of the ruling Egyptian family. These stories reinforced the legitimacy of the reigning rulers.

Records of religiously motivated revolution by the oppressed class is absent in ancient Near East history.[96] Akhenaton's religious "revolution" was the "only one revolution [albeit initiated by a king] in Egyptian histo-

---

[87] Louis Lawrence Orlin, *Life and Thought in Ancient Near East* (Ann Arbor: University of Michigan Press, 2007), 186.
[88] Orlin, *Life and Thought in Ancient Near East*, 188. Heinz, for example, details how Sargon of Akkad radically changed established traditions in the institution of imperial rule. See Heinz, "Sargon of Akkad."
[89] Ronald J. Leprohon, "Royal Ideology and State Administration in Pharaonic Egypt," in Sasson, *Civilizations of the Ancient Near East*, 1:274.
[90] Frankfort, *Kingship and the Gods*, 35.
[91] Frankfort, *Kingship and the Gods*, 34.
[92] Murnane, "History of Ancient Egypt," 695.
[93] Murnane, "History of Ancient Egypt," 696.
[94] Murnane, "History of Ancient Egypt," 698.
[95] Murnane, "History of Ancient Egypt," 699. For their Assyrian counterpart, see Bradley J. Parker, *The Mechanics of Empire*, Neo-Assyrian Corpus Project (Helsinki: University of Helsinki, 2001), 32.
[96] Jon Manchip White, *Everyday Life in Ancient Egypt* (New York: Peter Bedrick, 1991), 162.

ry."[97] Due to Akhenaton's revolution, Egypt's stability was shaken by threats from the priestly and military groups. Akhenaton suppressed oppositions by force.[98] The ensuing civil unrest attests to the power of religion both as an instrument of political control and destabilization.[99]

Similarly, no peasant revolt has been attested in Mesopotamia.[100] The view that the king was mandated by God to institute justice failed to translate to social norms. Though the law was known to have come from the deity, no accepted moral principle upholds it.[101]

In Mesopotamia, even Sennacherib was censured by the Assyrians when he destroyed Babylon's religions. His son Esarhhadon, in the process of consolidating his power, rebuilt Babylon. A propaganda text traced to this time called the Sin of Sargon portrays Esarhhadon as the reconciler of Babylonian and Assyrian gods.[102] During the Neo-Babylonian period, Nabonidus's preference of the worship of Sin over Marduk is believed to be the reason for Nabonidus's exile in Taima.[103]

The propagandistic nature of official records from ancient Egypt and Mesopotamia has to be taken into consideration, and similarly with regard to Israel's literature.[104] Ancient Near Eastern literature promotes the hegemonic worldview. It was the rulers' interests that motivated the writing and preservation of the memory of the past. State-sponsored rituals reconciled communities to existing sociopolitical and environmental reality.[105]

---

[97] John Baines, "Kingship, Definition of Culture, and Legitimacy," in *Ancient Egyptian Kingship*, ed. David Bourke, David O'Connor, and P. Silverman (Leiden: Brill, 1994), 28.
[98] Turner, *Great Cultural Traditions*, 231–32.
[99] Turner, *Great Cultural Traditions*, 230–31.
[100] Marc Van De Mieroop, *The Ancient Mesopotamian City* (New York: Oxford University Press, 1999), 35.
[101] Frankfort, *Kingship and the Gods*, 278.
[102] Erle Leichty, "Esarhaddon, King of Assyria," in Sasson, *Civilizations of the Ancient Near East*, 2:952.
[103] Aul-Alain Beaulieu, "King Nabonidus and the Neo Babylonian Empire," in Sasson, *Civilizations of the Ancient Near East*, 2:975.
[104] J. N. Postgate, "Royal Ideology and State Administration in Summer and Akkad," in Sasson, *Civilizations of the Ancient Near East*, 1:395. See also Levirani, *Ancient East*, 31.
[105] Walter Brueggemann, *Redescribing Reality: What We Do When We Read the Bible* (London: SMC, 2009), 2. See also Peter Berger, *The Sacred Canopy: Elements of a Sociological Theory of Religion* (New York: Doubleday, 1967).

3.
THE IMPACT OF THE ANCIENT NEAR EASTERN WORLD(VIEW)S ON ISRAEL

The Hebrew Bible is national literature produced by ancient Israel to assert its identity and aspirations. Political, economic, and sociological pressures on the preexilic, exilic, and postexilic Jews shaped the literature of ancient Israel. Israel articulated its identity and national ideology in the face of the totalizing drive by imperial nations. Such were the conditions under Assyrian, Babylonian, and Persian powers.[1]

Literally living at the edge of great civilizations, Israel, a small and weak nation, had the temerity to construct a body of literature to support its social construction. The sociopolitical reality of the ancient Near East is significant for understanding Israel's texts.

Recent sociocultural theories affirm that human thought is stimulated by material experiences. However, human beings have the capacity to deal creatively with physical reality and transform those in meaningful ways. The main questions therefore are: How had life in Israel been shaped by the social and political situations that Israel was subjected to as a colonized nation? How did Israel respond to the ancient Near Eastern powers? And consequently, how might the early prophets be understood?

---

[1] Max Weber, *Ancient Judaism* (New York: Free Press, 1952), 359. Blenkinsop says of the postexilic politics, "The allusion to military conscription, forced labor, and the requisitioning of livestock recall references elsewhere to the heavy burden of taxation during the Persian Period (Ezra 4: 13; 7:24; Neh 5:4). One of the worst aspects of imperial policy under the Archaemenids was the draining of local resources from the provinces to finance the imperial court, the building of magnificent palaces, and the interminable succession of Xerxes in 486 BCE. For this reason, then, the situation is one of great distress. The prayer is therefore, by implication, an inspiration toward political emancipation as a necessary precondition for the fulfillment of promises." See Joseph Blenkinsopp, *Ezra-Nehemiah Old Testament Library* (London: SCM, 1988), 307–8.

The Land and Life of Ancient Israel

Located in the narrow strip of land connecting the cradles of the world's great civilizations, the Israelites traced their roots to Mesopotamia and Egypt. Israel confessed its humble beginnings as wanderers and slaves (Deut 6:21; 26:5). Most of the Israelites were shepherds and farmers, former slaves, captives as well as *apirus, shosus,* Medianites, and/or Kenites from the desert.[2]

The Israelite community is associated with the three hundred or more villages that emerged in the central Canaanite highlands in the thirteenth century BCE.[3] Based on archeological findings, scholars have concluded that the Israelite villages in the hill-country were simple and impoverished.[4] In contrast, cities in the plains like the Philistines and Canaanite city-states left behind evidence of advanced material culture.[5] The Canaanite people have a history going as far back as the earliest civilizations (ca. 3000 BCE).[6] Benefiting from contacts with diverse peoples that passed through the highways in the plain, Canaanite civilization as seen in their architecture, musical instruments, pottery, and early use of copper and iron was advanced for the age. But due to the natural geographical division of the land, the Canaanite city-states did not have a centralized government.

Biblical history suggests that the highland communities later embraced monarchy following the prevalent statist system.[7] This was possible because at this time no nation had the power to assert dominance in Palestine. The imperial states in Egypt and Mesopotamia were weak. To the north, the power of the Hittites had waned. Hence, Israel had to deal with only the

---

[2] John Bright, *The History of Israel*, 3rd ed. (Philadelphia: Westminster, 1981), 130–31. The "shosus" were armed bandits, and the "apirus" were those who refused to be a part of the existing city-states. See also Robert B. Coote and Keith W. Whitelam, "The Emergence of Israel: Social Transformation and State Formation following the Decline in the Late Bronze Age Trade," in *Community, Identity, and Ideology Social Science Approaches to the Hebrew Bible*, ed. Charles E. Carter and Carol L. Meyers (Winona Lake: Eisenbrauns, 1996), 349.

[3] William G. Dever, "How to Tell a Canaanite from an Israelite," in *The Rise of Ancient Israel*, ed. Herschel Shanks (Washington DC: Biblical Archeology Society, 1992), 49.

[4] Dever, "How to Tell a Canaanite from an Israelite," 42.

[5] Dever, "How to Tell a Canaanite from an Israelite," 40.

[6] Flanders, Crapps, and Smith, *People of the Covenant*, 228.

[7] Bunimovits states that this was possible because of the imperial power vacuum at his time. See Shlomo Bunimovitz, "On the Edge of Empires—Late Bronze Age (1500–1200)," in *the Archeology of Society in the Holy Land*, ed. Thomas E. Levy (Virginia: Leicester University Press, 1995), 325–27.

smaller nations around her, mainly the Philistines, Phoenicians, Edomians, Arameans, and the Amalekites (2 Sam 8:1–11).

Jerusalem's location may have been the most important factor that ensured its continuing survival. With the resurgence of the power of Egypt, the cities in the plains suffered destruction in the tenth century. Archeology attests to the destruction wrought by the Egyptian pharaoh Sheshonq in 925 BCE.[8] Located in the central highlands, Judah was less desirable and accessible. But a more powerful empire emerged in the northeast.

Israel and Judah under the Neo-Assyrian Empire

The Neo-Assyrian kingdom (934–609 BCE) was established as a strong kingdom by the tenth century BCE. Ahaz called on the Assyrians to rid Judah of the combined Syro-Israelite forces that were forcing him to join their anti-Assyrian coalition in 735 BCE. Second Kings 16:8 mentions that all treasures from the temple and royal treasuries were given as tribute to Tiglath-pileser I.

From then on, Judah had to raise the annual tribute and in addition raise goods and supply troops and labor on Assyria's demand. Such exactions would have plunged Judah into social and economic crisis. The imperial policy of exacting wealth from vassal states had the effect of greater pressure to create surplus wealth in local economies. The masses ultimately bore the brunt of colonial burden. The internationalization of trade had the same effect. As traders are protected by those in power, exchange is always in their favor. Heavy taxation had the effect of siphoning wealth towards the control of fewer people. The plight of the majority became more desperate.[9]

The years 734–722 BCE was a tumultuous time in Israel. Tiglath-pileser attacked in response to the Syro-Israelite rebellion. Menahem became a vassal king of Assyria. He voluntarily paid tribute levied upon the rich, possibly because of drained national treasury (2 Kgs 15:17–19). Pekah, who may have represented an anti-Assyrian faction, assassinated Pekaiah, Menahem's successor. Consequently, Tiglath-pileser attacked Israel. Part of Israel's territory was annexed to Assyria and part of the population was exiled (2 Kgs 15:29). Samaria was retained as a vassal state of Assyria. Gile-

---

[8] Finkelstein cites carbon dating pointing to later date for cities that had been identified with Solomon's kingdom, while the cities destroyed by Shesonq were associated with the revived Canaanite cities. See Israel Finkelstein, "The Great Transformation: The 'Conquest' of the Highland Frontiers and the Rise of Territorial Israel," in Levy, *Archeology of Society in the Holy Land*, 349–67.

[9] R. H. Lowery, *The Reforming Kings: Cults and Society in First Temple Judah*, JSOTSup 120 (Sheffield: Sheffield Academic, 1991), 134, 211–12.

ad, Megiddo (including Galilee), and Dor were annexed as provinces. Pekah too was assassinated. Hoshea submitted to Assyria and paid tribute. When Tiglath-pileser died, Hoshea sided with Egypt and rebelled again, as revolts by subject states closer to Assyria broke out. Shalmaneser V launched an attack against Samaria. Hoshea was taken to Assyria as a captive.[10]

The Israelite leadership centered in Samaria still attempted to withhold tribute in 720.[11] Shalmaneser's son, the new king Sargon II, claimed the credit of putting an end to the Northern Kingdom.[12] The Assyrian army could have unleashed its cruelty upon the defeated city.[13] Of the Samarian hill country, one of the administrative provinces, the deportation of 27,280 people claimed by Sargon would have constituted 27 percent of the population. The loss of a third of Samaria's population is affirmed by archeological evidence.[14] Estimates of the population of Israel by this time vary from 300,000–700,000 people.[15] Israel ceased to be an independent political entity. The Assyrians settled people from Cuthah, Avva, Hammat, and Sepharvaim in Samaria (2 Kgs 17:24). Samaria was annexed as an Assyrian province, and its inhabitants both native and foreigners were taxed as Assyrian citizens.[16] Religious monuments and steles that projected and commemorated the dominance of Assyria would have been installed in the north. Assyrian constructions in Israel would have entailed forced labor.[17]

---

[10] Frank Moore Cross, *From Epic to Canon: History and Literature in Ancient Israel* (Baltimore: John Hopkins University Press, 1998), 173.

[11] Brad Kelle, "What's in a Name? Neo-Assyrian Designations for the Northern Kingdom and Their Implications for Israelite History and Biblical Interpretation," *JBL* 121 (2002): 661–66.

[12] Morton Cogan, *Imperialism and Religion: Assyria, Judah and Israel in the Eighth and Seventh Centuries B.C.E.* SBLMS 19 (Atlanta: Scholars Press, 1974), 49–50.

[13] K. Lawson Younger Jr., "The Deportation of the Israelites," *JBL* 117 (1998): 212. The book *Battles of the Bible* underscore the fact that Samaria then without a king and leader still held out against the Assyrian siege for three years—"the most famous last stands against overwhelming odds in the annals of antiquity." See Chaim Herzog and Mordecai Gichon, *Battles of the Bible* (Pennsylvania: Stackpole, 1997), 196.

[14] Rainer Albertz, *From the Beginning to the End of the Monarchy*, vol. 1 of *A History of Israelite Religion in the Old Testament Period* (Louisville: Westminster John Knox, 1992), 87.

[15] Edwin Yamauchi, "The Eastern Jewish Diaspora under the Babylonians," in *Mesopotamia and the Bible: Comparative Explorations*, ed. Mark W. Chavalas and K. Lawson Younger Jr. (Grand Rapids Michigan: Baker, 2002), 356. Albertz estimate it at 300,00–350,000. See Rainer Albertz, *Israel in Exile: The History and Literature of the Sixth Century B.C.E.* (Atlanta: Society of Biblical Literature, 2003), 87.

[16] Cogan, *Imperialism and Religion*, 49–50.

[17] Cogan, *Imperialism and Religion*, 57–60.

It was not Assyria's policy to impose the worship of Ashur in Assyrian provinces—2 King alludes to a degree of religious freedom enjoyed by the people (2 Kgs 17:27-33). But the recognition of the supremacy of Ashur over other gods would have been required.

Of those deported, the military personnel, administrators, priests, merchants, and skilled workers may have had better opportunities. The majority would have been employed as agricultural workers. State laborers would have been given a ration of one liter of barley per day, the minimum nutritional requirement for subsistence. Others were resettled in frontier areas to survive on their own among foreigners.[18]

Judah was an ally of Assyria in the early years of Hezekiah following Uzziah and Ahaz.[19] Prior to Hezekiah, there are no records of tribute to Assyria in the Bible or in Assyrian records. Peaceful ties with an imperial power would have fostered trade and brought wealth to Judah, wealth that Hezekiah turned over to Sennacherib (2 Kgs 18:13-37) when it became a vassal state. The religious reforms instituted by Hezekiah could be in preparation for staging a revolt.[20] After thirty years of being a tributary state, Judah attempted to join or supported an anti-Assyrian coalition between 704 and 702, initiated by Merodach-Baladan from Babylon.[21] Hezekiah's preparation was made possible by the broad support from surrounding towns and villages. Such actions prompted Assyrian attack on the outlying towns of Judah. Sennacherib launched campaigns against Jerusalem twice—in 701 and in 688-687.[22] The first campaign prompted Hezekiah's surrender and submission. In the second, Sennacherib's force suffered a severe setback and was compelled to return to Assyria. The more than two hundred years of Assyrian dominance and the resettlement of the north with foreigners mean that the Assyrian influence in Judah was significant.

Judah barely survived the Assyrian invasions. The whole land of Judah was ravaged. Micah 1:8-15 laments the Assyrian path of destruction and its

---

[18] K. Lawson Younger Jr., "Recent Study on Sargon II, King of Assyria: Implications for Biblical Studies," in Chavalas and Younger, *Mesopotamia and the Bible*, 296-99.

[19] See also Marvin Sweeney, "The Portrayal of Assyria in the Book of Kings," in *The Bible as a Human Witness to Divine Revelation: Hearing the Word of God through Historically Dissimilar Traditions*, ed. Randall Heskett and Biran Irwin (New York: T&T Clark, 2010), 274-84.

[20] Obed Borowski, "Hezekiah's Reforms and the Revolt Against Assyria," *BA* 58.3 (1995): 148-55.

[21] Carl D. Evans, "Judah's Foreign Policy from Hezekiah to Josiah," in *Scripture in Context: Essays on the Comparative Method*, ed. Carl D. Evans, William W. Hallo, and John B. White (Pennsylvania: Pickwick, 1980), 160-61. Evans argues for a single campaign against Judah by Sennacherib.

[22] William H. Shea, "Sennacherib's Second Palestinian Campaign," *JBL* 104 (1985): 401-18.

aftermath. Archeological studies point to "dramatic evidence of destruction" in "nearly all excavated areas" in Palestine.[23] Uncovered sites in Judah point to settlements reduced to half the number prior to Assyrian campaigns.[24] Of its cities, only Jerusalem was spared from destruction upon the payment of tribute demanded by Assyria (2 Kgs 18:13–16). Assyria also employed psychological warfare instigating victims to defy their leaders and surrender, with promises of rewards for defectors.[25]

The most readily felt impact of ancient empires was the required annual tribute. Assyria demanded considerable payments of precious metals and luxury goods that emptied royal coffers. In addition, war indemnities had to be paid in cases of revolts.[26] Siege by the imperial army and the resulting defeat would have disrupted agriculture and trade, caused death, and destroyed the infrastructure.[27]

Samaria's defeat and destruction created a deep impression on Judah. Refugees from the north flocked to Judah. Tales of horrors would have been passed around. With the incorporation of what remained of Israel into the empire of Assyria, the subjugated Judean kingdom had to deal with the full ramifications of Assyrian imperial aggression alone.

The emergence of nationalistic aspirations at a time when Assyrian power was at its peak had disastrous consequences for Judah. Except for Jerusalem, all the cities in Judah were destroyed. Manasseh inherited an economically drained and territorially reduced kingdom. Though faulted for his pro-Assyrian stance and thus blamed for the fall of Jerusalem and the Babylonian exile (2 Kgs 21:2–15), Manasseh may not have been a willing Assyrian puppet. Second Chronicles 33:11–13 hints that at some point of his reign, Manasseh participated in an uprising against Assyria.[28] Having failed and knowing the reality of Assyrian power, Manasseh naturally would have played the role of a willing vassal upon being restored to his position.

Manasseh had a long reign, fifty-five years (2 Chr 33:1) including his coregency with Hezekiah. As the Assyrians did not impose their religion, the mention of the proliferation of foreign cults in Jerusalem (see Zeph 1:8–12)

---

[23] Thomas E. Levy, ed., *The Archeology of Society in the Holy Land* (London: Leicester University Press: 1998), 431.
[24] Albertz, *Israel in Exile*, 89.
[25] Yigael Yadin, *The Art of Warfare in Biblical Lands in the Light of Archeological Study*, vol. 2 (New York: McGraw-Hill, 1963), 319.
[26] Norman K. Gottwald, *The Politics of Ancient Israel* (Louisville: Westminster John Knox, 2001), 223–24.
[27] Gottwald, *Politics of Ancient Israel*, 223–25.
[28] Anderson, *Understanding the Old Testament*, 361–62.

must be read as reflective of the embrace of the dominant power's religion and surviving syncretistic worship, on the one hand, and, on the other, the account's disapproval of Manasseh's religious policy or both.

The Assyrian Empire in the eighth and seventh centuries BCE was the largest territorial imperial extent in the ancient Near East.[29] Judah would have at first felt the economic benefits of free trade. The more superior Assyrian material culture set the standard of living among the elite. The intermingling of population, the free flow of information through travel and trade, and the amalgamation in the army of soldiers coming from different ethnic groups contributed to the progress of acculturation both in way of life and religion.[30] Aramaic became the international language—the language associated with prosperity and personal advancement.

There would have been disillusionment on the part of the people and worshippers of Yahweh due to the destructive consequences of Hezekiah's nationalistic policies. Syncretism and political pragmatism gained ground.[31] The worship of Assyrian gods was expected among wealthy Judeans, who welcomed the religion of the dominant power for reasons of political and economic expediency.[32]

Assyria lost control of Palestine towards the last quarter of the seventh century. But at this time, Egypt regained power and wielded its military capability in Palestine. With Babylonian power established in Mesopotamia, Judah was caught in the middle of an international power play. Caught between the colliding superpowers, Judah was also under threat from smaller nations surrounding Israel. The prophets point to the desolation and plunder of Jerusalem at the wake of the Babylonian invasion particularly by Edom, Egypt, Tyre, Sidon, and Philistia (Joel 4:4).

Judah's foreign policy became the most important aspect of Judean politics. Party rivalries were intense.[33] Amon, the son and successor of Manasseh, was murdered.[34] Amon had continued Manasseh's foreign policy, and his killers may have been in favor of Egyptian or Babylonian submission or may have been zealous Yahwists and/or militant nationalists.[35]

---

[29] Cogan, *Imperialism and Religion*, 92–95.
[30] Cogan, *Imperialism and Religion,* 93–95. See also Cogan, "Judah under Assyrian Hegemony," 403–14.
[31] Cogan, "Judah under Assyrian Hegemony," 413.
[32] Cogan, *Imperialism and Religion*, 96.
[33] Abraham Malamat, "The Historical Background of the Assassination of Amon, King of Judah," *IEJ* 3(1953): 26–29.
[34] Evans presumes the existence of pro-Assyrian and anti-Assyrian parties in Judah. Evans, "Judah's Foreign Policy from Hezekiah to Josiah," 169.
[35] Gottwald suggests that the group was "anti-Assyrian." See Gottwald, *Hebrew Bible*, 370, while Tomoo Ishida identifies them to be anti-Assyrian and pro-Egyptian. Ishida proposes that that the people of the land averted political collision between

However, none of these factions prevailed. A middle force, "the people of the land" (*'am ha ares*, 2 Kgs 21:24), killed those responsible for the king's death and installed a young king.[36] The "people of the land" became an important power player.[37] A young Davidic heir Josiah was installed as king. Once again, Judah courted and narrowly escaped Assyrian reprisals.

Manasseh managed to stay in power amidst political turmoil when the people had to bear enforced Assyrian tribute. No revolt erupted in his reign. It is remarkable that Manasseh did not figure in any of the eighth-century prophetic writings.[38] The precarious situation of Judah under Assyria was evident in the shedding of innocent blood in Jerusalem. Manasseh's sacrifice of his own son may be taken as a sign of Assyrian accommodation or of desperation. Manasseh did not have the courage to stand for his people (2 Kgs 21:2). His weak leadership brought the nation to the depths of apostasy.

The EP lost hope of recovery after the death of Josiah. Manasseh had reversed the reforms initiated by Hezekiah. The depths of apostasy to which Judah sank were irreversible. The king's apostasy was seen as the main reason for Judah's fate. Manasseh, the apostate king, was responsible for the incomprehensible reality, the destruction of Jerusalem.[39]

The EP were against imperialism. Aside from expressly prohibiting treaty with other nations, the EP commended Hezekiah and Josiah, the kings who resisted foreign vassalage. Israel's cultural and literary traditions emerged to resist imperialism. They are products of a community's consciousness of colonial victimization.

The threat posed by Assyria against Israel and Judah was the catalyst for literary activity that resulted in the composition of Amos, Hosea, Isaiah, and Micah, as well as ritual texts such as the core of the book of Deuteronomy and in the subsequent EP. Hence the Northern Kingdom takes a

---

the two groups in instituting a program of national reform under a descendant of David. See Tomoo Ishida, *History and Historical Writing in Ancient Israel*, Studies in Biblical Historiography (Leiden: Brill, 1999), 21.

[36] Albertz, *Israel in Exile*, 201.

[37] In his analysis of the meaning of the term "people of the land," Tomoo Ishida concluded that the term refers to the people of Judah in general and those who held power over determining the Davidic successor in "cooperation with or in opposition to the inhabitants of Jerusalem." See Ishida, *History and Historical Writing*, 96.

[38] Phillip J. King, *Jeremiah: An Archeological Companion* (Louisville: Westminster John Knox, 1993), 18.

[39] See Stuart Lasine, "Manasseh as Villain and Scapegoat," in *The New Literary Criticism of the Hebrew Bible*, ed. J. Cheryl Exum and David J. A. Clines, JSOTSup 143 (Sheffield: Sheffield Academic, 1993), 163–83.

prominent place in the early and the latter prophets, and, according to Schniedewind, the whole Hebrew Bible.[40]

Schniedewind's proposition is supported by Daniel Block's study of the role of language in the formation of national identity. Block proposes that a common language is the result, rather than the catalyst, of developing national identity.[41] The use of Hebrew was ancient Israel's assertion of its identity as a people. Founded on the rule of their God Yahweh, Israel asserted the validity of its social construction against that of the Assyrians.[42]

But as the prophetic books relate (2 Kgs 19:5–7; 21:9–10; Isa 8:1–17, 30:8–11), the people and the national leadership were, at first, not receptive of the words of the Lord. The prophetic traditions could have been the basis of critique of the imperial accommodation by the governing class, who would have justified the same on the basis of imperial demands and the consequences of revolt. With the decline of Assyrian power at the time of Josiah, anti-imperial sentiments and pronationalist voices found a hearing.

Judah Caught in Imperial Battles

Josiah is portrayed in the EP as having continued antipolitical accommodation policy. He advocated the worship of Yahweh alone and implemented a reform program (2 Kgs 23). The Northern Kingdom was given importance. An all-Israel identity was promoted.[43] Justice, an important theme in Deuteronomy, is a significant theme in the EP.[44]

Josiah extended his reform over the former Israel, which in his time have been annexed as Assyrian province. Further reforms were done according to the provisions of "the book of law" that was found in the temple in his eighteenth year. Josiah burned cultic images and vessels (2 Kgs 23:4, 6) related to Canaanites and Assyrians. The sacred places and worship shrines to other gods and goddesses were desecrated and destroyed, and their religious practitioners deposed including spirits practitioners (2 Kgs

---

[40] William M. Schniedewind, *A Social History of Hebrew: Its Origins through the Rabbinic Period* (London: Yale University Press, 2013), 77.

[41] Daniel I. Block, "The Role of Language in Ancient Israelite Perception of National Identity," *JBL* 103 (1984): 321–40.

[42] Otto Eckart, "Political Theology in Judah and Assyria: The Beginning of the Hebrew Bible as Literature," *SEÅ* 65 (2000): 59–76.

[43] This is the proposition of Theodore Mullen Jr. in *Narrative History and Ethnic Boundaries: The Deuteronomistic Historian and the Creation of Israelite National Identity* (Atlanta: Scholars Press, 1993). Though Mullen recognizes the existence of preexilic materials in DH, he identifies the exile as the life context of identity in response to cultural and political imperialism.

[44] Peter T. Vogt, "Social Justice and the Vision of Deuteronomy," *JETS* 51 (2008): 35–44.

23:5, 7-14, 24). These actions were possible because of the weakness of Assyria. Josiah's reforms followed the pattern of reforms done by Hezekiah.[45] Worship was centralized in the Jerusalem temple. Priests who were not connected with the temple in Jerusalem were disenfranchised (2 Kgs 23:5-20). The reform was not only directed against Assyrian cults, but also against syncretistic worship in Judah and in the former Israel.

The reform movement by Josiah received broad support. The leaders included the prophetess Huldah, the prophets Zephaniah (1:1-5, 2:4), Isaiah (Isa 8:23-9:6), Jeremiah, and Hosea, and their disciples.[46] This movement was sustained through the exile. This movement could be the equivalent of what we today may call nationalist or resistance movement.[47] Armed resistance was certainly part of it, traced back to the time of Hezekiah. The figure and content of the book of Joshua fits this context of production. The same can be said of the figure of King Josiah. Josiah personified the ideal Davidic ruler lending support to the reform and the reconstruction of united Israel.[48]

While Assyrian retreat from Palestine might be seen as relief from foreign control, this was a time when Judah had to do delicate balancing act between two colliding imperial powers to survive.[49] Judah would have felt more than ever the impact of colonialism. The pressure on Judah is reflected in the "intensifying polarity" between the pro-Babylonian and pro-Egyptian factions in the Davidic court in which the prophets figure prominently.[50] Political leaning and ideology became the main criteria for

---

[45] Hezekiah also placed central importance to Jerusalem as he called even the Northern Kingdom to celebrate Passover feast in Jerusalem (2 Chr 30:1-3) and gave importance to priests and Levites working in the temple (2 Chr 31:1, 16-17).

[46] Albertz, *History of Israelite Religion*, 201-2. Crüsemann also presupposes the existence of such a movement. F. Crüsemann, *The Torah: Theology and Social History of the Old Testament Law*, trans. A. W. Mahnke (Minneapolis: Fortress, 1996).

[47] Norbert F. Lohfink, "Was There a Deuteronomistic Movement?," in *Those Illusive Deuteronomists the Phenomenon of Pan-Deuteronomism*, JSOTSup 268 (Sheffield: Sheffield Academic, 1999), 59.

[48] Richard D. Nelson, "Josiah in the Book of Joshua," *JBL* 100 (1981): 531-40.

[49] Abraham Malamat, "The Kingdom of Judah between Egypt and Babylon: A Small State within A Great Power Confrontation," in *Text and Context: Old Testament and Semitic Studies for F. C. Fensham*, ed. W. Claassen, JSOTSup 48 (Sheffield: JSOT, 1988), 118-19.

[50] Dutcher-Walls study of laws that restrict the kings power in Deuteronomy particularly 17:16-17 concludes that its provenance was in a "particular faction" in preexilic Judah who wanted to proscribe the king from staging revolts. Other explanations do exist such as Gottwald's proposal of a decentralizing stream in Israel's traditions traced to the early premonarchy. Patricia Dutcher-Walls, "The Circum-

differentiating between false and true prophets.⁵¹ Ultimately the nationalists, who unlike Jeremiah advocated resistance to Babylon, prevailed.⁵² At this period, Judah was more preoccupied by external affairs than with its own. It was the bone of contention between two rival powers.⁵³

Resistance to colonial powers explains the policy pursued by Josiah, especially in the event of a peace treaty between the superpowers Egypt and Assyria. Having thrown off Assyrian yoke, Josiah attempted to prevent the extension of Assyrian and Egyptian power in Judah by attacking Necho who supported the Assyrian ally.⁵⁴ Some biblical historians presuppose that Judah sided with Babylon. But 2 Kings makes no mention of a treaty between Judah and Babylon. Taking cue from Josiah's actions, however, it would be unlikely that a Judean king who has just asserted independence and nationalist reforms would be eager to be a vassal to another, knowing what vassalage would entail. Deuteronomy 17:16 explicitly prohibits "going back to Egypt." It is also to be noted that Judah rebelled very early into Babylonian rule. Further, the EP critique rulers on account of their accommodating attitude towards foreign servitude.⁵⁵ Josiah's militant resistance to foreign subjugation is underscored in this light.

The oppressed and leaderless peoples of the north may have welcomed Josiah's initiatives. There must be some form of resistance and resentment against Assyria in the north.⁵⁶ It is to the common experience of subjugation, oppression, and threat of destruction that the developing unity and identity may be traced.⁵⁷ The affinity between Judah and Israel even after the division of the kingdom is presumed in the invitation to the northern tribes during the Passover celebration at the time of Hezekiah (2 Chr

---

scription of the King: Deuteronomy 17:16–17 in Its Ancient Social Context," *JBL* 121 (2002): 601–16.
⁵¹ Malamat, "Kingdom of Judah between Egypt and Babylon," 124.
⁵² Burke O. Long, "Social Dimension of prophetic Conflict," *Semeia* 21 (1981): 30–53.
⁵³ Malamat, "Kingdom of Judah between Egypt and Babylon," 124. See also Gottwald, *Hebrew Bible*, 372–73.
⁵⁴ Antti Laato, *Josiah and David Redivivus: The Historical Josiah and the Messianic Expectations of Exilic and Postexilic Times* (Sweden: Almqvist and Wikell International, 1992), 74, 79.
⁵⁵ Nadav Na'aman, "The Deuteronomist and Voluntary Servitude to Foreign Powers," in *Ancient Israel's History and Historiography: The First Temple Period Collected Essays*, vol. 3 (Winona Lake: Eisenbrauns, 2006), 270–71.
⁵⁶ "Overwhelming" archeological evidence point to "devastating invasions of Palestine in the eight century BCE." Levy, *Archeology of Society*, 431.
⁵⁷ Ernest W. Nicholson, *Deuteronomy and Tradition* (Oxford: Basel Blackwell, 1967), as cited by Steven Grosby, *Biblical Ideas of Nationality Ancient and Modern* (Winona Lake: Eisenbrauns, 2002), 43.

30:11).[58] This link is alluded to in 2 Chr 34:9 and Jer 41:3–5, which mention men from the north who were with Gedaliah in Mizpah and the coming of eighty men with offerings to the temple. The tribes of Ephraim and Manasseh are also attached to the sanctuary in Jerusalem.[59] The Samaritans' desire to help build the temple, to the ultimate exclusion of both private and state pagan cults, is significant in this respect.[60] Nehemiah 7:61–62 further mentions Israelites among the returnees whose ancestry could no longer be traced.

Evidently, the EP reflect anti-imperial sentiments that had gained popularity. It critiques kings accommodating to Assyria and with them those who support assimilation and political accommodation among the elite. This stance brought Judah in collision with both Egypt and Babylon. War could have been expected. City walls were built in consideration of its capacity to withstand attacks. The fortification of the city walls during the Assyrian hegemony attests to the preoccupation with security.[61]

In addition to being at the receiving end of invasion and bearing the cost of war against Egypt and Babylon, Judah suffered the exigencies of massive Egyptian and Mesopotamian armies marching through its land. With armies equal or even more than its total population, Judah as a vassal state endured supply and labor requisitions. Such impressive demonstration of the power and might of the surrounding nations would have a chilling effect among the people of Judah and their leaders. It served as warning against revolt. A submissive people might have been cowed to submission. But Judah defiantly stood her ground. Josiah, the ideal king, could not tolerate the presumptive move by the Egyptian pharaoh in passing through Israel's territory to aid Assyria. In the process, Josiah's good reign was cut short. Second Kings mentions the heavy tribute imposed by pharaoh Necho, which must have been exacted from the people (2 Kgs 23:34–35) as the state treasury had been drained. Soon the Babylonians conquered Egypt and took control of Palestine. But this development did not affect the continuing Mesopotamian influence on Judah since Babylon shared with Assyria the same language, religion, and political policies.[62]

---

[58] Cross, *From Epic to Canon*, 176–77.
[59] Cross, *From Epic to Canon*, 177–79.
[60] Morton Cogan, *Imperialism and Religion*, 109–10.
[61] Yadin, *Art of Biblical Warfare*, 289.
[62] Paul E. Dion, "Deuteronomy 13: The Suppression of the Alien Religious Propaganda in Israel during the Late Monarchical Era," in *Law and Ideology in Monarchic Israel*, ed. Baruch Halpern and Deborah W. Hobson (Sheffield: Sheffield Academic, 1991), 199–204.

Judah under Babylonian Empire

Egypt pursued an alliance with Judah against Babylon when Babylonian supremacy was established.[63] In less than three years of Babylonian vassalage, Jehoiakim rebelled. But he did not live to see the consequences of his rebellion. Jerusalem was besieged, and upon its surrender, the young successor to the Davidic throne, Jehoiachin, was taken to Babylon along with the leading citizens of the city. Nebuchadnezzar carried whatever was left of the temple vessels to Babylon.

Four years later, Judah was again drawn into resistance against Babylon alongside neighboring states: Edom, Moab, Ammon, and Phoenicia. This alliance may have been instigated by Egypt.[64] The incidents narrated in Jer 27 and 29 show Zedekiah's weakness. He succumbed to the pro-Egyptian faction in Jerusalem against the advice of Jeremiah to submit to Babylon.

Messengers were deployed to warn kingdoms of approaching army. The news of an attack force must have been followed by frantic attempt to fortify cities and store grains and supplies. In case of revolts, attacks were anticipated. Tension and fear grip the nation as defenders were conscripted, and all activities were channeled towards the defense of a city. This would have been the situation of Judah as it was caught like a pawn pushed and shoved about by the imperial power players Babylonia and Egypt.

Nebuchadnezzar acted decisively. After a siege of about three years, the wall was breached. The Babylonian army commander unleashed his troops to wanton destruction and violence in Jerusalem. The temple, the palace, and all significant buildings in Jerusalem were destroyed and burned. Those who survived were taken as captives to Babylon—the ruling and elite class, military officials, and religious leaders—leaving the land to the poorest of the people. Vinedressers and farmers were left behind presumably to ensure sustained production. This points to the survival of reconstructed smaller towns and villages that would have been population centers in the exilic times.[65]

The book of Lamentations depicts the suffering, death, and desolation caused by the siege. Second Kings 24:1–2 mentions that aside from the Babylonians, Judah's neighbors—the Arameans, the Moabites, and the Ammonites—participated in the plunder of Judah. A significant portion of the people fled to other lands throughout the Mediterranean world. Still, Jewish hopes and aspirations were tied up with their homeland and people. After all, they shared the same fate of being under foreign powers.[66]

---

[63] Malamat, "Judah between Egypt and Babylon," 124.
[64] Malamat, "Judah between Egypt and Babylon," 126.
[65] Matthews and Benjamin, *Old Testament Parallels*, 160.
[66] Gottwald, *Hebrew Bible*, 421.

Judah and Jerusalem were in ruins. Archeological evidence points to a widespread and overwhelming destruction and depopulation.[67] The number of deportees from Judah is estimated at 30,000[68] or about 10 percent of the population,[69] and those who died could be a third or one half of its former population.[70] Death during war times was also caused by starvation, disease, and exposure.

Deportation means long marches for captives sometimes bound and suffering abuse. This especially happens after a long, drawn-out siege and when an attacked city produces little booty for the attacking force.[71] Deported citizens would have been treated differently than fighters.[72]

There were zealous Yahweh worshippers left in Judah.[73] This group continued some form of Yahweh worship that did not include animal sacrifice. The "non-Temple piety" in the Hebrew Bible is attributed to this community.[74] They were considered syncretistic, like the Elephantine community in Egypt, by returning exiles. This points to the presence of remnants of pro-Babylonian and nationalist parties.[75] The pro-Babylonian party was connected with the advancement of reform, which the prophet Jeremiah supported. Ahikam, who pleaded for Jeremiah's life, was a part of this group. The Babylonians coopted this party in setting up a Babylonian sponsored governing structure in Jerusalem.[76]

---

[67] Salo Wittmayer Baron, *A Social and Religious History of the Jews*, vol. 1, 2nd ed. (New York: Columbia University Press, 1952), 105. See also Levy, *Archeology of Society in the Holy Land*, 431. Ephraim Stern confirms, "The results of all these excavations and surveys clearly affirm that Judah was almost entirely destroyed and that its Jewish population disappeared from most of the kingdom, except perhaps Benjamin." Ephraim Stern, "The Babylonian Gap: The Archeological Reality," *JSOT* 28 (2004): 273–77.
[68] Yamauchi, "Eastern Jewish Diaspora," 362.
[69] Yamauchi, "Eastern Jewish Diaspora," 356–57.
[70] Saul S. Weinberg, "Post-exilic Palestine: An Archeological Report," *Proceeding of Israel Academy of Sciences and Humanities* 4.5 (1971): 79. See Yamauchi, "Eastern Jewish Diaspora," 363; Albertz, *Israel in Exile*, 90.
[71] Karen Rhea Nemet-Nejat, *Daily Life in Ancient Mesopotamia* (Boston: Hendrickson, 1998), 237.
[72] Julian Reade, "Ideology and Propaganda in Assyrian Art," in *Mesopotamia: Power and Propaganda; A Symposium on Ancient Empires*, ed. Mogens Trolle Larsen, vol. 7. (Copenhagen: Akademik Forlag, 1979), 334.
[73] Daniel Smith-Christopher, *The Religion of the Landless: The Social Context of the Babylonian Exile* (Bloomington: Meyer Stone, 1989), 33.
[74] Smith-Christopher, *Religion of the Landless*, 33.
[75] Albertz, *Israel in Exile*, 91.
[76] Albertz, *History of Israelite Religion*, 201–2.

However, life in Palestine was far from the picture of recovery under Gedaliah portrayed in Jer 40:7–12. Lamentations depicts a complete breakdown of social order:[77] properties had been taken over by foreigners (5:2), forced labor was imposed (5:5, 8,13), extortion was rampant (5:4), rape (5:11), humiliation, and persecution were widespread (5:12). This was the result of Babylonian measures following Gedaliah's death.

The ruined temple, city, and walls of Jerusalem would have been a constant reminder of the people's subjugation and could have evoked the people's resentment against Babylon's might. Disorganized, without a means for defense, and with the walls destroyed, the people left in Palestine were vulnerable to attacks and raids of the people around them and the harassment of colonial officials. With the national leaders gone, village leaders and family heads continued their roles in practicing religious and cultural traditions. Such practices are to be taken as assertion of their identity against the dominant power.[78]

Of the Jewish communities in Egypt, the Elephantine community is most known. Documents traced to the community mention suffering from abuses. They had adjusted to the Egyptian society but adhered to their worship of Yahweh along with a female deity, 'Anat-yhw'—a faith linked to preexilic syncretistic Israelite faith.[79]

The exiles in Babylon enjoyed a degree of freedom to build houses, farm, and raise their families. Some Jewish settlements mentioned in the book of Ezekiel and Jeremiah were in Chebar, Tel-abib, Tel-melah, Tel-harsha, Cherub, Adan, Immer, Casiphia, and Ahava (Ezek 1:3; 3:15; Ezra 2:59; 8:17, 21). Isaiah 42:22 and 51:23 allude to the cruel treatment and victimization to which the exiles were subjected. This is a common experience among conquered population but also among the Babylonian masses. Babylon maximized profit through heavy taxation.[80] But the exiles were left free to earn a living by farming and use their skills, making it possible for some to prosper. Many of the exiles experienced in temple treasury prospered as merchants and traders in Babylon. The exiles were left relatively free to form communities based on kinship and the practice of their religious traditions.[81]

However, the effects of the destruction of the government and religious institutions, and the power vacuum created by the Babylonian exile had continuing effects on the Jews as a people. The dispersion attests to the pre-

---

[77] Albertz, *Israel in Exile*, 93.
[78] Berquist, *Judaism in Persia's Shadow*, 17.
[79] Albertz, *Israel in Exile*, 97–98.
[80] Berquist, *Judaism in Persia's Shadow*, 17.
[81] Oesterly and Robinson, *Hebrew Religion*, 43–46.

cariousness of life in Palestine and in diaspora.[82] The Jews had to find ways of coping and surviving in foreign conditions.

The Jews need to assimilate in order to survive. Zephaniah 1:12 reflects uncertainty that must demand adjustment to the changed environment. But many might have persisted in their beliefs and way of life.[83] The strength of Jerusalem and land traditions is evident, in that the Babylonian Jewry decided against building a temple in Babylon or sacrificing animals raised in Babylonian soil.[84] The force of Deuteronomic polemics for Jerusalem as the sole place of worship had become normative. This was a way of resisting foreign influence and asserting religious identity and land claim.

Periodic family gatherings also ensured the survival of Jewish identity in Babylonia. As with the Jews left in Palestine, family and clan gatherings became an important social force among the Jews in the diaspora.[85] Identity based on ethnicity was strengthened during Babylonian and Persian domination. Family distinction was given more importance than the land of origin. Family purity valued highly by the Jews was sustained as the Babylonians settled ethnic groups together.[86]

The context of the empire provided the catalyst for ancient Israel's social reconstruction based on lineage. It emerged as a *mechanism of survival* for the Judeans. The structural change to family-based leadership was an adaptation of the Jewish community. Rituals were family centered.[87] Ceremonial and religious rites that were already in practice in preexilic times became important marks of distinction: circumcision, dietary laws, and the Sabbath.[88] The Jewish exiles looked up to the leadership as presiders of covenant rituals of old. Covenanting rituals like the Passover and Sabbath observances stressed loyalty to Yahweh and the distinctiveness of the Israelites as a people.

Many Jews fared well in Babylon, but they were living as outsiders in a foreign country. The loss of identity and dislocation and being objects of discrimination cannot be trivialized. Westerners have a tendency to gloss over the biblical experience of conquest and exile.[89] The trauma of siege, defeat, destruction, and exile experienced by ancient Israel can be related to

---

[82] Baron, *Social and Religious History of the Jews*, 108–9.
[83] Baron, *Social and Religious History of the Jews*, 118.
[84] Baron, *Social and Religious History of the Jews*, 122–23, 127–28.
[85] Baron, *Social and Religious History of the Jews*, 125.
[86] Albertz, *Israel in Exile*, 100.
[87] Smith-Christopher, *Religion of the Landless*, 119–20, 149.
[88] Albertz, *Israel in Exile*, 107–8.
[89] Daniel L. Smith-Christopher, *A Biblical Theology of Exile*, Overtures to Biblical Theology (Minneapolis: Fortress, 2002), 103–4.

posttraumatic stress disorder. Even the imprisonment of a leader, the bearer of national aspirations, could have staggering effects to the whole nation.[90] Psalm 137 speaks of paralyzing rootlessness, disorientation, and of sadness. However, recent studies on posttraumatic stress disorder call attention to a fuller appreciation of the historical and social implications of the siege of Jerusalem, the deportations, and executions.[91] It is worth noting that deportations and executions did not only happen under the Babylonians, but, as Hebrew Bible faith summaries attest, was the confessed experience of the Israelites under Egypt, Assyria, Babylonia, and Persia (Deut 26:5-8; Josh 24:5-12; 1 Sam 12:6-12; 1 Kgs 8:33-51).

Postexilic Israel

With the change of imperial hand from Babylon to Persia came the shift from theocratic imperialism that aimed for homogenization to a universal empire that allowed diversity. Persia coopted religious elites of subjugated nations. Sheshbazzar and Zerubbabel were identified as leaders of the returnees. By their names, they may have assimilated to Mesopotamian conditions. These leaders were not members of the Davidic dynasty.[92]

Political expediency would have motivated collaboration.[93] Jewish leaders would have been educated in Persian lore, if not pressured to promote the interest of Persia. Since they saw Persia as "liberator," many Jews, in the beginning of Persian rule, sympathized with Persia. The name "God of Heavens" was appropriated to Yahweh, in accordance to Persian religion.[94] Cyrus was hailed as "the Lord's anointed." These are evidences of the attractiveness of Persian political propaganda. Persian interventionism can be presumed in the banning of the reestablishment of the Davidic monarchy and the persistence of insurrectionary movements.[95] Zealous worshipers of Yahweh and the Jerusalem priestly hierarchy branded the "people of the land" and the Samaritans heretics. By virtue of their Zadokite blood, the returnees asserted their sole prerogative as temple officials.[96]

---

[90] Albertz, *Israel in Exile*, 104.
[91] Daniel Smith-Christopher, *Biblical Theology of the Exile*, 95.
[92] Geo Widengren, "The Persian Period," in Hayes and Miller, *Israelite and Judean History*, 518. See also Baron, *Social and Religious History of the Jews*, 520. Baron takes the adoption of Babylonian names as hints of assimilation and cultural adaptation.
[93] Carl Schultz, "The Political Tensions Reflected in Ezra Nehemiah," in Evans, Hallo, and White, *Scripture in Context*, 235.
[94] Baron, *Social and Religious History of the Jew*, 130.
[95] Baron, *Social and Religious History of the Jew*, 130-31.
[96] Martin Noth, *The History of Israel* (New York: Harper), 338-39.

Actually, these conflicts were caused by Persian enacted policies rather than group rivalry.[97] The conflict between the Samarians, the Judeans left in the land, and the returnees was caused by differing social configurations.[98] The crisis faced by the exiles as the minority created an in-group solidarity and the formation of ethnic identity.[99] The former religious leaders among the returnees, for whom the law functioned as identity maker, must have observed some laxity in the practice of the law among those who remained in the land.

Persia's policy of tolerance was a political reaction in view of Judah's strategic location.[100] Tolerance was a strategy towards strengthening the empire's hold on peripheral territories. A strong Jewish state would be a source of revenue and a base of defense, and it would promote a positive view of the empire.[101] But the Jews were not all eager to go back to their homeland. The harsh reality of rebuilding their lives in a ruined city daunted many.[102] In addition, the creation of a new Persian base in the south generated hostile attitudes and created tension among Judah's neighbors.[103] They opposed the reestablishment of Jerusalem as a Persian base in Palestine.

When Cambyses, the son of Cyrus, died in an attempt to usurp power, several colonies revolted. In Judah, the revolutionary spirit heightened people's expectation for the coming of the messiah who would realize restoration prophecies. It hastened the completion of the temple.[104] Darius stamped out the revolts, and the policies of Cyrus were continued. Jews in Jerusalem were left alone so long as the interests of Persia was not disturbed.

Exile and the Hebrew Bible

The loss of land and government structure, the destruction of the temple and the threat of loss of faith, and the experience of subjugation and defeat by the exiles and those left in Palestine were the main impetus in the production, collection, and preservation of Hebrew Bible materials. Imperial politics was a major issue in the conflicts among the returnees, the people

---

[97] Evans, Hallow, and White, *Scripture in Context*, 172.
[98] Smith-Christopher, *Religion of the Landless*, 64–65.
[99] Smith-Christopher, *Religion of the Landless*, 64–65.
[100] Baron, *Social and Religious History of the Jews*, 131.
[101] Baron, *Social and Religious History of the Jews*, 26.
[102] See Smith-Christopher, *Biblical Theology of the Exile*, 59.
[103] Smith-Christopher, *Biblical Theology of the Exile*, 59.
[104] Widengreen, "Persian Period," 518.

of the land, the Samarians, the Ammonites, and the local governors.[105] Political leaning served as the main distinction between the returnees and those who remained. The Persians who needed a loyal Judea capitalized on the leadership of the returnees, in view of the restiveness of the outlying subject states particularly Armenia, Sardis, and Egypt in the west. In addition, Athens has established a base close to Mount Carmel.[106]

It is generally held that the exile group played a central role in gathering and putting together the literary traditions that fostered Jewish identity and ushered the development of Judaism.[107] Yet it must be noted that the prophetic books are critical of both the Jerusalem elite and temple worship (Isa 65:1–7; Jer 7:9, 18, 31; 44:3, 17–19).[108]

Because Persia was an imperial state faced by political problems, altruistic motivations should not be expected. Nevertheless, Persian imperial policy gave space for the survival and nurture of the postexilic Jewish communities under the strong leadership of Nehemiah. Social inequality was addressed, and the Sabbath and the cultic laws centered on the temple were upheld.

Understanding the conflict between the Jewish parties along political interests alone as a reason for the canonization of the EP will not suffice. There were zealous nationalists left in the land, who had been Yahwists. Remnants of Jeremiah's group and other loyal Yahwists with him were considered pro-Babylonia. This group favored submission to Babylon. A clear categorization of parties along political and religious leanings is hardly possible. Rather, religious and antiempire sentiments served as uniting factors among the exiled and the Palestinian Jews. Coalitions against the imperial powers were after all common even among former enemy nations.

Resistance against Persia was evident even among the former exiles. The break-up of mixed marriages, for example, was a part of "defense structuring" or "boundary maintenance." It is a common survival strategy among minority and exiled groups resisting foreign environment. Other components of cultural resistance employed by the Judean community were the

---

[105] Schultz, "Political Tensions Reflected in Ezra Nehemiah," 224, 232–35.
[106] Schultz, "Political Tensions Reflected in Ezra Nehemiah," 235.
[107] Widengren, "Persian Period," 531. Lester L. Grabbe states that the gathering and editing of a large part of the Hebrew Bible including DH, the Pentateuch, and the prophets, was done in this time when the second temple has already been built, though he presupposes the existing materials. Lester L. Grabbe, "The History of Israel: The Persian and Hellenistic Period," in *Text in Context: Essays by Member of the Society of Old Testament Study*, ed. A. D. H. Mayes (Oxford: University Press, 2000), 408–10.
[108] John Halligan, "Unsolved Mysteries: The Second Temple," in *Sense and Sensitivity: Essays on the Reading of the Bible in Memory of Robert Caroll*, ed. Alastrair G. Hunter and Phillip R. Davies, JSOTSup 348 (Sheffield: Sheffield Academic, 2002), 152–53.

concern for ritual purity, the formation of kinship links, and the separation (*badal*, בדל) construct. This use of בדל is a key to discovering the priestly theology of religious or cultural resistance (or a spirituality of resistance). Religion was employed to accomplish political ends, namely, avoidance of assimilation. But then again, religion in the ancient times was not considered private or having to do with otherworldly concerns. Religion for the ancients was the foundation political ideology.

The Impact of Imperialism on Israel and Its Literature

The peoples and lands of Syria and Palestine served as information highway between established civilizations. Life in Canaan flourished during the periods of stagnation among ancient empires (1207–1112; 1074–909; 824–809; 782–745). The difficulties brought by imperial impositions and aggression shaped Israel's faith and literature.

It was under the threat posed by dominant powers that the Hebrew Bible was composed and canonized. The exile(s) of the north and the south were the most important stimulus that led to the composition, collection, and canonization of the Torah, the Prophets, and the Writings. Deuteronomy, the initial authoritative text, can be traced to the time when deportations and the catastrophic end of Israel were still fresh, and Judah was caught between life and death choices due to Egyptian and Babylonian imperial pressures. It eventually gave rise to the EP literature.

Domination and oppression characterize the context of EP. At the time of the Assyrians, the Northern Kingdom was destroyed. Deportations and resettlement of Samaria by other peoples spelled the end of the identity and the nation of Israel. Judah, under the leadership of King Hezekiah and King Josiah resisted Assyrian assimilation. Josiah fought Egyptian army north of Palestine. Even in military weakness, Judah's kings revolted against Babylonian power. The ideological basis for reform became the canon and foundation for subsequent writings. Other prophetic figures that produced writings that touched on God's dealings with Israel and other nations came about.[109]

The dominating rule of empires and the consequent effects on a subjugated people was the context of the Hebrew Bible.[110] Prophetic literature stood in opposition to the triumphalist mode of imperial and royal ideology.

---

[109] David L. Petersen, *The Prophetic Literature: An Introduction* (Louisville: John Knox, 2002), 39.

[110] Jacob L. Wright, "Introduction," in *Warfare, Ritual, and Symbol in Biblical and Modern Context*, ed. Brad E. Kelle, Frank Ritchel and Jacob L. Wright (Atlanta: Society of Biblical Literature, 2014), 2.

These books draw attention to the plight of those at the receiving end of domination.[111] The impact of imperial nations on Israel's literature is attested in its form and content.[112]

Violence and warfare and the resulting social suffering were significant factors that shaped Israelite religion.[113] Israel's rituals were a strategized form of resistance by a group facing domination. In view of repression and coercion, Israelite resistance was ritualized.[114] Warfare was a central motif in Israelite thought due to Israel's experience of wars and the struggle to survive amidst much stronger military powers.[115]

Imperialism was the dominant force in the ancient Near East. From the point of view of the empire, the reigning king was always legitimate. He was not accountable to any moral code or power. All rebels and challengers to the king's rule were considered the king's enemies, and the gods were clearly on the side of the king. Hence, the war fought by the king against those who would not submit or those who revolt were all holy wars sanctioned and fought by the gods. War endeavors presuppose ancient concepts of time, space, and reality, where the imperial center was considered the ordered reality, secured and civilized according to the empire's prescriptions. At the periphery was chaos, where the uncivilized barbarians lived in the darkness. Imperial expansion should be seen as a mission of expanding the reign of the deity against chaos, reenacted and actualized as the kings fought and subdued the periphery towards annexation to the ordered center.

It is tempting to see the empire as the one spreading peace and order in an otherwise chaotic world of the ancients characterized by conflicts and the unknown in its periphery. Empires facilitated trade, advanced technology, and spread knowledge. Indeed, Assyrian imperialism gave the push towards the production of a body of literature that "saved" Israel.[116]

---

[111] Hobbs, *Time for War*, 197.

[112] J. Andrew Dearman, *Religion and Culture in Ancient Israel* (Peabody: Hendrickson, 1992), 99. See also Duane L. Christensen, *Transformations of the War Oracles in Old Testament Prophecy Studies in the Oracles against the Nations* (Montana: Scholars Press, 1975), 74; Petersen, *Prophetic Literature*, 18.

[113] T. M. Lemos, "Forging a Twenty-First Century Approach to the Study of Israelite," in Kelle, Ames, and Wright, *Warfare, Ritual, and Symbol*, 279.

[114] Lemos, "Forging a Twenty-First Century Approach," 279.

[115] Edgar W. Conrad, *Fear Not Warrior: A Study of 'al tîra Pericopes in the Hebrew Scriptures* (Chico, CA: Scholars Press, 1985), 148–49.

[116] Aberback, *Imperialism and Biblical Prophecy*, 8. He writes, "It is hard to see Tiglath Pileser III, Sargon II or Sennacherib as an unwitting savior of Judah, but there is reason to believe that this was so. For in a sense, Assyrian imperialism forced upon Judah the discipline of monotheism and its teachers, the prophets. If left alone, Judah might have abandoned its faith and submitted to paganism which dominated the Near East, making it far more vulnerable to assimilation and disappearance."

The Hebrew Bible was produced as resistance literature and in turn shaped Israel as a nation.[117] Three important factors are necessary for the development of nationhood, and all three factors—*vernacular literature, struggle against external threat*, and *state formation*—were present in ancient Israel. External factors were determinative of Israel and Judah's life,[118] but they were after all still a colony, with some degree of self-determination.[119]

Taking the political mechanism and ideology of the empire into the study of the EP, it is remarkable that Israel created a porous boundary welcoming the foreigners or refugees (*gerim*) and that Judaism was not a missionary religion. Royal theology may echo triumphalism. But the EP appear to discern the dominating aspect of centralized power as it identified Solomon's oppressive and liberal religious policies as well as Manasseh's complicity as the main causes for the split of the kingdom, eventual end of the Northern Kingdom, and destruction of Jerusalem.

The exodus from Egypt and the exile in Babylon are central events in the EP.[120] These events point to the context of subjugation and suffering brought by the imperial powers. Available historiographic data and employment of social-scientific and political theories in analyzing the politics of ancient Israel point to the legacy of resistance in ancient Israel. Jewish identity developed out of the faith and way of life of preexilic Judah.[121] In view of international pressures, Israel had chosen to resist homogenization. In the cultivation of writing and literacy, Jewish leadership paved the way for the production and transmission of the Hebrew Bible.[122]

---

[117] Adrian Hastings, *The Construction of Nationhood*: Ethnicity Religion and Nationalism (Cambridge: Cambridge University Press, 1997), 2.
[118] World-Systems theorists such as Christopher Chase-Dunn, Immanuel Wallerstein and Shmuel Eisenstadt, assert that in imperial context, nations cannot be studied in isolation. See Christopher Chase-Dunn and Peter Grimes, "World-Systems Analysis," *Annual Review of Sociology* 21 (1995): 387–417. See also Berquist, *Judaism in Persia's Shadow*, 247. Brueggemann says in this regard "Perhaps it must be concluded that the vision emerging from Moses is viable only in an international community whose passion for faith is knowingly linked to survival in the face of dominant, hostile culture.... Such situations of risk do seem to call forth radicalness. Conversely, situations of cultural acceptance breed accommodating complacency." See Walter Brueggemann, *The Prophetic Imagination* (Minneapolis: Fortress, 2001), 22.
[119] Berquist, *Judaism in Persia's Shadow*, 10. What Berquist says of the Persian period can also be applied to the period of Assyrian and Babylonian imperialism.
[120] Smith-Christopher, *Biblical Theology of the Exile*, 104.
[121] Smith-Christopher, *Biblical Theology of the Exile*, 247.
[122] Smith-Christopher, *Biblical Theology of the Exile*, 247–49.

Resistance to imperialism formulated in religious, cultural, and political theology was the main impetus for the composition and preservation of the Hebrew Bible. Israel outwardly submitted but seethed with resistance eventually bequeathing a purposeful, resistance text against imperialism. A tiny and weak nation, Israel utilized everything within her means to survive and outlive mighty empires, and it succeeded.

4.

RESISTANCE IN THE EARLY PROPHETS

The context of imperialism is significant for reading the early prophetic books. Parallel to the function of literature in advancing dominant ideology,[1] ancient Israel also advanced nationalist literature, and in Hebrew.[2] The Assyrian Empire's connection with the EP is reflected in its "imitation" and "subversion" of Assyrian literary genres and content. Yahweh takes the place of the suzerain, and Deuteronomy imitates the "curses" for disloyalty.[3] The loyalty oaths in Deuteronomy insist on exclusive loyalty to Yahweh alone.[4] Deuteronomy 12:18-27; 14:22-29; 16:1-17 are "subversive, anti-imperial, and anti-Assyria" with land claim being prominent in these texts. Deuteronomic festive meal rituals appear to mimic Assyrian victory feasts extolling Yahweh as a warrior. All adult men are required to be present in

---

[1] Machinist, "Literature as Politics," 455-82.
[2] Stephen Chapman points to the Qumran texts as an "unambiguous witness to an ancient stage of the Hebrew Bible." See Stephen B. Chapman, *The Law and the Prophets: A Study in Old Testament Canon Formation* (Tübingen: Mohr Siebeck, 2000), 210. See also Peter Ackroyd, "Biblical Interpretation of the Reign of Ahaz and Hezekiah" in *In the Shelter of Elyon: Essays on Ancient Palestinian Life and Literature in Honor of G. W. Ahlström*, ed. W. Boyd Barrick and John R. Spencer, JSOTSup 31 (Sheffield: JSOT, 1984), 255-56.
[3] Mark G. Brett, "Reading as a Canaanite: Paradoxes in Joshua," in *Interested Readers: Essays on the Hebrew Bible in Honor of David J. A. Clines*, ed. James K. Aitken, Jeremy M. S. Clines, and Christl M. Maier (Atlanta: Society of Biblical Literature, 2013), 239; See also Mordecai Cogan, "Literary-Critical Issues in the Hebrew Bible from an Assyriological Perspective: Additions and Omissions," in *Mishneh Todah: Studies in Deuteronomy and Its Cultural Environment in Honor of Jeffrey H. Tigay*, ed. Nili Sacher Fox, David A. Glatt-Gilad, and Michael J. Williams (Winona Lake: Eisenbrauns, 2009), 403; Weinfeld, *Deuteronomy and the Deuteronomic School*, vii, 57, 146; Stephen A. Kaufman, "A Reconstruction of the Social Welfare Systems of Ancient Israel," in Barrick and Spencer, *In the Shelter of Elyon*, 282-83; Dutcher-Walls, "Circumscription of the King," 610.
[4] Otto, "Political Theology in Judah and Assyria," 62-65. See also Michael Chan, "Isaiah 10:5-34 and the Use of Neo-Assyrian Royal Idiom in the Construction of an Anti-Assyrian Theology," *JBL* 128 (2009): 717-33.

these feasts. The absence of the king in such meals and the backdrop of Yahweh as the host are conspicuous.[5]

The idea of divine intervention in history through retribution, a theme of the EP, is a reflection of the worldview of the ancient Near East. But Israel gave more emphasis on historical divine intervention.[6] While the cyclical view of history is observed in the Deuteronomic summaries of Israel's actions in the book of Judges (Judg 2:18–19), Yahweh's power and direction of the historical process is emphasized.[7]

The parallels between Deut 13 and Neo-Assyrian treaties point to the submissive attitude of the vassal and the threat of merciless treatment of those who are disloyal. In Deuteronomy the overlord is the God of Israel and not the king of Assyria.[8] Deuteronomy insists upon undivided loyalty to Yahweh alone. This is underscored by stories in the EP, for instance, the zealous faith demonstrated by Elijah against the worshippers of Baal.

Assyrian influences in the EP may be taken as a hint of the provenance of these materials.[9] In addition, the references "to this day" (Deut 3:14; 10:8; 11:5; Josh 5:9; 7:26; 8:28; 9:27; 13:13; 14:14; 15:63; 16:10; 22:3, 9; 24:15, 25; Judg 1:21, 26; 2 Kgs 10:27; 16:6; 17:21; 20:17, etc.) presuppose the existence of the temple, the Judean state, and the fall of the Northern Kingdom. A study of the phrase point to "the late-seventh or early sixth century BCE, during or shortly after the reign of Josiah."[10]

---

[5] Peter Altmann, *Festive Meals in Ancient Israel: Deuteronomy's Identity Politics in Their Ancient Near Eastern Context* (Berlin: de Gruyter, 2011), 98, 128ff., 133–34, 211–12.

[6] H. W. F. Saggs, "The Divine in History," in *Essential Papers on Israel and the Ancient Near East*, ed. Frederick E. Greenspahn (New York: New York University, 1991), 21, 28.

[7] Saggs, "Divine in History," 30.

[8] Simo Parpola, "Assyria's Expansion in the Late Eighth and Seventh Centuries and Its Long-Term Repercussions in the West," in *Symbiosis, Symbolism, and the Power of the Past: Canaan, Israel, and Their Neighbors in the Late Bronze Age to the Romans; Proceedings of the Centennial Symposium W. F. Albright Institute of Archaeological Research and American Schools of Oriental Research, Jerusalem, May 29–31*, ed. William Dever and Seymour Gitin (Winona Lake: Eisenbrauns, 2003), 99–111. Parpola cites the following authors who propose the same connection: B. M. Levinson, J. Pakkala, E. Otto, H. U. Steymans.

[9] There is wide support for the Assyrian connection of Deuteronomy and much of DH among biblical scholars. See Coogan, *Old Testament*, 181–83; J. G. McConville, *Deuteronomy*, Appollos Old Testament Commentary 5 (Leicester, England: Intervarsity Press, 2002); Dion, "Deuteronomy 13," 198–99.

[10] Jeffrey C. Geoghegan, *The Time, Place, and Purpose of the Deuteronomistic History* (Providence, RI: Brown Judaic Studies, 2006), 142.

Thematic connections such as the Davidic ruler theme and subsequent worship-centralization ideologies are also linked with Assyrian destruction of the Northern Kingdom.[11] Materials such as the conquest, the Gibeonites' deception, and the story of the "Golden Age" under David and Solomon are traced to the time of national resurgence under Josiah when Assyria lost control over Judah and Josiah pursued nationalistic policy. Through these stories Israel imagined a lost past.[12]

The disappointment brought by the death of Josiah, the subsequent vassalage to Egypt, and eventually the destruction of Jerusalem and exile to Babylon called for an update of the historical account. Exilic redaction transformed the materials to "a sermon on history addressed to Judean exiles."[13] The editor's restraint in the narration of the fall of Jerusalem contrasts with the previous writer's hortatory style.[14]

Some recent works propose that Deuteronomy is more a product of Josiah's reform than its cause.[15] Deuteronomy is read as an assessment of the nation's faith, centered on the temple and kingship, from the context of the exile. This reading underlines "cult-oriented traditions" and traces such to aristocratic priestly circles in Jerusalem.[16] The absence of anti-Babylonian sentiments in the EP and its commendation of the Judean kings who stood up against Assyria are rationalized on two grounds. First, it is a way through which the writer underscored the hand of God behind the Babylonian triumph over the vanquished Jews. Second, as deportees the writer(s) might have wanted to win the favor of the Babylonians or at least not to arouse their hostility. I propose that the account is a Babylonian sponsored history. The restraint in the account in 2 Kgs 25:21 is attributed to the unpleasantness of recounting a recent painful event in Judah's history.[17] The

---

[11] Israel Finkelstein, "Archeology in the Third Millennium: A View from the Center," in *International Organization for the Study of the Old Testament Congress Volume Basel 2001*, ed. A. Lemaire (Leiden: Brill, 2002), 338.

[12] Finkelstein, "Archeology in the Third Millennium," 338–41.

[13] Cross, *Canaanite Myth and Hebrew Epic*, 287.

[14] Cross, *Canaanite Myth and Hebrew Epic*, 288.

[15] See Ronald E. Clements, "The Book of Deuteronomy: Introduction, Commentary, and Reflections," in *The New Interpreter's Bible*, ed. Leander E. Keck, vol. 2 (Nashville: Abingdon, 1998), 279–82.

[16] See Raymond F. Person Jr., *The Deuteronomic School: History, Social Setting, and Literature* (Atlanta: Society of Biblical Literature, 2002), 152. Person however notes the difficulty of determining the compositional stages in the EP because it underwent extensive revision and expansion by redactors sharing common vocabulary and theology making it difficult to delineate their respective works.

[17] Thomas C. Römer, *The So-Called Deuteronomistic History: A Sociological, Historical and Literary Introduction* (New York: T&T Clark, 2007), 162–64.

exilic context suits reading the account under the "prophecy and fulfillment" scheme.[18]

Other scholars push the writing of the EP to the period of the Persians who may have commissioned a work that documents their rule and supports their legitimacy.[19] Scribes may have written it not as a record but as a source of identity.[20] The compositions of Deuteronomy, the prophetic books, and the Pentateuch were "survival mechanisms" of the exiled Jews, a source of identity to resist assimilation.[21] Hence the origin and growth of the EP, which also spurred the whole Hebrew Bible, is traced to the emergence of identity consciousness.[22]

From a sociocultural premise, the EP addressed the dangers of assimilation that could result in religiocultural annihilation. This is supported by the content and form of the EP. As part of the "primary history" (Genesis–2 Kings), the EP describe the evolving nature of Israel, distinct from the imposed culture and religion of the suzerain.[23] In general, the propositions above point to the EP as a product of ancient Israel under colonial control.

The Assyrian connection of much of the EP provides insights to its understanding. Linked with Deuteronomy as a polity, the EP resist international political arrangements. Though oppressive, Assyrian religious toleration gave Israel the space to construct religious themes. This served as the backbone of Israel literary construction. Babylonia and Persia would not have tolerated such a blatant repudiation of colonial power.[24]

---

[18] Robert Polzin, *Deuteronomy, Joshua, Judges*, part 1 of *Moses and the Deuteronomist: A Literary Study of the Deuteronomic History* (New York: Seabury, 1980), 9, 72.

[19] Jon L. Berquist, "Identities and Empire: Historiographical Questions for the Deuteronomistic History in the Persian Period," in *Historiography and Identity (Re)formulation in the Second Temple Historiographical Literature*, ed. Louis Jonker, (New York: T&T Clark, 2010), 8.

[20] Berquist, "Identities and Empire," 9.

[21] Theodore Mullen Jr., *Ethnic Myths and Pentateuchal Foundations: A New Approach to the Formation of the Pentateuch* (Atlanta: Scholars Press, 1997), 59.

[22] Mullen, *Ethnic Myths and Pentateuchal Foundations*, 71.

[23] Mullen, *Ethnic Myths and Pentateuchal Foundations*, 71.

[24] Robert R. Wilson, "Deuteronomy, Ethnicity, and Reform," in *Constituting the Community: Studies on the Polity of Ancient Israel in Honor of S. Dean McBride Jr.*, ed. John T. Strong and Steven S. Tuell (Winona Lake: Eisenbrauns, 2005), 116. Moshe Weinfeld also notes that while Assyria and Babylonia allowed the existence of vassal kingdoms, Persia did not permit "political independence to small peoples." See Moshe Weinfeld, *Normative and Sectarian Judaism in the Second Temple Period* (London: T&T Clark, 2005), 234.

Further, the religious reforms and governance in Deuteronomy make sense in Assyria's time.[25] Deuteronomy functioned as a society's constitution.[26] It was produced in a time when an apparatus for the production of national literature existed—in the preexilic Judah.[27]

Furthermore, the canonical position of EP requires structural authority. Otherwise, it would have been accepted and adopted because it was popular.[28] State mechanism and conducive sociopolitical environment existed in preexilic Judah and was absent in the exilic and postexilic periods. The time of preexilic Judah fits as it was a time when classical Hebrew was prevalent—the late Judean monarchy or the late eight through the sixth centuries BCE.[29]

Moreover, the arguments for the threat of assimilation, experience of colonial victimization, identity crisis, and the postcolonial situation in the exile also fit with the short interlude when Judah was free from colonial control at the decline of Assyria as an empire. Judah became a vassal of Egypt later and subsequently to Babylon. Judah's assertiveness against Assyria and Babylon points to the existence of a national ideology. From another perspective, the absence of restoration passages in the EP and its presence in the book of Jeremiah is proof that the account has attained a fixed status by the time restoration ideas were entertained by the exilic community.[30]

Situating the EP in the life struggles of the exiles underscores the prominence of the empire. But attributing it to exilic writers disregards the

---

[25] Wilson, "Deuteronomy, Ethnicity, and Reform," 113–15.
[26] Wilson, "Deuteronomy, Ethnicity, and Reform," 123. See also Dean S. McBride Jr., "Polity of the Covenant People," in Strong and Tuell, *Constituting the Community*, 17–34.
[27] Christopher A. Rollston, *Writing and Literacy in the World of Ancient Israel: Epigraphic Evidence from the Iron Age* (Atlanta: Society of Biblical Literature, 2010), 89, 134–35. Citing preexilic and postexilic epigraphic evidence, Schniedewind argues that dating the composition of a large part of the Hebrew Bible to exilic and postexilic periods do not correspond to social and political situation. See William Schiedewind, "Aramaic, the Death of Written Hebrew, and Language Shift in the Persian Period," in *Margins of Writing, and Origins of Culture*, ed. Seth L. Sanders, Leslie Schramer, and Thomas Urban, University of Chicago Oriental Institute Seminars 2 (Chicago: University of Chicago Press, 2006), 140–42.
[28] Kofoed says "Stalinistic power is needed to impose a literature. See Jens Bruun Kofoed, *Text and History: Historiography and the Study of the Biblical Text* (Winona Lake: Eisenbrauns, 2005), 107.
[29] Schniedewind, "Aramaic, the Death of Written Hebrew," 41.
[30] Yair Hoffman, "The Deuteronomist and the Exile," in *Pomegranates and Golden Bells: Studies in Biblical, Jewish, and Near Eastern Ritual, Law, and Literature in Honor of Jacob Milgrom*, ed. David P. Wright, David Noel Freedman, and Avi Hurvits (Winona Lake: Eisenbrauns, 1995), 675.

extensive work done on the EP that observes preexisting materials in the narrative. The proposition of exilic origins also overlooks the importance accorded by the EP to the Northern Kingdom. Judah was central in the exile and postexilic period, when Israel was a remote memory, particularly in the face of the destruction of Jerusalem and the temple. But the EP chose a name that encompasses, if not commemorates the lost kingdom in the North—Israel.

From a literary point of view, the EP have always been regarded as a composite work.[31] The variety of sources that have been included is multi-faceted. Biblical scholars have discerned varying themes[32] that point to a complex process. As a whole the account lends itself to varying historical and redactional reconstructions. But essential coherence and connection of the EP with Deuteronomy is widely recognized.[33]

Considering differing opinions that locate the account to preexilic, exilic, and postexilic periods, the EP must still be located to what Norman Gottwald broadly termed as "Jewish colonialism"—"a period when the Jews were subservient to powerful empires."[34] Though Gottwald particularly used the term for the exilic time, the period from the last quarter of the eighth century to the Babylonian and Persian period can be broadly called colonial period when Israel and Judah were under imperial control.[35] Indeed Israel and Judah had been under Egypt, Assyria, Babylonia, and Persia. This is the historical period recounted in the EP—the context of production, reception, and canonization. The EP addressed the ramifications of being a colonial state. Hence, the EP display awareness of imperial propaganda, the reality of political subjugation, and the need for internal cohesion. As Daniel Smith-Christopher states, "Too much can be made of the difference between

---

[31] David Damrosch, *The Narrative Covenant: Transformations of Genre in the Growth of Biblical Literature* (San Francisco: Harper & Row, 1987), 307. See Robert Alter, *The Art of Biblical Narrative* (New York: Basic Books, 2011), 132.

[32] Such as Noth's doxology of judgment, Von Rad's prophecy fulfillment, Wolf's hope, Weinfeld's royal ideology, Cross's synthesis of the three and as propaganda for reform, and Person, Berquist, and Mullen's exilic and postexilic community's institutionalization.

[33] Of the more recent studies, see Erik Eynikel, *The Reform of King Josiah and the Composition of the Deuteronomistic History* (Leiden: Brill, 1996).

[34] I am using Gottwald's term to mean the broad historical period when Judah and Israel were controlled by imperial powers through political intervention, economic oppression, and military coercion, beginning with the subjugation of King Hoshea of Israel and the time of King Hezekiah of Judah. Gottwald used the term to mean the Jewish situation from 586–63 BCE. Gottwald, *Hebrew Bible*, 421.

[35] Smith-Christopher, *Biblical Theology of Exile*, 109. See also Deist, *Material Culture of the Bible*, 77.

'preexilic' and 'postexilic' in the entire period (as Thomas Thompson has quipped, 'there was exile ... often!')."[36]

Purpose and Central Themes

The EP is inseparable from the Torah.[37] Within the Hebrew Bible, the prophetic message is understood along the lines set by Deuteronomy's exhortation of obedience to the law.[38] Deuteronomy portrays Moses as the prophet *par excellence* (Deut 5:25-27; 18:16-18).[39] The early and latter prophets serve as Yahweh's spokespersons giving instructions on the practice of the torah to the Israelite community. Their proclamations function as means for actualizing the will of God.[40] Deuteronomy, the last of the Torah, paves the way for Joshua and the other prophets. Joshua, the successor of Moses, is the first of the respected figures such as Samuel, Nathan, Ahijah, and Elijah. Joshua as a figure and book play the important role of a hinge that binds the succeeding prophetic figures and books to the Torah.

Biblical tradition locates the prophets at the periphery of the society in relation to the rise of the monarchy. Opposition and pressure towards silencing the prophets in favor of supporting rulers' policy is observable in Isa 29:9-12.[41] In Israel, opposition by the ruling establishment pushed prophetic ministry underground.[42] Prophets were voices that clamored for a more egalitarian social structure both in Israel and Judah.[43] The prophets

---

[36] Smith-Christopher cites Thomas L. Thompson, "The Exile in History and Myth: A Response to Hans Barstad," in *Leading Captivity Captive*, ed. L. L. Grabbe, JSOTSup 278 (Sheffield: Sheffield Academic, 1998), 101-19. Smith-Christopher, *Biblical Theology of Exile*, 109.

[37] Otto Kaiser, "The Law as the Center of the Hebrew Bible," in "Sha'arei Talmom" *Studies in the Bible*: *Qumran and the Ancient Near East Presented to Shemaryahu Talmon*, ed. Michael Fishbane and Emanuel Tov (Winona Lake: Eisenbrauns, 1992), 96-97.

[38] Norbert Lohfink, "Distribution of the Functions of Power: The Laws Concerning Public Office in Deuteronomy 16:18-18:22," in *A Song of Power and the Power of Song: Essays on the Book of Deuteronomy*, ed. Duane L. Christensen (Winona Lake: Eisenbrauns, 1993), 351.

[39] See also Nicholson, *Deuteronomy and Tradition*, 77.

[40] Lohfink, "Distribution of the Function of Power," 351.

[41] J. J. M. Roberts, *The Bible and the Ancient Near East* (Winona Lake: Eisenbrauns, 2002), 284, 287.

[42] Lohfink, "Was There a Deuteronomistic Movement?," 49. The critique that the prophets lack class consciousness but only condemned religious sins reveal the lack of understanding of the ancient worldview where there is no separation between religion and politics.

[43] Robert R. Wilson, *Prophecy and Society in Ancient Israel* (Philadelphia: Fortress, 1980), 252.

condemn the tributary mode of production.[44] They served as the voices of the downtrodden against the rich and powerful.

Reform movements in Judah can be traced to the northern Ephraimite prophets, whose advocacy for reform was met with hostility by the political and religious establishment both in Israel and Judah.[45] In the south, violence committed against Jeremiah was the result of the intensifying conflict between the central southern prophets and the Ephraimite reform prophets with Jeremiah calling the central proestablishment prophets false prophets. The destruction of Jerusalem and the exile vindicated the Deuteronomic interpretation of history that predicted God's judgment for social inequity.[46]

The prophetic books give importance to the Exodus tradition.[47] In these books Israel's distinctiveness as the people of Yahweh justifies Israel's existence and its destruction as well.[48] As Yahweh's covenant people, social justice has been set as the standard of practice for Israel (Deut 16:18–20). Though the EP give importance to Judah, it addresses the people as a whole—Israel.[49]

Deuteronomy indicts the failure of Israel's leaders responsible for leading the nation to apostasy. The account is a critique of the ruling establishment. But foreign nations too are condemned. The prophets call Israel to keep faith in Yahweh in face of powerful empires.[50]

As the first of the EP, Joshua endorses the law as a way of maintaining Israel's distinct way of life as a covenant community. The conflict between Yahwism and Canaanite religion is depicted in Joshua. It zealously affirms Israel's covenant obligations. It further asserts the claim of each Israelite to a family plot (*nachalah*), as it firmly establishes Israel in the land of Canaan.

Deuteronomy as National Polity

Deuteronomy is the cornerstone of the EP. It is the basis for the institutions that govern the life of the people: its leadership, its laws, its worship, and

---

[44] Norman Gottwald, *The Hebrew Bible in Its Social World and Ours*, SemeiaSt 25 (Atlanta: Scholar's Press, 1993), 356–57.
[45] Wilson, *Prophecy and Society*, 304.
[46] Wilson, *Prophecy and Society*, 306.
[47] John E. Harvey, *Retelling the Torah: The Deuteronomistic Historian's Use of Tetrateuch* (London: T&T Clark International, 2004), 11–12.
[48] Brian Peckam, *The Composition of the Deuteronomistic History* (Atlanta: Scholars Press, 1985), 60, 62.
[49] David Frankel, *The Land of Canaan and the Destiny of Israel: Theologies of Territory in the Hebrew Bible* (Winona Lake: Eisenbrauns, 2011), 7.
[50] Aberback, *Imperialism and Biblical Prophecy*, 13. Aberback cites Isaiah Berlin who called this faith centered culture "a culture on wheels."

the prophetic office.[51] It sets forth ideals upon which the Israelite community should be founded. It commanded the centralization and standardization of Israelite religious practice (Deut 16–24). As the words of Moses himself, Deuteronomy established the foundation that will ensure the survival of the nation.[52] The choice is presented as a life and death situation. Such a crisis in Israel's life can only be connected with imperial threats.[53]

Internally as a polity, the Deuteronomic Code (Deut 12–26) subverts the parallel Assyrian documents. Deuteronomy 16, for instance, appears like a copy of Esarhaddon treaty with Israel, but Yahweh takes the place of the Assyrian king. It insists that Israel owes exclusive allegiance to Yahweh alone.[54] The power of the king in Deuteronomy is circumscribed (Deut 17:14–20). God, not the king, owns and grants land. Yahweh, not the king, fights battles. The king is not a "son of God" but a brother of the people.[55] He must not exalt himself (17:18–20), and he is prohibited from taking a harem and acquiring wealth. The practice of justice is made the condition for continued occupation of the land (16:19–20).

Only Yahweh is recognized as sovereign over Israel.[56] Yahweh's will must be followed in all aspects of the nation's life.

The Early Prophets, Worship, and Social Construction

The sovereignty of Yahweh is the basis for Israel's ethics and way of life. This is the purpose and content of worship rituals.[57] Although the EP accept that sacrifice is "customary for worship," it is not a central element in Israelite faith. The temple is the place where people pray and the place for the promulgation of divine justice.[58]

---

[51] Weinfeld, *Deuteronomy and the Deuteronomic School*, 168. See also Gordon J. Wenham, "The Deuteronomic Theology of the Book of Joshua," in *Reconsidering Israel and Judah: Recent Studies on the Deuteronomistic History*, ed. Gary N. Knoppers and J. Gordon McConville (Winona Lake: Eisenbrauns, 2000), 203.
[52] McBride, "Polity of the Covenant People," 21.
[53] Dearman, *Religion and Culture in Ancient Israel*, 150–52.
[54] Römer, *So-Called Deuteronomistic History*, 81.
[55] McConville, *Deuteronomy*, 34. See also Peter T. Vogt, *Deuteronomic Theology and the Significance of Torah: A Reappraisal* (Winona Lake: Eisenbrauns, 2006), 230.
[56] Diana Edelman, introduction to *Deuteronomy–Kings as Emerging Authoritative Books: A Conversation*, ed. Diana Edelman (Atlanta: Society of Biblical Literature, 2014), 2–13.
[57] David Janzen, *The Social Meaning of Sacrifice in the Hebrew Bible: A Study of Four Writings* (Berlin: de Gruyter, 2004), 158–59. Martin Noth observes DH's disinterest in cult.
[58] Martin Noth, "The Central Theological Themes," in Knoppers and McConville, *Reconsidering Judah and Israel*, 24–25.

The Jerusalem polemics emphasize the unity of Israel and sole rule of Yahweh.[59] The word of the Lord governs the history of Israel—that is a prophetic view of history.[60] Consequently, loyalty and obedience to Yahweh in all aspects of the nation's life is the central demand in the EP. This encompasses the political, economic, and sociocultural spheres. The political implication of faith is illustrated by how independent pericopes function in the narrative. For instance, the story of Naboth illustrates the sociopolitical implications of the EP's national program.[61] The story may have come from the court records of Jeroboam II (786–46 BCE), and may have functioned as legitimation of the bloody revolution that catapulted Jehu to power.[62] The passage may be regarded as a reliable source of a religious conflict exacerbated by social conflict that erupted in a revolution. The prophets Elijah (2 Kgs 9:25–26) and Elisha (2 Kgs 10:1–6) were actively involved in this conflict.[63] Prominent in the Elijah and Elisha stories are the prevalence of foreign cult and consequently of famine and poverty in Israel. The story illustrates the consequences of a king's disobedience of the law.

The core of Deuteronomy served as sources of the teachings of the EP.[64] Stories that portray revolution as a legitimate reaction against religious apostasy and oppressive rule by those in power such as Solomon (1 Kgs 11:29–31; 2 Kgs 9:6–9) were woven into the narrative. The books advocate a radical social program that emphasized the inviolable rights of the people for their family plot (*nachalah*, 1 Kgs 21:3). In the Elijah-Elisha stories attention is called to the plight of the victims of injustice—the poor, the widows, and the orphans at the periphery of society. These social ills are projected as the consequence of the embrace of a foreign cult. The prophets' approach to faith practice is non-ritual,[65] summarized as doing what is good and right (Mic 6:8).[66]

---

[59] McConville, *Deuteronomy*, 35. See also Weinfield, *Deuteronomy and the Deuteronomic School*, 312.
[60] McConville, *Deuteronomy*, 15.
[61] Allen Dwight Callahan, "The Arts of Resistance in an Age of Revolt," in *Hidden Transcripts and the Arts of Resistance: Applying the Work of James C. Scott to Jesus and Paul*, ed. Richard A. Horsley (Atlanta: Society of Biblical Literature, 2004), 29–40.
[62] Georg Fohrer propose that the narrative about Jehu's revolution may have come from the ninth century close to the actual events. Fohrer, *Introduction to the Old Testament*, 232.
[63] Albertz, "Social History of Ancient Israel," 361.
[64] Gottwald, *Hebrew Bible*, 352.
[65] Noth, "Central Theological Themes," 26.
[66] Noth, "Central Theological Themes," 29.

Prophetic resistance to the dominant culture is prominent in these stories. Yahweh's rule in Israel served as the foil against aggressive assimilationist drive by the dominant power in Israel's national institutions: the monarchy, the temple, and even the prophets. The worship of Yahweh is portrayed as the core principle that sustains life in Israel.

Collective Identity in the Early Prophets

The EP define the identity of the groups and communities comprising Israel. From an ideal beginning of "all Israel" in conquest, Israel is pictured as a loose federation of tribes (Judges), which for a short period became one nation, only to split on account of political and economic issues. The EP give importance to the kinship and religious ties that bind the tribes and thereafter Israel and Judah. The prophets in both the north and the south stressed that both kingdoms are obligated to uphold its covenant with God. For its failure to do so, the Northern Kingdom suffered God's judgment. Though the south survived the north for about 130 years, it suffered the same fate. The account stresses that Israel and Judah deserved the punishment attendant to their covenant with God.

The EP also call attention to Assyrian and Babylonian imperialism. They recount the destruction of the Northern Kingdom and the Assyrian impositions on Judah. They commend kings who resisted Assyrian vassalage. Hence, they underscore the effects of imperialism in Israel. A noncompromising stand against imperialism that is stressed as faith in Yahweh was the criterion for community membership (Josh 2, 24) not ethnic characteristics (ancestry and culture). Claiming common ancestry and shared suffering, kinship among the tribes constituting Judah and Israel was promoted.[67] The accounts construct an identity based on national "brotherhood" taking priority over clans and tribes. Hence, Israel's social structure is different as the king is a brother of the people.[68] The accounts provide the basis for the process of "identity formulation" grounded on the Mosaic tradition.

As Israel resisted oppression and assimilation, their shared experience resulted in the conceptualization of kinship. The worship of Yahweh justified the existence of a social configuration that gives central importance to justice. Yahweh was projected as the center and the source of life for Israel

---

[67] Kenton L. Sparks, *Ethnicity and Identity in Ancient Israel* (Winona Lake: Eisenbrauns, 1998), 283.
[68] Mark Brett, "National Identity as Commentary and as Metacommentary," in Jonker, *Historiography and Identity*, 39.

that makes her distinct from other nations. Faith in Yahweh functions as the "symbolic vehicle of Israel's will to existence."[69]

Ethnic consciousness developed from Israel's experiences of oppression and their struggle against domination. The emergence of ethnic consciousness has roots in social pressure. Israel's self-definition and group loyalty was shaped by attachment to a more egalitarian way of life.[70] The distinctive materials supplied in the accounts pertain to the self-identification of Israel as a nation, its description of its origin and organization, its definition of boundaries and characteristics, and its distinction from other peoples and nations.[71] The phrase "enemies on all sides" pertain to the nations surrounding Israel. In the EP, Egypt is presented as an enslaving nation, and Assyria and Babylonia as cruel invaders. Israel recognized its affinity with the surrounding nations such as the Ammonites and Edomites, but Israel's Yahwistic faith separated it from these nations. Only those willing to enter into a covenant with Yahweh became a part of Israel.[72]

Israel's confession of Yahweh having mastered an imperial power like Egypt led to the assertion that Israel's security rests on right relationship with Yahweh. From Judah, Isaiah declared that Yahweh's sovereignty encompasses these empires.[73] Israel's declaration of Yahweh's superior power was anti-imperial in nature. It led to the theology of divine retribution through which Yahweh avenged the wrongs done to his people.[74] Assyrian religious tolerance must have shaped Israel's national ideology towards religiosity, rather than ethnic sentiments. Israel claimed a common ancestry

---

[69] Grosby, *Biblical Ideas of Nationality*, 100–101. Grosby cites Mircea Eliade, *The Sacred and Profane: The Nature of Religion*, trans. Willard R. Trask (London: Harcourt, 1987); Anthony Smith, *The Ethnic Origins of Nations* (Basil: Blackwell, 1986); John Armstrong, *Nations before Nationalism* (Chapel Hill: University of North Carolina Press, 1982). Patricia Dutcher-Walls, in studying the laws that restrict the kings' power in Deut 17:16–17, concluded that its provenance was in a "particular faction" in preexilic Judah who wanted to proscribe the king from staging revolts. Pursuing such a policy will make the king powerless to launch any form of revolt. Such a policy accordingly will benefit the said faction. While Dutcher-Walls's ideological connection do makes sense, other explanations exist such as Gottwald's proposal of a decentralizing stream in Israel's tradition traced to the early premonarchic traditions. See Dutcher-Walls, "Circumscription of the King," 601–16.
[70] Willa Mathis Johnson, "Ethnicity in Persian Yehud: Between Anthropological Analysis and Ideological Criticism," in *Society of Biblical Literature 1995 Seminar Papers*, ed. Eugene H. Lowering Jr. (Atlanta: Scholars Press, 1995), 181.
[71] Peckam, *Composition of the Deuterononmic History*, 60, 62.
[72] Sparks, *Ethnicity and Identity in Ancient Israel*, 92.
[73] Sparks, *Ethnicity and Identity in Ancient Israel*, 220.
[74] Sparks, *Ethnicity and Identity in Ancient Israel*, 221.

and strong kinship ties, as well as shared memories of the past, a common way of life, and a peoplehood based on collectively affirmed religion. This further led to a common language and nationality.[75]

The prophetic narratives identify the unity of the south and the north as Israel. Among the many law codes that must have been known in Judah, the humanitarian Deuteronomic law was emphasized as the central identifying mark of the people of Israel. Further, in face of varieties of Yahwistic practices, the EP assert the worship of one God—Yahweh—in one legitimate sanctuary to achieve unity in identity. The identification process points to a collective identity crisis, a crisis that may have been precipitated by external pressures to assimilate.[76] Israel's destruction is therefore justified on account of their adoption of ways of the nations around them instead of being faithful to Yahweh (2 Kgs 17:12–18).

As historiography the EP legitimize the foundational institutions of the people of Israel: its religion, political organization, laws, and norms. The account reflects on the dynamics and processes of constituting a people distinct from the peoples of the ancient Near East. The account therefore sets the mark for a people as a distinct social group. As history, the EP recount the life of Israel and assert the importance of law for its continuing future. It anchors ancient Israel on Yahweh and in the land of Israel.

Israel needed a unified religious identity to survive the onslaught of foreign influences.[77] Knowledge of history leads to identity formation. Joshua as a book builds and strengthens group identity.[78] It insists on independent polity and distinct identity in the context of imperial drive for assimilation and aggression that caused social and economic problems.[79] Within Israel itself, community membership was open to all groups in Palestine, as the story of Rahab and the Gibeonites attests.[80] It is remarkable that Israel's historical narratives construct an identity that at the same time recognizes the diversity of the groups that constitute Israel. The polemics against foreigners in Deuteronomy are to be understood in the context of

---

[75] R. Schermerhorn, *Comparative Ethnic Relations* (New York: Random House, 1970), 12. See also Martin Rose, "Deuteronomistic Ideology and Theology of the Old Testament," in *Israel Constructs Its History: Deuteronomistic Historiography in Recent Research*, ed. Albert de Pury, Thomas Römer, and Jean-Daniel Macchi (Sheffield: JSOT, 2000), 444.
[76] Römer, *So-Called Deuteronomistic History*, 111.
[77] Luis Jonker, introduction to Jonker, *Historiography and Identity*, xi–xv. See also Rose, 445–46.
[78] Richard D. Nelson, *Joshua: A Commentary* Old Testament Library (Louisville: Westminster John Knox, 1997), 9.
[79] Jose E. Ramirez Kidd, *Alterity and Identity in Israel: The* גר *in the Old Testament* (Berlin: de Gruyter, 1999), 283, 323.
[80] Kidd, *Alterity and Identity in Israel*, 116.

imperial aggression. International sociocultural and political pressures in the ancient Near East led to the emergence of Israel's faith-based identity characterized by humanitarianism and social justice.[81] Hence, the EP's way of constituting Israel was pluralistic.[82] Various ethnicities and subcultures were subsumed in a covenant relationship with Yahweh.

Colonial oppression is not peculiar to Israel. The Hebrew Bible and ancient Near East history attest that other nations around Israel also revolted against foreign occupation. But it was Israel that composed a body of literature to define its identity and society. In the midst of foreign oppression, Israel produced a body of literature that constructed a society apart from imperial control. The common experience of being victims of imperial aggression, particularly under the Assyrians, gave rise to a collective consciousness in Israel and Judah. Literary compositions such as the EP were a way of resisting colonial rule. It prohibited treaty-making with other nations and instigated rebellion against unjust and ungodly rulers (1 Kgs 11:29-33; 12:16-17). Consequently, victimization of the weak is addressed in the EP. The stance against imperial aggression in face of Israel's weakness is pictured in detail in 2 Kgs 18. Surrounded by the mighty Assyrian army, there appears to be no help for Judah. The narrative lingers in the Assyrian polemic against Jerusalem and Yahweh in 2 Kgs 18:13-37 as it does in narrating the David and Goliath story (1 Sam 17:12-31). The passage portrays Assyrian officials' insolence against Yahweh. A humbled Assyrian army is portrayed stricken in the subsequent chapter (19:33-37), with Sennacherib later killed by his own son. The book of Kings presents the Assyrian empire as a presumptive invader.[83]

Overlapping themes form the identity of Israel: the *temporal* describing *when* "Israel" was formed, the *spatial where* it happened, and the myth of common *ancestry* (in the Torah). In addition three important ethnic elements are present in the EP: "the creation of a sense of solidarity," "distinctive cultural characteristics," and "shared history."[84]

Resistance through nationalist education and national commemorations strengthen collective consciousness and national identity. Nationalist endeavors give importance to culture, language, and history of the oppressed nation that may include a memory of a glorious past. Civil

---

[81] Kidd, *Alterity and Identity in Israel*, 116.
[82] John Van Seters, *In Search of History: Historiography in the Ancient World and the Origins of Biblical History* (Winona Lake: Eisenbrauns, 1997), 359.
[83] Sweeney, "Portrayal of Assyria in the Book of Kings," 284.
[84] Mullen, *Ethnic Myths and Pentateuchal Foundations*, 69-70.

resistance develops national consciousness and collective identity.[85] This is affirmed by a comparative study of postcolonial identity formation in Hong Kong and Taiwan. Bond-feeling and group recognition is strengthened by civil and society resistance power.[86] These elements are present in the EP.

Taking white-Afrikaner-speaking people in South Africa who have forged an African identity as a model, Ferdinand Deist proposes that Israel's identity construction worked because of the presence of "a degree of ethnic/cultural continuity between Judah and Yehud, a fair deal of shared memory, and the existence of traditional monuments and festivals that served as the venue for the publication of the interpreted history."[87] It can be categorically stated that ancient Israel's identity was strong to have withstood such massive external threats.[88]

Ethnic formation is a signaling strategy through which a group defends itself and its resources.[89] In face of dominant power, such a "signal" may invite reactions. Analyzing the cost of ethnic configuration and its advantages, Richard E. Blanton proposes that advantages outweigh the cost in contexts where "the weak periphery is in danger of being incorporated into a more dominant system, in the context of intercultural trade; and in internal situation of a poorly functioning or failed state."[90]

In connection with the book of Joshua, recognized historians such as E. Hobsbawm and T. Ranger consider Joshua as traditions that shape communal values.[91] Hobbs links invented traditions with social change. It is an element of "self-justification" through an appeal to the past.[92] Historiographical in form the EP shape identity. Modern education in history has been recognized to have a significant impact on national identity formation.

---

[85] Maciej J. Bartkowski, *Recovering Non-violent History: Civil Resistance in Liberation Struggles* (Colorado: Lynne Rienner, 2013), 3.

[86] Tina Chan, "National Identity Formation in a Postcolonial Society: Comparative Case Studies on Hong Kong and Taiwan," http://www.tisr.com.tw/wp-content/uploads/2012/05/National-Identity-Formation-in-a-Post-colonial-Society.pdf.

[87] Deist, *Material Culture of the Bible*, 74–75.

[88] Rosita Albert, Edina Schenieveis, and Iva Knobbe, "Strengthening, Hiding or Relinquishing Ethnic Identity in Response to Threat: Implications for Intercultural Relations," *Intercultural Communications Studies* 14 (2005): 107–18.

[89] Fredrik Barth, ed., introduction to *Ethnic Groups and Boundaries: The Social Organization of Culture Difference* (London: Allen & Unwin, 1969), 9–38.

[90] Richard E. Blanton, "Theories of Ethnicity and the Dynamics of Ethnic Change in Multiethnic Societies," *Proceedings of the National Academy of Sciences of the United States of America* 112.30 (2015): 9176–81.

[91] E. T. Ranger Hobsbawm, *Invention of Tradition* (Cambridge: Cambridge University Press, 1984), 1. As cited by T.R. Hobbs, *Time for War*, 63.

[92] Hobbs, *Time for War*, 63.

The Early Prophets as National Ideology

Israel's intellectuals from different sectors and parties must have written the books of the EP.[93] Yet, though the writers belonged to the upper class, they critique the governing class and the monarchy. The succession narratives and the court histories expose the nations' leaders to public scrutiny and criticism. Conversely, the flight of ordinary people, the soldier Uriah (2 Sam 11:1–27), the neighbor Naboth (2 Kgs 21:1–29), and the widows and the poor are given attention. Politics in its gory and scandalous details is portrayed for what it is in the succession narratives. The shocking consumption and ambitions of Solomon is censured. The oppressive nature of the kingship was made explicit. Consequently, the powers of Israel's kings have been circumscribed. With its critique of the ruling elite and preferential tendency to focus on the issues of the peasants,[94] it is probable that prophetically inclined intellectuals wrote these narratives.[95]

---

[93] Patricia Dutcher-Walls, "The Social Location of the Deuteronomists: A Sociological Study of Factional Politics in Late Pre-Exilic Judah," in *Social-Scientific Old Testament Criticism*, ed. David J. Chalcraft (Sheffield: Sheffield Academic, 1997), 356. Lemche propose that only about 5 percent of ancient peoples can read and write. Niels Peter Lemche, *The Old Testament between Theology and History* (Louisville: Westminster John Knox, 2008), 312. Rollston argues that literacy in ancient Israel is confined to the elite, and some would have been bilingual. Rollston, *Writing and Literacy in the World of Ancient Israel*, 89, 134. With Rollston are James Crenshaw, Susan Niditch, and Phillip R. Davies who finds little evidence of high literacy rate in ancient Israel.

On the other side of the argument are those who propose broad literacy in ancient Israel particularly in the late monarchy period: William B. Schniedewind, E. W. Heaton, Andre Lemaire, Simon B. Parker. See James Crenshaw, *Education in Ancient Israel: Across the Deafening Silence* (New York: Bantam Doubleday, 1998); Philip R. Davies, *Scribes and Schools: The Canonization of the Hebrew Scriptures* (Louisville: Westminster John Knox, 1998); David W. Jamieson-Drake, *Scribes and Schools in Monarchic Judah: A Socio-archeological Approach*, The Social World of Biblical Antiquity 9 (Sheffield: Almond, 1991); E. W. Heaton, *The School Tradition of the Old Testament: The Hampton Lectures for 1994* (Oxford: Clarendon, 1940); Susan Niditch, *Oral World and the Written World* (Louisville: Westminster John Knox, 1996); and Simon B. Parker, *Stories in Scripture and Inscriptions: Comparative Studies in Northwest Semitic Inscriptions and the Hebrew Bible* (New York: Oxford University Press, 1997).

[94] Noth, "Central Theological Themes," 30.

[95] Rose, "Deuteronomistic Ideology and Theology," 443–44. See also, Lowery, *Reforming Kings*, 215.

Resistance

Resistance against Assyria was an important unifying element in the formation of Israel as a nation. Hence the EP assail Ahaz's complicity with Assyria. They bewail the destruction of the Northern Kingdom Israel, justifying it as a result of disobedience in adopting foreign worship (2 Kgs 17:7–18). But they critique Assyria's arrogance, as it taunts its failure to conquer Jerusalem (2 Kgs 18:17–19:37). The incorporation of northern traditions with that of the south was a result and proof of the renewal of affinity between Judah and what remained of Israel in the north. There would have been sympathy for Hoshea in Judah. The EP have a less negative assessment of Hoshea (2 Kgs 17:2). The decline of Assyria and the reformation led by Josiah paved the way towards the conceptualization and attempt to reestablish "all Israel" as a nation based on prophetic teaching.[96]

The Deuteronomist ideology rallied "all Israel" towards unity in defense of the land by proposing the following themes as basis for unity: "(1) that only Yahweh be worshipped in all land of Israel; (2) that only the law of Yahweh be obeyed in the land of Israel and by the people of Israel; and (3) that Jerusalem be the religious center of the nation of all Israel."[97]

Affinity between small nations Judah and Israel continued in the two hundred years of separate existence, in the common worship of Yahweh and in the shared colonial victimization, even as separate identities also developed. Eventually, Assyria annexed Israel as a province. Relatively isolated, Judah alone had to contend with a very powerful threat. The Assyrian threat must have been so overwhelming that the EP retained only a thread of hope for survival.[98]

References to Israel's weakness in the face of much bigger and more powerful nations abound in the EP. Israel's powerlessness is emphasized in Deut 7:1, 7:7, 8:17; 9:1–2. The EP present Israel's consciousness of her puny situation.[99] Consequently, the imperial power as the subject and object of the prophetic narratives comes out clearly, not only in the examination of its sociohistorical location, but also in its content and form.

---

[96] Grosby, *Biblical Ideas of Nationality*, 44.
[97] Grosby, *Biblical Ideas of Nationality*, 44.
[98] Norbert Lohfink, "Which Oracle Granted Perdurability to the Davidides," in Knoppwers and McConville, *Reconsidering Israel and Judah*, 421–44.
[99] Walter Dietrich, "Martin Noth and the Future of the Deuteronomistic History," in *The History of Israel's Traditions: The Heritage of Martin Noth*, ed. Steven McKenzie and M. Patrick Graham, JSOTSup 182 (Sheffield: Sheffield Academic, 1994), 168. See also Zimmerli, *Old Testament Theology in Outline*, trans. David E. Green (Atlanta: John Knox, 1978), 45.

Nationhood

The EP is national historiography. It served as a nationalist literature that critiqued the governing class and foreign domination. In the EP, Israel is presented as a ruthlessly oppressed people who assert their own against mighty nations.[100] Imperialism is both the stimulus and object of the narrative. The EP advocate "cultural independence" and "creates national consciousness."[101]

The economic, political, social, religious, and cultural dimensions of imperialism are addressed in theological terms.[102] The EP also address internal problems and critique Israel as a people and especially its leadership.[103] The EP justify the existence of a small and weak nation such as Israel. They affirm a worldview and social structure founded on Yahweh's will, in contrast to the blanket authority and privileges enjoyed by non-Israelite rulers.[104]

Both propaganda and subversion are found in the EP. The EP prefer monarchy but condemn the kings as the cause of Israel's downfall. The EP unite the religious traditions of Israel in Jerusalem and in the temple, yet they prophesy Israel's destruction as well as portray a society where everyone can practice and teach the law. The EP lay a very strong claim on the land, but they also make its possession conditional.

No institution or person in Israel is beyond critique. The EP do not allow a monolithic view of society. For instance, the royal theology that claims unconditional promise to the Davidic dynasty was censured but not silenced. In the EP the place of rituals and priesthood is recognized, but the EP emphasize social justice as central covenant requirement. The writers did not impose a single interest in the narratives.[105] The EP display an

---

[100] Frank S. Frick, "*Cui Bon?*"—History in the Service of Political Nationalism: The Deuteronomistis History as Political Propaganda," *Semeia* 66 (1995): 89; Lowery, *Reforming Kings*, 216.

[101] Lowery, *Reforming Kings*, 216.

[102] Lowery, *Reforming Kings*, 216. See also Andrew D. H. Mayes, "Deuteronomistic Ideology and the Theology of the Old Testament," in de Pury, Römer, and Macchi, *Israel Constructs Its History*, 472; and Coogan, *Old Testament*, 181.

[103] Rex Mason, *Propaganda and Subversion in the Old Testament* (London: SPCK, 1997), 84.

[104] Nahum M. Sarna, "Naboth's Garden Revisited (1 Kings 21)," in *Tehillah le-Moshe Biblical and Judaic Studies in Honor of Moshe Greenberg*, ed. Mordechai Cogan, Barry L. Eichler, and Jeffrey H. Tigay (Winona Lake: Eisenbrauns, 1997), 120.

[105] Martin Noth, *The Deuteronomistic History*, 2nd ed., JSOTSup 15 (Sheffield: Sheffield Academic, 1981), 142. See also Rudolf Smend, "The Law and the Nations: A Contribution to Deuteronomistic Tradition History," in Knoppers and McConville,

openness that allows readers to reflect on what "makes an ideal society with no endorsement and rejection" of royal, prophetic, and other ideologies.[106] The accounts transcend narrow class, religious, and political interests and espouses a militant faith. They stand up to imperial powers and critiques rulers who would collaborate with imperial powers. As a historical writing, the EP present an open-ended story. The narrative shows restraint in drawing conclusions, thus presenting possibilities of imagining the future by interweaving different even contradictory themes. The assessment of the EP as mere ideology ignores the observation of contradictory themes that serve as dialogical and critical voices that undermine or oppose authoritarian dogmatism.

Land

Another element that is prominent in EP is the theme of land. In the narrative, the concept of being a people is closely tied up with the land. The identity of the people is connected to an identified territory.[107] Land is an important element of nationhood, but the early prophetic narratives make the possession of the land conditional. It prescribes a relationship with the land that is founded on law observance.[108] With the law understood as doing what is just, the account sets justice as the condition for nationhood.

Land serves as the "life-force" of a nation, embodies its spirit, and shapes its way of life.[109] Similarly ancient Israel understood its call as a nation of Yahweh in the land given by Yahweh. The emphasis on obedience to God, as crucial to the realization of God's blessings, is connected with the gifts of land and nationhood. The interconnectedness of its covenant with God, the land of Canaan, and Israel as a people is vital in understanding Yahweh's requirements on Israel.[110]

Vernacular

Another remarkable element of the EP as national ideology is their use of vernacular language. The Hebrew Bible, and the EP in particular, is written

---

Reconsidering Judah and Israel, 110; Wenham, "Deuteronomic Theology of Joshua," 194–203. Von Rad, *Old Testament Theology*, 1:346ff.
[106] James R. Linville, "On the Authority of Dead Kings," in *Deuteronomy–Kings as Emerging Authoritative Books: A Conversation*, ed. Diana Edelman (Atlanta: Society of Biblical Literature, 2014), 203–22.
[107] Rose, "Deuteronomistic Ideology and Theology," 444; Grosby, *Biblical Ideas of Nationality*, 70, 84.
[108] Zimmerli, *Old Testament Theology in Outline*, 65.
[109] Grosby, *Biblical Ideas of Nationality*, 27.
[110] Frankel, *Land of Canaan*, 38–39.

in Hebrew except for six chapters in Daniel and some verses in Ezra, which were written in Aramaic. Hebrew has affinities with other ancient Near East languages, but it acquired Canaanite elements.[111] Written in Hebrew, the historical narrative became the bearer of Israelite thought and culture. The Hebrew language as a cultural medium is an important factor in the efficacy of the Hebrew Bible as an anti-empire tool. Hebrew is the old name of the Israelites, which connotes: "the dwellers beyond the River," or the *apiru* mercenaries, or the wanderers who refused the yoke of established states in Palestine.[112]

Aramaic, on the other hand, was the language and writing system used by the Assyrians as the tool to advance imperial interests in the west as opposed to Akkadian—the prestige language of the empire.[113] As an imperial policy the use of Aramaic as the language of education was enforced. The Assyrians were aware that native language could be used as a tool to undermine the empire.[114] Sargon claimed to have made "one mouth" out of people of "foreign tongues and divergent speech"; this implies not only speaking one language but that the subjugated peoples have been made mouthpieces of the imperial power. The use of Aramaic language in colonial administration served at the same time to indoctrinate local administrators.[115] Assyrians as a policy sent administrators to subjugated peoples to indoctrinate them in Assyrian ideology.[116] The reference to the Assyrian treaty in Deuteronomy appears to have been an outcome of this policy of indoctrination that goes back to the time of Shalmanezer III (858–824 BCE). Aramaic flourished from the seventh century onwards, and branched out into two, the east and the west, by the sixth and fifth centuries BCE.[117] Western Aramaic was spoken in Palestine by the first century CE.

Language was a part of the emerging Israelite identity as Aramaic had been the language of international relations in Asia Minor.[118] Ordinary Israelites did not understand Aramaic at the time of Hezekiah (2 Kgs 18:26). But necessity would have required the business and governing classes, and

---

[111] Matthew Black, "The Biblical Languages," in *The Cambridge History of the Bible from the Beginnings to Jerome*, ed. P. R. Ackroyd and C. E. Evans (Cambridge: Cambridge University Press, 1970), 1.
[112] Bernhard W. Anderson, *Understanding the Old Testament*, 4th ed. (Quezon City, Claretians, 1986), 39.
[113] Schniedewind, *Social History of Hebrew*, 83–84.
[114] Schniedewind, *Social History of Hebrew*, 85.
[115] Schniedewind, *Social History of Hebrew*, 86.
[116] See Shawn Zelig Aster, "Transmission of Neo-Assyrian Texts in Judah in the Late Eighth Century BCE," *HUCA* 78 (2007): 1–44.
[117] Quoted from Kofoed, *Text and History*, 162.
[118] Moisés Silva, *God, Language and Scripture* (Grand Rapids: Zondervan, 1990), 68.

the exiles later, to learn the language. The EP describe a society where communication shifted from oral to written and the broad segment of the Judean society was literate (see Deut 6:7–9).[119] The EP's use of Hebrew speaks of the sociocultural location of their writers and is connected to their purpose. It was a deliberate attempt to preserve or perpetuate the Israelite worldview in the vernacular spoken by ordinary people. It was a move towards indigenization to counter assimilation.

The adaption of Aramaic as the language would have taken hold among the government officials, educated elite, the merchants, and even the ordinary people in Israel and Judah after centuries of Assyrian domination. By the time of Josiah, the Israelites would have been under Assyria for more than one hundred years, discounting the previous years when Judah was an ally of Assyria. By necessity, Judah's elite must have spoken Aramaic. Government records, literature, and commercial exchanges would have been done and recorded in Aramaic. The mechanism of imperial propaganda would have repressed the publication of indigenous literature. Later, as a minority, Jewish exiles had to speak the imperial language to survive in foreign lands. But Hebrew thought and language survived through all these in the Hebrew Bible.

The language problem would have been more acute in the exilic and postexilic times, particularly among the educated as it went against the grain of cultural trend for the elite to be unassimilated to the dominant culture. Colonial rulers would have intervened in the elite's education and scribal institutions. Among the exiles in Babylon Aramaic was used for communication, the Aramaic square script for writing, but the Hebrew language was still used in biblical texts.[120] The use of Hebrew language as a cultural medium in the Hebrew Bible is significant. Although Aramaic was the universal language since the time of the Assyrians, the exiles retained facility of their indigenous language in a foreign land.[121]

If the time of Manasseh was the high mark of Assyrian assimilation, the reform platform would have resorted back to the language of older Hebrew literature such as the Yahwist, over against Aramaic, the language of education and learning at the time of the Assyrians. The choice would have been more deliberate in the exilic and postexilic times particularly among the exiles and diaspora Jews. Aramaic language would have made inroads into communication and writing as the EP reflect Assyrian form and content. Royal recorders must own Mesopotamian literature and documents written

---

[119] William Schniedewind, "Orality and Literacy in Ancient Israel," *RSR* 26 (2000): 330.
[120] Silva, *God, Language and Scripture*, 68.
[121] Phillip R. Davies, *In Search of Ancient Israel: A Study of Biblical Origins*, JSOTSup 148 (Sheffield: Sheffield Academic, 1992), 94–112.

86 | A Filipino Resistance Reading

in Aramaic pertaining to Israel and Judah. That the EP are written in Hebrew is significant. The fact that the writers had a collection of indigenous literature and were proficient in the vernacular despite more than a century of foreign rule to the degree that they are able to compose literature in Hebrew is remarkable.[122]

Contemporary evidences point to the pervasiveness of the dominant culture and the significant role of language in establishing hegemony. The case of the Philippines, colonized by the United States in the last years of the nineteenth century, where English remained the dominant language even after its independence from only forty-eight years of US colonial rule, speaks of the pervasiveness of language imperialism.[123]

Ideology and Historiography

The EP form a national narrative in Israel's language. The acceptability of this narrative was not for the reason of its "plausibility" as much as in its capacity to create an "alternative world."[124] It is precisely because of their "counter factual context" that the EP's relevance is seen in the postexilic imperial context. The narrative provided identity markers. At the same time it portrayed a pluralistic world where independent communities, clans, tribes, monarchies coexist as an alternative to the empire.[125] Some parts of the narrative were earlier materials that may have been composed at the time of the united monarchy. By that time, the identities and way of life of different peoples that made up Israel had to be adjudicated.[126] Though Israel adapted monarchy as structure, the prophetic narratives espouse a critical and prophetic view of the political structure. Ethnicity and culture were subsumed under the concept of covenant loyalty to Yahweh.

The EP narrative fueled resistance against imperial powers.[127] The same resistance is evident during the Persian period as seen in the passages from Ezra and Nehemiah against what has been considered a benevolent

---

[122] See Samuel Noah Kramer, "Sumerian Literature in the Bible," in *The Bible in Its Literary Millieu*, ed. John Maier and Vincent Tollers (Grand Rapids: Eerdmans, 1979), 283. See also Louise Hitchcock, "One Cannot Export a Palace on Board a Ship," *Backdirt* (Fall/Winter 2000): 6–7.

[123] G. Raja Seckhar, "Colonialism and Imperialism and Its Impact on English Language," *Asia Journal of Multidimensional Research* 1.4 (2012): 115.

[124] Berquist, "Identities and Empire," 10.

[125] Berquist, "Identities and Empire," 11.

[126] Machinist, "Literature as Politics," 480–81.

[127] J. David Pleins, *The Social Visions of the Hebrew Bible: A Theological Introduction* (Louisville: Westminster John Knox, 2001), 149–50.

empire.[128] Ideology cannot be clearly separated from theology. As ideology, the narrative justified the destruction and exile of Israel.[129] But it ensured the survival of Israel's identity as a people.

Israel's social construction is rooted in the land, but it is translatable. As a social vision, it was conceived to address the situation of marginalization and displacement. The EP narrative is a part of the canonized texts of an oppressed and colonized nation.[130]

To some extent, the early prophetic books can be called an ideology but not in the sense of "false consciousness." Neither are they a system of distorted ideas. Rather, they present systematized ideas based on a reality, particularly in an event of unprecedented national crises caused by imperialism that could make or unmake Israel. Ideology may not necessarily be bad.[131]

As historiography, the prophetic narratives use the thought and literary conventions of their time and place to address a crisis in a nation's life. To use modern criteria for historiography in a work of antiquity is to miss the point.[132] As Israel's history, the EP are Israel's accounts of its past in the way they want and for their purposes.[133] Historical verity should not be the central goal of the study of biblical materials for though in the form of historiography, the purpose of the material was not to document history.[134]

Israel's historiography is distinctly centered on the collective called Israel. Other ancient Near Eastern historical writings are centered on the king.[135] Further, the concept of ethnicity and nationality pertaining to a people is not a salient idea in ancient Mesopotamia.[136] The stress on nationality was the contribution of the EP.[137] With Deuteronomy as the fundamental law, a nation composed of diverse groups and cultures and with its own law and territory was created.[138]

---

[128] Smith-Christopher, *Biblical Theology of Exile*, 45.
[129] Mayes, "Deuteronomistic Ideology," 480.
[130] Mayes, "Deuteronomistic Ideology," 480.
[131] K. Lawson Younger Jr., *Ancient Conquest Accounts: A Study in Ancient Near Eastern and Biblical History Writing* (Sheffield: JSOT, 1990), 51.
[132] See Baruch Halpern, *The First Historians: The Hebrew Bible and History* (San Francisco: Harper & Row, 1988), 118, 234.
[133] Hallo, "Biblical History in Its Near Eastern Setting," 8.
[134] Hallo, "Biblical History in Its Near Eastern Setting," 8.
[135] Van Seters, *In Search of History*, 355. See also Reade, "Ideology and Propaganda in Assyrian Art," 342.
[136] Grosby, *Biblical Ideas of Nationality*, 32–37.
[137] Grosby, *Biblical Ideas of Nationality*, 47.
[138] Grosby, *Biblical Ideas of Nationality*, 26.

The EP narrative is a self-critical history (Deut 32).[139] Repentance is an important theme (1 Kgs 8:46–53; 2 Kgs 22:13), and the account evokes shame connected with guilt as a way of instilling alternative values.[140] With Israel's history ending in the exile, the new generations were being called to a way of living that advocates nonconformity.[141]

Israel's social construction is inclusive of those at the periphery. The emerging Israelite community adopted a common metanarrative. Among the exiles the concepts of "Total Exile" and "Empty Land" served to instill the gravity of the national tragedy creating social cohesion and identity.[142] The EP applied the term "all-Israel" to open membership to the assimilated northern Israel.[143]

As a nation in the ancient Near East, Israel's worldview connected with its social environment. But Israel's conception of God made it stand out. The conditional nature of its covenant with God made operative through the law is significant. The attribution of political power on Yahweh alone apart from any nation or potentate set Israel's God apart. It also provided the counterpoint for Israel's self-critique.[144] As a whole the EP resisted and subverted imperial hegemony.[145]

---

[139] Richard Elliott Friedman, "From Egypt to Egypt: Dtr 1 Dtr 2," in *Traditions in Transition Turning Points in Biblical Faith*, ed. Baruch Halpern and Jon D. Levenson, (Winona Lake: Eisenbrauns, 1981), 191.
[140] Smith-Christopher, *Biblical Theology of the Exile*, 120.
[141] Smith-Christopher, *Biblical Theology of the Exile*, 121.
[142] Ehud Ben Zvi, "Total Exile, Empty Land and the General Intellectual Discourse of Yehud," in *The Concept of Exile in Ancient Israel and Its Historical Contexts*, ed. Ehud Ben Zvi and Christoph Levin, BZAW 404 (Berlin: de Gruyter, 2010), 167.
[143] Ben Zvi, "Total Exile, Empty Land," 100–101. See also Robert P. Carroll, "Removing an Ancient Landmark: Reading the Bible as Cultural Production," in *Borders, Boundaries and the Bible*, ed. Martin O'Kane, JSOTSup 313 (Sheffield: Sheffield Academic, 2002), 17.
[144] Grosby, *Biblical Ideas of Nationality*, 99.
[145] Davies, *In Search of Ancient Israel*, 87. See also Millard C. Lind, *Yahweh Is a Warrior: The Theology of Warfare in Ancient Israel* (Telford, PA: Herald, 1980), 168. Lind proposes, "For the Deuteronomist, Yahweh's kingdom is founded not upon military power, nor upon manipulation of power through diplomacy, nor upon concentration of wealth that husbands national and social resources, nor upon human wisdom that enables one to make decisions in relation to all the above for one's national advantage. Yahweh's kingdom founded rather upon Yahweh's promise and miraculous act, upon his covenant structure of the Torah and prophetic word; and Israel's future depends solely upon her present faith and obedience to this structure. Thus the tension between the way of the nations and the way of Yahweh in regard to the question of political power is at the heart of the Deuteronomist's message."

5.
EARLY PROPHETS AS RESISTANCE LITERATURE

Imperialism has three central doctrines: the doctrine of power (which it seeks to expand through religion, politics, and military drive); the doctrine of profit; and the doctrine of the superiority of its own civilization (justifying its expansion as an altruistic mission).[1] For an imperial power to take hold, it must be established with hegemonic ideology. Hegemony is a nonviolent form of "control exercised through the whole range of dominant cultural institutions and social practices, from schooling, museums, and political parties; to religion, architectural forms, and the mass media."[2] In the context of the ancient Near East, written texts established the sociopolitical structure.[3] Colonial manipulation of education, communication, and culture was geared towards the justification of domination.[4]

Power and Resistance

Basically, greed for economic surplus, its protection when acquired, and the desire for more propels imperialism.[5] Towards such end, military build-up becomes a necessity to protect and expand the power structures. With the sway of hegemonic knowledge and control through established structures, submission is secured. To the degree that power is used to dominate, control, and exploit, it is expected that resistance will emerge and increase.

Barbara Harlow credits Ghassan Kanafani, a Palestinian writer, for first applying the term "resistance" to describe the literature in modern day occupied Palestine, which corresponds to the situation of ancient Israel.[6]

---

[1] Thornton, *Doctrines of Imperialism*.
[2] Anathea Portier-Young, *Apocalypse against Empire: Theologies of Resistance in Early Judaism* (Cambridge: Eerdmans, 2011), 11. Citing Timothy Mitchell's summary of Gramsci's concept of hegemony in "Everyday Metaphors of Power," *Theory and Society 19* (1990): 553.
[3] Machinist, "Literature as Politics," 478.
[4] Thiong'O', *Decolonizing the Mind*.
[5] Turner, *Great Cultural Traditions*, 300.
[6] Barbara Harlow, *Resistance Literature* (New York: Menthuen, 1987), 2. Barbara Harlow cites Ghassan Kanafani, *Literature of Resistance in Occupied Palestine: 1948–*

Ancient Israel experienced violent invasions, economic oppression and exploitation, destruction of its material achievements, resettlement, and exile. Assyria, Egypt, Babylon, and Persia intervened in the life and the political structure of Judah. They asserted their ideological hegemony, installed preferred leaders, and exploited the economy of the conquered. In the context of imperial control, Harlow emphasizes the significance of the political and "armed struggle," as well as the struggle for historical and literary production.[7] A people's way of life plays a significant role in resisting colonialism and sustaining the larger struggle for liberation.[8] Kanafani stresses the "extreme importance of cultural form of resistance as no less valuable than the armed resistance itself."[9]

The asymmetry of power that lies behind domination makes resistance inevitable.[10] While Harlow situates resistance literature in the context of movements fighting imperial domination through armed, legal, or peaceful means, resistance can include the ways through which the oppressed refuse to accept and comply with the impositions of imperial power—their assertion of their way of life.[11] Cultural resistance counters the effects of domination.[12]

Sociologist James Scott, who studied Malaysian folk resistance, coined the term "hidden transcripts," which decoded the resistance of the weak on a day to day basis.[13] Ordinary people resist the hegemonic knowledge that supports dominance and the mechanisms through which power is made effective. Power exercise through discourse, institutionalization, and acts of coercion conversely produces calculated resistance expressed in various ways such as humor, ritualism, folklore, laziness, passivity, and silence.[14] Other identified resistance strategies are mimicry, sly civility, colonial non-

---

1968 (Beirut: Institute for Arab Research, 1981), 2.
[7] Harlow, *Resistance Literature*, 7.
[8] Harlow, *Resistance Literature*, 10.
[9] Harlow, *Resistance Literature*, 11.
[10] Michael Foucault, *The History of Sexuality: An Introduction*, vol. 1 (Harmondsworth: Penguin, 1990), 92–97.
[11] Portier-Young, *Apocalypse against Empire*, 6.
[12] Ania Loomba, *Colonialism/Postcolonialism*, 2nd ed. (New York: Routledge, 1998), 155. See also Edward W. Said, *Culture and Imperialism* (New York: Alfred Knauf, 1993), xii.
[13] See James C. Scott, *Domination and the Arts of Resistance: Hidden Transcripts* (New Haven: Yale University Press, 1990), 106.
[14] See for example Vicente Rafael, *Contracting Colonialism* (Quezon City: Ateneo de Manila University Press, 1988). Rafael cites an example of Filipinos finding funny words in the Spanish homily of Padre Damaso in Rizal's *Novel Noli Me Tangere*. Also note the proverbial indolence of the Filipinos in colonial literature.

sense, and hybridity.[15] Coded resistance creates a strong sense of identity and solidarity among colonized peoples.[16] However, powerlessness confines resistance to ways that may not bring reprisals. Resistance limits the exercise of power and changes power relations.[17] It is a way of protecting sociopolitical arrangements threatened by power structures.[18] The continuing practice of a people's "religious, cultural, and social practices" is resistance.[19] Mimicry and sly civility, for example, exposes the silliness of the colonial project. Similarly, hybridity invalidates the colonial and racist project of "purity."[20]

On the level of social construction, social vision functions as a critique of the status quo.[21] Hence, the prevalence of domination established by hegemonic knowledge, on one hand, and the observed revolts and movements for the liberation, on the other, establish resistance as it draws the battle lines. Texts coming from the underside that empower the weak, though not openly oppositional, may be considered a form of resistance. As propaganda works in subtle ways, subversion of the established order in the face of repressive power must be coded and refined, especially in literature, and so is the case of the Hebrew Bible as national literature. To some degree resistance is determined by the varied expressions of domination.[22] Horsley applying Scott's "hidden transcripts" states: "these indignities of submission, humiliation, forced deference, and punishment that generate the anger, indignation, and frustration (that) fuels resistance with passion, energy, and cunning."[23]

---

[15] Homi K. Bhabha, *The Location of Culture* (London: Routledge, 1994), 88–138.
[16] Deist, *Material Culture of the Bible*, 81. The emergence of the Filipino identity from shared suffering under the Spanish occupation can be cited as an example.
[17] Portier-Young, *Apocalypse against Empire*, 7. She quotes Jack M. Barbalet, "Power and Resistance," *British Journal of Sociology* 36 (1985): 531–48, particularly 539.
[18] Portier-Young, *Apocalypse against Empire*, 8–9. She cites Klaas Walvaren and Jon Abbink, "Rethinking Resistance in African History," in *Rethinking Resistance: Revolt and Violence in African History: An Introduction*, ed. Jon Abbink, Mirjam de Bruijn, and Klaas van Walvaren (Leiden: Brill, 2003), 8.
[19] Portier-Young, *Apocalypse against Empire*, 9.
[20] Bhabha, *Location of Culture*, 122–15.
[21] Jonathan E. Dyck, "A Map of Ideology for Biblical Critics," in *Rethinking Contexts, Rereading Texts: Contributions from the Social Sciences to Biblical Interpretation*, ed. Daniel M. Carroll, JSOTSup 299 (Sheffield: Sheffield Academic, 2000), 124.
[22] Vincent L. Wimbush, introduction to *Interpreting Resistance, Resisting Interpretations of Resistance: A Colloquy on Early Christianity as Rhetorical Formation*, Semeia 79 (1997): 6.
[23] Richard Horsley, ed., *Hidden Transcripts and the Arts of Resistance: Applying the Work of James C. Scott to Jesus and Paul* (Atlanta: Society of Biblical Literature, 2004), 8.

The goal of resistance literature is liberation. Acts of resistance such as the enactment of rituals and composition of literature aim to assert national identity and undermine hegemony. Resistance paves the way for reconfiguration of reality outside imperial control, thus empowering the oppressed in standing up for a cause. As Edward Said states, "The slow and often bitterly disputed recovery of geographical territory which is at the heart of decolonization is preceded—as empire had been—by the charting of cultural territory."[24] But often, the past is lost and cannot be recovered. What remains has been stamped with imperial imprint, thus the need for reimagination and reinvention. The importance of cultural resistance is indispensable in the reconstitution of the victimized community.[25]

In this regard, Scott considers the educated "assimilated" sectors to be more threatening because they are schooled in the thought and ways of those in power. They can therefore use the "master's tools to dismantle the master's house."[26] As subtle means of cultural and religious manipulation in everyday life are felt, resistance intensify.[27] Articulating and promulgating counter discourse and cultural expressions are therefore important forms of resistance to hegemony.[28] Where articulated and shared, it creates in-group solidarity and identity that undermines hegemony and eventually spill out to organized resistance.

Domination by the few at the center is accomplished by the cooperation of leaders that serves as centers of power in colonies. To justify the resulting inequality and overcome resistance, ideology projects the center as the source of ordering power against chaos. This is made effective through the enactment of rituals and supporting ideology. Such hegemonic construction projects those at the center in positive light and those at the periphery as inferior, barbaric, or enemies.[29] Imperial ideology presents those at the center as the gauge against which the colonized must measure up. Subject peoples are depicted as strange, exotic, and subhuman comparable to animals. Hence, the need to subjugate and civilize and, if need be, annihilate them.

In relation to the Hebrew Bible, Hobbs observes the use of similar imperialist epithets in Israel's literature against Israel's enemies, but the Hebrew Bible also uses the same epithets to Israel and Judah as basis for a

---

[24] Said, *Culture and Imperialism*, 209.
[25] Said, *Culture and Imperialism*, 209. Said quotes Basil Davidson, *Africa in Modern History: The Search for a New Society* (London: Allen Lane, 1978), 155–56.
[26] A concept popularized by Audre Lorde.
[27] Portier-Young, *Apocalypse against Empire*, 12.
[28] Portier-Young, *Apocalypse against Empire*, 12.
[29] Portier-Young, *Apocalypse against Empire*, 12.

"theology of defeat."[30] He traces this radical stance to the prophets who redirected the polemics to Israel for becoming like its enemies.[31]

The significance of the Hebrew Bible as resistance literature was observed by Robert Alter who, referring to biblical writers, stated: "they wrote with an intent, frequently urgent awareness of fulfilling or perpetuating through the act of writing a momentous revolution in consciousness."[32] Literature production is a way of subverting hegemonic knowledge.[33] Ancient Israel did not only produce resistance literature, but also canonized and transmitted it. Citing Charles Altieri in relation to literary canons, Stephen Chapman in his study of the Hebrew canon formation mentions three important functions of literary canons: (1) to institutionalize an on-going cultural process of idealization; (2) to establish the source of social authority by providing a cultural "grammar"; and (3) to set the "projective dimensions" for contemporary writing by new authors and critics.[34] Indeed in the EP Deuteronomy set the process of cultural idealization, provided the cultural grammar, and set the standard for Hebrew literature production.

For Israel, Deuteronomy's ideal society served as an alternative against the status quo under an imperial state.[35] But tradition must be accepted for the sense of nationality to take hold.[36] Accepted tradition changes and generates change over history.[37]

It is from social change that nations are born, constructed through popular literature that creates a shared culture.[38] Shared culture is evident in ancient Israel. A particular example of how the EP served as resistance literature is detailed by Walter Brueggemann, who expounds Deut 15:1–18 as a way of "imagining all social life away from coercion and competition to compassionate solidarity."[39]

---

[30] Portier-Young, *Apocalypse against Empire*, 188–90.
[31] Portier-Young, *Apocalypse against Empire*, 196.
[32] Alter, *Art of Biblical Narrative*, 155.
[33] Loomba, *Colonialism/Postcolonialism*, 63.
[34] Chapman, *Law and the Prophets*, 96. Chapman cites Charles Altieri, "The Idea and Ideal of a Literary Canon," *Critical Inquiry* 10 (1983–1984): 37–60.
[35] Barrie Bowman, "Future Imagination: Utopianism in the Book of Jeremiah," in *Jeremiah (Dis)placed: New Directions in Writing/Reading Jeremiah*, ed. A. R. Pete Diamond and Louis Stulman (New York: T&T Clark International, 2011), 244.
[36] T. S. Eliot, "Tradition and the Individual Talent," in *Selected Essays*, new ed. (New York: Hardcourt, Brace & World), 2–11.
[37] Grosby, *Biblical Ideas of Nationality*, 45–46.
[38] See Benedict Anderson, *Imagined Communities*, new ed. (London: Verso: 1983), particularly 9–46.
[39] Walter Brueggemann, *Sabbath as Resistance: Saying No to the Culture of Now* (Louisville: Westminster John Knox, 2014), 44–45.

Portier-Young's examination of how apocalyptic literature counters imperial discourse is applicable to the EP: "a radical relocation of ultimate power, countering imperial claims to ultimate power by asserting God's power and power given by God to the faithful."[40] Such assertion paved the way for the weak "to imagine and engage in effective resistance." In addition to the discourse on power, the text could also employ discursive strategies such as critical inversion "that reimagined a world governed not by empires, but by God."[41] The EP's historiography "critiques ruling powers, claims a greater power than that available to current temporal rulers, and assures the audience of divine providence; it projects an end to current rule, countering imperial claims to ultimacy; and it frames hope for the faithful in terms of justice, reversal, and good age to come."[42]

The Hebrew Bible as a whole function as resistance literature as it *redescribes* the world. That is, constructing it alternatively by creating an "alternative consciousness, dismantling the dominant consciousness, and delegitimizing the existing order towards it rejection, and the generation of anticipation and direction of energies towards the construction of a new order."[43]

Another forensic approach applicable to the EP as resistance literature is what Daniel Smith-Christopher identified as "mechanisms of survival" common to communities who have lost land and social infrastructure. These communities resort to survival strategies such as: adapted structure and leadership pattern, institutionalization of rituals, the production of folktales as expression of social existence, and the creation of "resistance literature."[44] Under a dominant power, a minority group resorts to means of resistance that maintain their identity through group consolidation and boundary-making. These actions are ways of self-preservation or resistance. Resistance is self-evident, "because it is the Judeans *who successfully maintained their identity that were responsible for the biblical texts we are concerned with. This is therefore not only social reality, but it is the social reality reflected in the texts.*"[45]

---

[40] Portier-Young, *Apocalypse against Empire*, 7–8.
[41] Portier-Young, *Apocalypse against Empire*, 15.
[42] Portier-Young, *Apocalypse against Empire*, 29.
[43] Walter Brueggemann, *The Prophetic Imagination* (Minneapolis: Fortress, 2001), 3.
[44] Smith-Christopher, *Religion of the Landless*, particularly 73–78.
[45] Smith-Christopher, *Religion of the Landless*, 73. Italics in the original.

Sanders affirms the "life-and-death situation" that spurred the formation of the canon and rues "selectivity" in stressing political factor to the "exclusion of all others" in canon formation.[46]

Taking into consideration the canonical function of the individual books in the EP, Knauf states that Joshua connects land with torah observance and establishes Israel as a covenant community to have inalienable right in the land.[47] Serge Frolov further states that Joshua played a "central role" in demonstrating that the land is a reward and that possession of the land is contingent on Yahweh's support.[48] Frolov also sees Joshua as having "counterbalanced" the royal-centered book of Kings with the picture of a united Israel under no king.

Amit sees the value of the book of Judges in its paradigmatic presentation of history that illustrates God's sovereignty, mercy, and justice. It also brings in the complex dynamics of relationships between the tribes in the north and the south and between insiders and outsiders.[49] Related to Amit's propositions is Susanne Gillmayr-Bucher's reading of the book of Judges as a way of establishing Israel's self-identity in terms of ethnicity, religion, and intertribal relationship and its views on leadership. Israel's collective identity in the book of Judges is "an inclusive point of view that embraces all of Israel in its memory, in order to (re)construct Israel. It reassures those who already know what is right and what is wrong and shows them different examples, thereby urging them to remember their past and at the same time to rise to the challenge to reinvent Israel."[50] Of 1–2 Samuel, Thomas O. Bolin reconstructs a scenario where the young boys were to read, memorize, and recite texts. The stories about Saul and David would have served as a way of learning desirable character traits of leaders or finding a model worth emulating.[51] The succession stories would have exposed the king's

---

[46] James A. Sanders, *From Sacred Story to Sacred* Text (Philadelphia: Fortress, 1987), 22–23.

[47] E. Axel Knauf, "Does "Deuteronomistic Historiography (DH) Exists?," in de Pury, Römer, and Macchi, *Israel Constructs Its History*, 390–82.

[48] Serge Frolov, "The Case of Joshua," in Edelman, *Deuteronomy—Kings as Emerging Authoritative Books*, 100–101.

[49] Yairah Amit, "Who Was Interested in the Book of Judges in the Persian-Hellenistic Period," in Edelman, *Deuteronomy—Kings as Emerging Authoritative Books*, 102–14.

[50] Susanne Gillmayr-Bucher, "Memories Laid to Rest: The Book of Judges in the Persian Period," in Edelman, *Deuteronomy—Kings as Emerging Authoritative Books*, 132.

[51] Thomas O. Bolin, "1–2 Samuel and Jewish Paideia in the Persian and Hellenistic Periods, in Edelman, *Deuteronomy—Kings as Emerging Authoritative Books*, 133–58.

character flaws and inconsistencies.[52] The religious policies of the kings, both internally and in relation to imperial nations, would have been studied and discussed among family groupings and scribal schools.

National polity and leadership, religious and cultural norms, ethnic and collective identity, and territorial claim are recurring and overlapping themes in the EP. The traditional reading of EP as teaching one God, one worship, in Jerusalem, are encompassed in the over-arching theme of creating a national vision of an ideal society outside imperial claim, with its own government, administering just laws on its land under God's rule.

The EP is resistance literature by the following arguments: One, imperial power was so pervasive throughout the period of its composition, redaction, transmission, and canonization. From the time of Manasseh or Hezekiah earlier, Josiah, the exile and the closing of the canon in the council of Jamnia, Judah's situation can be described as a subjugated state suffering from sociocultural threat, political and economic oppression, by occupying empires.

That resistance against occupying powers was alive and smoldering throughout the Assyrian, Egyptian, and Babylonian occupation is attested by the intermittent revolts and religiocultural reforms attempted in Judah and Israel. On this basis, Manasseh's rule was censured. He was a willing puppet of Assyria. But Hezekiah and Josiah were approved. In Israel, Hoshea found some favor from the prophetic historian who summarizes "He did what was evil in the sight of the Lord, yet not as like the kings of Israel who were before him" (2 Kgs 17:2).[53] Assyria was portrayed as insolent but impotent against Yahweh. Babylon was forever etched in the memory of Israel as the nation who dared to be like God (Gen 11:1–10) and who exiled and destroyed Israel's cherished institutions.

The loss of land and government structure, the destruction of the temple and the continuing threat of assimilation, and the experience of defeat and life in exile, both by Israel and Judah, served as the impetus in the production, collection, and preservation of the EP. The imperial threat to a

---

[52] Klaus-Peter Adam, "What Made the Books of Samuel Authoritative in the Discourses of the Persian Period? Reflection on the Legal Discourse in 2 Samuel 14," in Edelman, *Deuteronomy–Kings as Emerging Authoritative Books*, 170–82.

[53] The rest of the kings of Israel earned the censure "He did what was evil in the sight of the Lord; he did not depart all his days from any of the sins of Jeroboam son of Nebat, which he caused Israel to sin" (1 Kgs 15:26, 34; 2 Kgs 8:18) except for kings whose acts and death are described in more detail (Jeroboam I, Nadab, Joram, Jehu) or those whose reign are too short (Tibni, Shallum).

great extent determined the development of the biblical faith.[54] The occupation and invasion of colonizing powers were major issues in preexilic and exilic Judah. Persian colonial politics determined internal situation in the postexilic Judah.[55]

In sum, the EP resist domination in all its forms. Joshua stands as the first of the EP so closely attached to the Torah and solidly stands on a body of literature known for its stubborn insistence on Yahweh alone as the source of life and security for Israel. Prophets stand in opposition to the oppressive use of power serving as covenant "watchmen."[56] The EP categorically insists on justice as the foundation of a national polity. It condemns unjust rule of the powerful within Israel. It gives voices to the disenfranchised. The centrality of justice in opposition to the monopolization of wealth by the elite points to the EP's nature as resistance literature.[57]

Internal politics may have played a part in its production, but the EP cannot be simplistically understood as propaganda of the ruling elite or with any group in Palestine. Its over-all message transcends political and economic partisanship to embrace the whole nation. As literature, it scathingly presents an obstinate people who deserved its misfortunes holding the kings responsible. The nation's leaders are enjoined to observe the law and uphold justice especially in relation to the poor, the widows, and the orphans. Central to EP is the strengthening of community unity and identity. The community stands as one in covenant with God over and against empires.

Two, the existence of a reform movement grounds the EP on actual historical resistance movements against the presumptions of its governing class and externally against imperial aggression, economic exploitation, and cultural assimilation. Judah, with a broad support of its people, had repeatedly staged revolts against Assyria and three major revolts in the short period under mighty Babylonia.

While the EP's connection with Josiah's reform is not beyond question, it cannot be denied that the reform emerged from a small subjugated, defeated, exiled, and foreign-occupied Israel. The EP have been attributed to

---

[54] Schultz, "Political Tensions Reflected in Ezra Nehemiah," 224, 232, 234–35. Smith-Christopher provides a survey of the way the exile has been depicted as a historical event in biblical scholarship in Smith-Christopher, *Biblical Theology of the Exile*, 27–74.
[55] Schultz, "Political Tensions Reflected in Ezra Nehemiah," 235.
[56] Victor Matthews and Don Benjamin, *Social World of Ancient Israel 1250–587 BCE* (Grand Rapids: Baker, 2011), 212. In J. G. McConville's words, the EP "stands on guard against any royal hegemony over the people of Yahweh on the model of [ancient Near East] monarchies" (McConville, *Deuteronomy*, 35).
[57] James L. Mays, "Justice: Perspectives from the Prophetic Tradition," in Strong and Tuell, *Constituting the Community*, 61–61.

the "Yahweh alone movement" or a circle of scribes, wise men, or priestly exilic group. It is a testament to Israel's tenacity in continuing religiocultural resistance and in crafting a program for the survival of a people cherishing a self-critical polity, in as much as it subverts imperial control.

The EP were composed intelligently and purposefully in the service of Israel. Their efficacy as a national narrative is attested by the primary role they played in the Hebrew canon formation.[58] The composition projected a community living as an extended family under God's rule, observing God's law, and living a prosperous and blessed life in its land—in the most adverse situations.

The centrality of liberation is explicit in the EP as a promise. It enabled the community to imagine a reality and future apart from imperial imposition, resist assimilation, and struggle for national survival. Yet, the EP as a national ideology is critical of Israel as a nation and is unquestionably centered on Yahwistic faith. In the EP Israel magnifies Yahweh's power. In its humiliation and defeat, Yahweh is exalted. In the face of the unrivaled power of Egypt, Assyria, Babylonia, and Persia, the EP project Yahweh's unsurpassed might and glory. In the face of seemingly insurmountable odds, they speak of hope and victory. A small and weak nation, the biblical community thought of itself as constituting the people of Yahweh. Resistance is not confined to political and armed resistance, "we are in danger of making a serious mistake ... whenever we infer anything at all about the beliefs or attitudes or anyone solely on the basis that he or she has engaged in an apparently differential act."[59] That Israel survived the mighty empires of the ancient Near East speaks of the power of EP narratives as a resistance text.

Three, the centrality of resistance in EP is attested by the presence of elements of resistance literature held in common with other literatures produced by oppressed groups, ironically first coined in reference to Palestinians under Israeli occupation. Using military language familiar to empires, Israel claims the land as a grant by Yahweh the warrior to Israel,

---

[58] John Van Seters says of EP, that it "is a literary work of superb accomplishment." Van Seters, *In Search of History*, 359, 362. Meir Sternberg also says, "As regards sophistication, the Bible is second to none and no allowances need to be made of it. The opening and timing of gaps, the processing of information and response, the interlinkage of the different levels, and the play of hypotheses with sanctions against premature closure, the clues and models that guide interpretive procedure, the roles fulfilled by ambiguity: all these show a rare mastery of the narrative medium." Meir Sternberg, *The Poetics of Biblical Narrative: Ideological Literature and the Drama of Reading* (Bloomington: Indiana University Press, 1987), 230. See also Gottwald, *Hebrew Bible*, 260.

[59] Scott, *Domination and the Arts of Resistance*, 20, 23.

Yahweh's people. Israel is projected in the EP as the theocratic society under an inviolable treaty to Yahweh; in faithfulness to this treaty, Israel stands or falls. Yet centralized power within its own society is resisted as militantly as the broader form of international imperialism that draws surplus to the core center at the expense of those in the periphery. There is no room in the EP for accommodation to these mighty nations. Consequently, foreign vassalage and compromise is resisted.

These books praise the actions of Hezekiah and Josiah despite its catastrophic consequences to the national government. Strengthening identity and unity of an independent national entity, the EP empower resistance. They subvert hegemonic knowledge asserting the rule of an uncompromising deity. For the EP, Assyria is but the "rod of Yahweh's anger," and Babylon, an executor of God's judgment. Such an extravagant claim projects tiny Israel as Yahweh's invincible possession! Like a David who challenged Goliath, Israel challenges the imperial powers defiantly declaring: "who is this uncircumcised man who dares to defy the army of the living God?" The EP reveal a fatal flaw in the empire—it is not invincible. Their reticence in narrating the exile sends a powerful message concerning the violence of imperial aggression. The historical narrative ends with a hint of a taunt, Jehoiachin still lives under imperial sponsorship.

To sum up, central to resistance literature is (1) the creation of a national identity through historiography and folklore, (2) the creation of a viable national polity and leadership, (3) the enactment of cultural norms and rituals, and (4) the claim of national patrimony, which is fundamental to the Deuteronomistic historiography.

The EP's texts were cherished in subsequent periods under later empires. People's resistance against imperial Babylonia, Persia, and Greece is reflected in the untiring production of literature that nourished Jewish hope and aspiration for good life and freedom, and the preservation and transmission of its existing literature throughout the era of Greek and the Roman empires.

From a postcolonial perspective, the identity shaped by the prophetic narratives was not monolithic. Nor did it construct the other in terms of ethnicity, race, and religion. Rather it claimed the rule of an unseen God Yahweh made visible in a societal well-being. The EP paved the way for a dialogue between alternatives leaving adjudication and decision to the community of readers. Borrowing Bakhtin's term, the narratives allowed a "dialogic" process in identity formation. In Callahan's observation, "The expression of resistance in ancient Israel is not a question of great versus little tradition, but of competing interpretations of one complex common tradition."[60] Alexander Gracia Düttman notes that resistance in the form of

---

[60] Callahan, "Arts of Resistance," 31.

literature adheres to "principle of charity" that is "scandalously encompassing."[61] The EP point towards a community that is inclusive, dialogical, and pluralistic sharing a monotheistic faith.

Interpreting the Early Prophets Today

Class Interests

The EP dispute the idea that writings and ideology coming from the elite class automatically correlate with the social and economic interest of the group that produced it. Shared experience of economic exploitation and colonial oppression as the context of composing the early prophetic narratives is significant in the narrative. As a history the EP include issues that transcended class interests. The EP are a representation of the people's reality and struggles. As part of Scripture, the EP's acceptability to the Jews is beyond dispute.[62] Ideological manipulation would not have won acceptance in the absence of structural imposition and coercion. Particularly in the situation of the exile and Jewish diaspora, a national narrative with which Jews do not identify with would not have worked.

The ascendancy of the EP as national literature required a strong bureaucratic structure for its promotion and perpetuation.[63] There was no external authority to prop up the authority of the Enneateuch in the postexilic times.[64]

Mark Brett critiques the usual correlation of ancient Israel's historiography with the interest of its urban writers. He contends that historiography is an ineffective ideological tool.[65] Brett argues that even if it is assumed, as Deuteronomy suggests, that literacy was widespread in monarchic Israel, the existence of texts that restrict the power of the king (Deut 31:24–29) and the popularity of central prophets would serve as

---

[61] Alexander García Düttmann, "The Art of Resistance" (paper delivered in the context of the Literaturfestival Berlin on the 18th of September 2015; http://www.fourbythreemagazine.com/the-art-of-resistance.html).
[62] See Kidd, *Alterity and Identity in Israel*, 116.
[63] Jens Bruun Kofoed says of what it would entail for an authority to impose a text on a group, "it is very unlikely that a 'twisting' of a canonical tradition would have been accepted universally. It would have required almost superhuman—or at least 'Stalinistic'—powers of the Jews and keep alive such a tradition." See Kofoed, *Text and History*, 107.
[64] Frolov, "Case of Joshua," 95.
[65] Mark Brett, "Literacy and Domination: G. A. Herion's Sociology of History Writing," in *Social-Scientific Old Testament Criticism: A Sheffield Reader*, ed. David J. Chalcraft (Sheffield: Sheffield Academic, 1997), 122.

checks to the monarchy and the cult officials. In such an environment Brett says, "even if urban priests did manipulate the past, we can doubt whether this was an effective means of controlling the beliefs of the lower social strata."[66]

A quick survey of literature and art proves that human beings regardless of class have the capacity to go beyond personal interests and present the other side. Chapman, following Altieri, calls this capacity "self-subsumption."[67] This is a nature of literature such as the Hebrew Bible that is mostly glossed over on account of over-emphasis of its political agenda.[68] At any rate, even the poor and socially marginalized can be ideologues. It is reasonable, even desirable, to have a critical eye towards elitist ideology. But a wholesale dismissal of a literature because it is presumed to have come from the elite and is presumed to be elitist, without giving a serious analysis to the work in question is inapt. Ideological production has been the work of the educated and enlightened intellectuals. Karl Marx himself and most of the world's greatest minds came from the educated class. Paul Ricoeur attributes this to the human capacity for self-critique.[69]

Ricouer calls for an ideological analysis based on the projected social vision itself and not only on a presupposed materially determined ideology.[70] Aside from the capacity to rise above their self-interest, the scribes, who were indispensable part of the ancient states, were not members of the ruling elite. They were independent minded and more knowledgeable than the people they serve. They cannot be easily manipulated.[71]

Nor can the ideology of a particular group be simply dismissed. In the context of a collectivity, various groups even of opposing ideologies have valid claims in the overall scheme of things. As a text, the EP preserved a variety of views and ways of life anchored on their faith and transmitted it

---

[66] Brett, "Literacy and Domination," 124–25, 131–32. See Gary Herion, "The Role of Biblical Historiography in Biblical Thought: The Tendencies Underlying Old Testament Historiography," *JOST* 21 (1981): 25–57.

[67] Brett, "Literacy and Domination," 100. Chapman quotes Charles Altieri, *Canons and Consequences Reflections of the Ethical Force of Imaginative Ideals* (Evanston, IL: Northwestern University Press, 1990), 45.

[68] Smith, *Palestinian Parties and Politics*, and Coote and Coote, *Power, Politics, and the Making of the Bible*, are examples.

[69] Paul Ricouer, *Lectures on Ideology and Utopia* (New York: Columbia University Press, 1986), 313.

[70] Jonathan E. Dyck, "A Map of Ideology for Biblical Critics," in *Rethinking Contexts, Rereading Texts: Contributions from the Social Sciences to Biblical Interpretation*, ed. Daniel M. Carroll, JSOTSup 299 (Sheffield: Sheffield Academic, 2000), 122–24. See Ricouer, *Lectures on Ideology and Utopia*, 172–73.

[71] Davies, *Scribes and Schools*, 19.

to future generations of Jews.[72] The canonization, preservation, and transmission of EP, on the one hand, and its continuing relevance in the production and integration of a meaningful and workable order, on the other, is an argument for the validity of various ideologies. Transmission and canonization according to Phillip Davies provides a way of evaluating and distilling knowledge.[73]

Society and history distills knowledge. As an alternative to the conception of narrow class and ethnic interest, Chapman proposes an understanding of the Hebrew Bible towards the production of a "theological grammar" that sets forth ideals that "unsettled or even disconfirmed regnant ideologies."[74] Chapman deplores the seeming rejection, even smugness of biblical scholars that detect only "ideological" interest in the Hebrew Bible canon formation.[75] In the light of the comprehensive and translatable social vision of the EP, the critique that it is but a class ideology from some Western scholars fails to account for the dynamics of international and local politics in ancient Israel. The present biblical scholarship by virtue of the degree of education and required academic rigor can be categorized as a learned and comfortable class. Furthermore, it is dominated by Western, white, male scholars who are a part of dominant knowledge producers. It appears to be preoccupied by a drive to be objective and consistent. It rests on the argument that the interest of the dominant group was imposed on the EP—a reading which appears to critique but actually dominates the text.

The alleged ideological interest of the EP is refuted by its nature and content. The narrative transcends the ideological interests of the groups connected with producing it. In Duttman's words, the EP is "scandalously encompassing." This narrative presents differing voices and interests having legitimate claims in the over-all scheme of things as part of uniting Israel under Yahweh. The EP are resistance literature against dominant structures.[76] They are humanitarian in content. They critique both religious

---

[72] Polzin, *Deuteronomy, Joshua, Judges*, 26. Taking Deuteronomy as an example, Polzin notes the presence of "utterance within utterance within utterance within utterance," which results in "the deliberate representation in Deuteronomy of a vast number of intersecting statements, sometimes in agreement with one another, sometimes interfering with one another. This enables the books to be a repository of a plurality of viewpoints, all working together to achieve an effect on the reader that is multidimensional."
[73] Polzin, *Deuteronomy, Joshua, Judges*, 35.
[74] Chapman, *Law and the Prophets*, 97–98.
[75] Chapman, *Law and the Prophets*, 98–99.
[76] Richard Nelson, observing the "microredaction" present in Deuteronomy, attributed this to "dissident Jerusalem circle" in the time of Manasseh. This

and political establishments as they allow a dialogue among differing groups and interests. They are a humbled history that is critical of Israel's failures. Viewed in the context of the ancient Near East and internal Israelite politics, the EP's ideology gained ascendancy because the Israelite community owned it. It was not viewed as a representation of the narrow interest of the learned and comfortable. If ideological bias were to be ascertained, then EP were biased for Israel as it is a literary by-product of Israel.

Early Prophets as a Canonical Text

We have in the EP a canonical text. The EP's context, in addition to its composite nature and message as a whole, provides the parameters for interpretation. This narrative came out of a particular reality and serves a purpose that is linked to the interests of the people who produced it. It may not be taken as universally applicable. Chapman quotes Altieri to elucidate on the dynamics of particularity and the ways meaning transcends the canonical text such as the EP:

> the crucial enabling step is to insist on reading authors as I think most of them intended to be read: as agents constructing a version of experience with a claim to influence the ways generation of readers would view themselves and their world. This activity does not entail partly reading against historical specificity, so as to highlight those qualities of the work that transcend the conditions of the work's genesis. Highlighting transcendent qualities does not mean ignoring history, nor does it require denying the historical commitments of a given writer. We need the specificity of the work, need it to maintain an otherness with something different to say to us.[77]

There is a close link between historical particularity and transcendent meanings. From G. F. Snyman's view, context connects the text and its application. He quotes Edward Said, a Palestinian philosopher who said in defense of the Hebrew Bible that texts are often quoted apart from its function in its historical and social world.[78]

"underground reform theology" accordingly became the public policy favorable in the internal and international situation at the time of Josiah. See Richard Nelson, *Deuteronomy: A Commentary* (Louisville: John Knox, 2002), 8.

[77] Chapman, *Law and the Prophets*, 100. He quotes Altieri, *Canons and Consequences*, 45.

[78] Cited by G. F. Snyman, "Texts Are Fundamentally Facts of Power, Not of Democratic Exchange," in *Past, Present, Future: The Deuteronomistic History and the Prophets* ed. Johannes C. De Moor and Harry F. Van Rooy (Leiden: Brill, 2000), 279.

Preoccupation with the texts as support for presumed abstract truth paved the way for universal application. To the contrary, ancient Israel constructed its text for a particular purpose. While it is true that a text once inscribed acquires a life of its own, the language, symbols, and codes used anchor it in a life situation within which its function and meaning is interpreted. Imbedded in the text are the historical and cultural codes that serve as interpretation pointers. Such codes cannot be ignored. To disregard contextual meaning is to misinterpret the text. Snyman further quotes Edward Said insisting that textuality arises from concrete circumstances and "not anywhere at anytime."[79]

The context of EP has been exhaustively described in this work. The production, interpretation, transmission, and canonization were done in the context of domination. It is a text cherished by a weak and oppressed community so much so that Brueggemann characterized the Hebrew Bible message as social theodicy.[80]

Aside from anchoring the EP in a context of sociopolitical oppression and its composition as resistance texts against imperialism, it can be categorically stated that the EP was not composed as a tool for imperialism. In relation to northern Israel, EP's label for its program is "all Israel." It is based on historical identity that justifies an action by the remnant of the former nations to provide leadership and nurture hope of national reconstruction. It is remarkable in relation to imperialism that though Israel knew that Yahweh's actions in their behalf would have an effect on other nations, it barely dwells on it.[81] Judaism never became a missionary religion. This confirms the recognition of the particularity of Israel's social construction. The early prophetic history is Israel's literature not of other nations.

In addition to a solid contextual and canonical anchor as ground for the interpretation of the EP, Chapman's inquiry into canon is also relevant for interpretation:

> Canons are "entities" and, as such, additions to a given canon exhibit an "obligation" to interpret themselves in the light of the whole event even when they stand in tension with the received tradition ... this is especially

---

[79] See Edward Said, *The World, the Text, and the Critic* (Cambridge: Harvard University Press, 1983), 4.
[80] Walter Brueggemann, "Theodicy in a Social Dimension," in *Social-Scientific Old Testament Criticism: A Sheffield Reader*, ed. David Chalcraft (Sheffield: Sheffield Academic, 1997), 261.
[81] Noth, "Central Theological Ideas," 23; Noth, *Deuteronomistic History*, 136.

in the case of biblical canon, which has always been more of an "entity" than the sundry classics of the Western literary tradition.[82]

Chapman in short calls interpreters to "interpret the various parts of the biblical canon in the light of the whole."[83] To this I add the opinion of Levinson: "Properly understood, the canon is radically open. It invites innovation, it demands interpretation, it challenges piety, it questions priority, it sanctifies subversion, it warrants difference, and it embeds critique."[84] Along this line, Sanders observes that the canon is adaptable to different situations but its meaning is rooted in the community that produced it. Its meaning in a particular situation is related to the needs of the community which transmitted it.[85]

Isolating themes and interpreting the EP without taking into mind the differing perspectives represented by the whole work violates its essential composite and canonical nature.[86] Faithful interpretation of the EP takes into account particular themes and their function in the whole. In this respect, the prophetic and resistance meanings of the narrative and canon are significant.

What was canonized is not the writer's intention alone or a certain line of interpretation but the open-ended text. The text has enshrined inclusiveness and social justice as condition for the possession of the land. The land grant theme is pervaded with the warning of judgment. The text for the Jews spurred the process of establishing their identity and the values and norms of their community. It also guided them in marking the boundary of their community. It provided the community's thought categories and symbols that served as the building blocks for cultural cohesiveness and ethics. Diverse groups and peoples under the just rule of Yahweh made visible in the preservation of a faith and way of life that counters imperial impositions became the core of the prophetic history and way of life.

Pertaining to the EP, the canon functions to broaden but at the same time control the meaning of the text.[87] Canon necessitates hermeneutics to

---

[82] Chapman, *Law and the Prophets*, 105.
[83] Chapman, *Law and the Prophets*, 105.
[84] Bernard M. Levinson, "You Must Not Add Anything to What I Command You: Paradoxes of Canon and Authorship in Ancient Israel," *Numen* 50.1 (2003): 50.
[85] James A. Sanders, "Adaptable for Life: The Nature and Function of Canon," in *Magnalia Dei: The Mighty Acts of God; Essays on the Bible and Archeology in Memory of G. Ernest Wright*, ed. F. M. Cross, W. E. Lemke, and P. D. Miller (Garden City, NY: Doubleday, 197), 543–44. Sanders, *From Sacred Story to Sacred Text*, 23.
[86] Chapman, *Law and the Prophets*, 284.
[87] Edgar W. Conrad, "Changing Context: The Bible and the Study of Religion," in *Perspectives on Language and Text* Edgar, ed. W. Conrad and Edward G. Newing, (Winona Lake: Eisenbrauns, 1987), 396.

make it relevant. The canon generates hermeneutics and produces controlling texts. Consideration of the canonical function and purpose supports the interpretation of the EP as resistance literature. At the same time, canon rules out the "use of the text" in establishing hegemonic social control since it violates its canonical function in the critique of Israelite society and in resisting imperialism. Recognition of the resistance nature of the EP will serve to correct the over-emphasis on class and political factionalism as the main motivation for the textual production of the Hebrew Bible.

As a composite text, the EP functioned as resistance discourse in its emphases on Israel's worldview, culture, religion, political structure, and ethnicity. But it is not exclusive. It reflects the pluralism of the Hebrew canon as a whole.[88]

The recovery of the EP as resistance text is anchored in its historical or contextual function. This marshals interpretation towards resistance. The EP cannot be interpreted out of its context.[89] The context functions as a forensic lens that exposes ideologies in the text. Ideological interests linked with broad coalition of Yahwists, prophets, nationalists, resisters, and survivalist groups have surfaced in social-scientific studies on the EP. Putting all these together lead to a more holistic perspective and application of meaning.

With its acute experience of colonization, Israel's traditionists appear to have come to the insight that knowledge is intimately connected with the operation of power. Power works through language, literature, and culture. It is made effective by the institutions and structures of coercion that regulate daily lives. Hence, the EP put together a literary work that unifies the various groups of the Israelite society, and canonized it.[90]

Emerging in a world where texts were produced for hegemonic legitimation, Israel produced a collective text displaying similarities with those of its neighbors and colonizers but appropriated for Israel's purposes. Further, Israel developed mechanisms through which the rights of the different groups within the community might be safeguarded by bringing them into dialogue not only among themselves but with the obtaining history. The canon presumes the coherence of the text, encompasses dialogue and consensus within the community, and connects the text with the past and existing reality. Canonical reading requires faithfulness to the diversity of the text, to the contexts of interpretation, and to the liberating purpose of the text whether it be for the Jews or other oppressed communities. The

---

[88] Sanders, *From Sacred Story to Sacred* Text, 30.
[89] Gottwald, *Hebrew Bible in Its Social World and Ours*, 191.
[90] Gottwald, *Hebrew Bible in Its Social World and Ours*, 192.

text was communally owned, canonized, and transmitted to sustain its idea of an alternative society in the context of death-dealing domination.

The prophetic interpretation of Israel's history insists on the liberative activity of God in relation to a collectivity called Israel in time and space. The inseparable human and divine dimensions in history as witnessed by the EP served as a paradigm of how faith in God can be the source of identity and way of redefining reality that will resist the dominant materialistic culture, towards sustaining a life-affirming communal life among diverse communities.[91]

The social reality pervasively felt within and without Israel was the death-dealing imperial drive that squeezes surplus from peripheral societies and the vulnerable in the society, in favor of the center.[92] The ancient world's tributary form of production extracted surplus from the villages. It was the result of domination by powerful nations over smaller nations such as Judah and Israel in Canaan. Locally, colonial officials and collaborators profited from the impoverishment of the peasants as they forcibly imposed levies and were only too happy to grant high interests loans indenturing land and services to their advantages. Prophetic oracles attest to the deprivation, poverty, loss of land, and slavery that resulted from power asymmetry.[93]

Having stated the resistance function of the EP in the context of its main composition and the succeeding reception and transmission, the imperial origin and function of the conquest rhetoric in Joshua must also be unmasked. Assyria asserted its claims on the land of Canaan invoking that the supremacy and power of Ashur as the one who grants lands, manifest in actual military victory. Israel invalidated this claim by a counter assertion that Israel's God had secured the land of Canaan for Israel, pointing to the failure of Assyria to conquer Jerusalem. Subsequently, prophetic history justified defeat and exile by the Sumerian ideology of national God abandonment on account of its failure to keep its covenant obligation to its sole God as a suzerain. Current imperialist readings of the EP appear to have tapped to the original imperial location and function of the text. Analysis of the context, however, reveals the tenacity of the producers of the text in talking back to the empire using its language. In itself it is a courageous stand. In the EP, Israel dared to name itself as Israel with an identity, historical memory, independent polity, social aspirations, and territory.

Israel's narrative unmasks the ideology and mechanisms of coercion employed by Assyria. The EP address the impacts of imperial pressure upon

---

[91] Gottwald, *Hebrew Bible in Its Social World and Ours*, 184.
[92] Joseph Blenkinsopp, *Prophecy and Canon: A Contribution to the Study of Jewish Origins* (Notre Dame: University of Notre Dame Press, 1986), 147–48.
[93] Gottwald, *Hebrew Bible in Its Social World and Ours*, 351, 354–55.

peripheral societies. Literature production, along with other societal measures, sustained and ensured ancient Israel's survival. This is linked with the prominence of war in the EP.[94] But we must be mindful that prophetic militancy is a reaction against domination.[95] The purpose of creating unity to ensure survival in a life and death situation cannot be overlooked. The prophetic literature cannot be used to support dominance.

---

[94] Hobbs, *Time for War*, 197.
[95] Hobbs for instance says, "The answer, we suggest, is to be seen in the context of the same pressures for unity and a unified image of the past which emerge from our understanding of the military history aspects of the book of Joshua, namely the monarchy. Such dynamics are the products of an 'imperialistic ideology', which is basically religious in character." Hobbs, *Time for War*, 207.

6.

JOSHUA 1:1-9: LITERARY AND RHETORICAL OBSERVATIONS

Joshua is scripture for ancient Israel, part of a body of literature that empowered resistance against imperial drive. Written in Hebrew and containing concepts familiar to the people, the literature is a part of a national narrative that shaped the thought and way of life of Israel apart from imperial impositions. The book of Joshua, particularly Josh 1:1-9, has been employed to justify imperial expansion by the modern state of Israel and the Christian West. Interpreting Josh 1:1-9 in its context will lay the groundwork for the appropriation of the resistance meaning and function of this text in a receptor's context.

The Book of Joshua

Joshua points to the fulfillment of the covenant promise of land and nationhood (Gen 12:1-2, 7). It is the climax of the story from Gen 12 to Deuteronomy (Exod 3:8; Deut 6:23). Deuteronomy anticipates Joshua, as Moses the exodus leader and lawgiver passed his responsibilities to his successor Joshua (Deut 31:23; 34:9).

The dominant image of Joshua being Moses's successor is that of a prophet. Joshua's predecessor was the prophet par excellence. As a prophet, Joshua's primary task is to enforce the covenant (6:30-35; 24:1-27). In Pseudo-Philo Joshua is an ideal prophetic successor of Moses as well as a good warrior.[1] The prophetic image is merged with that of good ruler.[2] But the royal image in Joshua departs from the ancient Near Eastern kingship tradition. From being a warrior and vicar of God, the king becomes a covenant mediator.[3] The king is an example of obedience to Yahweh.[4]

---

[1] E. Noort, "Joshua of Reception and Hermeneutics," in *Past, Present, Future: The Deuteronomistic History and the Prophets* (Leiden: Brill, 2000), 204.
[2] J. Roy Porter, "The Succession of Joshua," in Knoppers and McConville, *Reconsidering Judah and Israel*, 162.
[3] See also H. Schiffman, *Texts and Traditions: A Source Reader for the Study of Second Temple Judaism* (Hoboken, NJ: Ktav, 1998), 39.
[4] Gerrald Eddie Gerbrandt, *Kingship according to the Deuteronomistic History* (Atlanta: Scholars Press, 1979), 190.

As the leader is a prophet, the book of Joshua presents history as the fulfillment of God's word proclaimed by the prophets. The book affirms Yahweh's sovereignty,[5] and the book must be understood as a voice that advocates the social ideals of the prophets.[6]

Taking these concepts in the context of the ancient Near East, the accounts in Joshua serve as a foil against Assyria's claim over the land and military drive to subjugate the people of Israel.[7] The empire is an agent of chaos that Israel fights. Yahweh overcame chaos in the crossing of the Sea of Reeds,[8] and the divine warrior is with Israel still. The call to arms is issued. The Jordan river gives way and the commander of the Lord's army appears (Josh 6:13-15). A new people who successfully establishes Yahweh's rule in the land is created.

Analyzing the book as literature, the distinction between "reporting speech and reported speech" can be observed.[9] Deuteronomy is reported speech and Joshua to 2 Kings is a narrative report. Supposedly the narrative report confirms reported speech, but in many instances the latter overrides the former.[10] This is a strategy of bringing into dialogue existing norms with lived experience. The literary context of Joshua anchors the meaning of narratives in its cultural and sociopolitical setting.[11] Its nature and content hint at its interpretation. In the book, Israel's history is constructed from idealized historical past that projects unity and common identity. Though Joshua presupposes Deuteronomy, the commands such as those about treaty and annihilation of the inhabitants were not interpreted legalistically. Thus the command for annihilation must be taken as a metaphor against assimilation, in consonance with the very strong condemnation of treaties especially with powerful kings.[12] In Joshua the command to annihilate the

---

[5] Deist, *Material Culture of the Bible*, 181–82.
[6] Blenkinsopp, *Prophecy and Canon*, 147. See also Gottwald, *Hebrew Bible in Its Social World and Ours*, 356–57.
[7] McConville, *God and Earthly Powers*, 26.
[8] A body of water that is the image of the primordial chaos in creation again stands between God's people and the promised land.
[9] Polzin, *Deuteronomy, Joshua, Judges*, 19.
[10] Polzin, *Deuteronomy, Joshua, Judges*, 22.
[11] Deist, *Material Culture of the Bible*, 112–13.
[12] Gordon Mitchell states, "The narrative and poetic world picture, interpret and explain the world people live in with reference to the implied linguistic categories, logical links, metaphors, cosmological orientation, social values, religious convictions, political, social and economic preferences. To understand the world presented in language necessitates an intimate knowledge of the categories, values, convictions, orientations and preferences of the relevant culture." Gordon Mitchell, *Together in the Land: A Reading of the Book of Joshua* (Sheffield: JSOT, 1993), 190.

inhabitants of Canaan is interpreted in a nonliteral way. Lived reality is given priority over stated norms. Exceptions to the law on ban are recounted. This supports a nonmilitaristic reading of Joshua. At the same time the stress on the law points to militancy based on the law. It is the observance of the law that will establish Israel in the land, not military superiority. But law interpretation in Joshua is flexible. Joshua appears to present alternatives in dealing with insiders who act like outsiders: driving them away or making them a part of the community through covenant, for those who will oppose them and those among them who will lead the people astray—annihilation as the story of Achan illustrates.

Attention to rhetoric is important in reading Joshua as literature. Repetition of words and phrases suggest thematic significance. The repetitions of "servant of the Lord"/"my servant," "be strong and be of good courage," and "being careful to act in accordance with all the law" are significant for understanding Joshua. The same is true when a designation or label is attached to a person.[13] In verse 1, Joshua is called Moses's assistant, the first of the divinely inspired liberators.[14]

Applying the dialogue of ideals and lived reality found in the book, the promise of land is affirmed by divine speech and the book narrates its fulfillment. God's actions are seen in miracles: the fear of the Canaanites, the successful Jordan crossing, the fall of Jericho, the sun standing still, and the victory of the Israelites. The Israelites were established in the land, but the book also portrays Joshua and the Israelites to have violated the expressed commands not to make any treaty with the inhabitants of the land and to exterminate Canaanites. Rahab the prostitute's confession of faith in Yahweh and aid to the spies show her to be a believer of Yahweh and therefore an insider. The accounts justify a treaty by deception by the Gibeonites (2:8–14; 9:27). They cannot be exterminated. The solemn nature of an agreement made in the name of Yahweh made the treaties inviolable. Though Joshua has established Israel in the land, yet there still are lands to be occupied (13:1–6). While Joshua obeyed the command to exterminate everyone (Josh 10:28, 30, 32, 33, 34, 37, 38, 40; 11:11, 12), many Canaanites remained in the land (13:13; 15:15). Yet the wars of conquest have ended and the fighters from the two and a half tribes settled east of Jordan were allowed to go home. In the farewell address (23:5), Joshua affirms the fear-inspiring act of Yahweh. Yahweh has driven powerful nations before Israel, and will drive away the remaining inhabitants from the land. The book of Joshua affirms seemingly contradictory claims: the extermination of the inhabitants of the land, on one hand, and, on the other, the existence of Canaanites whom Israel are bound to protect by treaties. Contradictory tra-

---

[13] Mitchell, *Together in the Land*, 180.
[14] Mitchell, *Together in the Land*, 180–81.

ditions are in dialogue in Joshua. In the final chapter the covenant making ceremony resolve the issue as the Israelites who were portrayed to be Canaanites had chosen to serve Yahweh alone in Josh 24. Reality is messy, defying neat categorization.

The narratives mimic imperial violence.[15] But in doing so, they open imperial ideology to critique and expose the violence of the empire. The conquest account in Joshua depicts violence as colonial nonsense. A people cannot just be exterminated. Violence cannot win. An alternative occupation account is presented in the book of Judges. Still, each of the battles in Joshua are premised on the formation of powerful Canaanite coalitions that Israel had to contend with (10:5; 11:5). The stories of violent conquest are best understood as metaphor against syncretistic Israelite religion, depiction of colonial nonsense and mimic, or defensive propaganda when the survival of Israel is at stake.[16] Serving as foil to literal understanding of the conquest that follow are the stories of the defection by Rahab, treaty-making with the Gibeonites, and the conquest of Jericho. The conquest of Jericho calls for a critical reading of the conquest stories. Jericho was demolished by ruckus making.

The tribal land allotments ground each of the twelve tribes in the land as a grant from Yahweh. In the book of Joshua, the foundational practices of Israel's life as a covenant community was established. Israel has common ethnicity, bound together by historical memory, and united by a covenant with Yahweh. Though Joshua projects land claim, ethnicity, common way of life and worship as elements of Israel's developing identity, their relationship with Yahweh stands out as the defining identity marker in Joshua (Josh 2:8–14; 6:25; 24).[17]

---

[15] Bhabha says of mimicry, "It is a form of colonial discourse that is uttered inter dicta: a discourse at the crossroads of what is known and permissible and that which though known must be kept concealed; a discourse uttered between the lines and as such both against the rules and within them." See Bhabha, *Location of Culture*, 89.

[16] Bernard M. Levinson, *Deuteronomy and the Hermeneutics of Legal Innovation* (Oxford: Oxford University Press, 1997), 149.

[17] This is attested by the prominence of the covenant concept in the DH, the prophets, and the Old Testament as a whole. Israel's consciousness of being a covenant people is self-evident. Hawk asserts, "However, many aspects of the book subvert these assertions and thus prohibit the reader for viewing ethnic purity, correct practice, or possession of land as essential marks of Israelite identity.... As a whole, Joshua thus has the remarkable effect of illustrating the relative character of a national identity, founded on territorial claims, kinship bonds, or proper religious practices. The essence of Israel's identity, we learn in the final, climactic episode, is rather YHWH's exclusive choosing of Israel and Israel's exclusive choosing of YHWH

Affinity and dissimilarity with the former Canaanites are stressed with regards to the people that constitute Israel.[18] The strongest censure is directed towards the dominant Canaanite culture finding its most virulent expression in the call to Holy War. The same stance is directed to insiders who act as outsiders (like Achan). The conquest may be understood as cultural repudiation of the imperialist ways and values.[19] As a people's literature Joshua is a powerful narrative against imperial ideology.[20]

Joshua affirms the social and cultural values of Israel. Strongly expressed polemics against powerful foreign nations and their way of life may be taken as geographic claims and anti-imperial rhetoric using irony and hyperbole.[21] Israel counts itself as a nation among other nations. By all means Israel must resist colonization. In this regard, the king is entrusted with the responsibility to make the covenant effective. The worship of Yahweh and egalitarianism are to be the norm in Israel. Israel is bound to Yahweh by an exclusive inviolable covenant relationship that is the central assertion of the stories. Israel's main obligation is to always choose Yahweh.[22]

Following Joshua and the stress on the unity and obedience of all Israel is the book of Judges. Judges presents Israel as disparate tribes loosely bound by a covenant with Yahweh. It projects a common expectation of mutual help in times of war. It stresses loyalty to Yahweh and ethics based on brotherhood (1:3; 5:14–18; 8:1; 10:17–18; 14:3; 19:18–20, 30; 20:21). In contrast with the book of Joshua, Judges depicts a time when Israel had no leaders and "everyone did what was right in their own eyes" (Judg 21:25). In times of crisis, leadership is conferred to someone who has recognized charisma (Deborah, Jephthah, Othniel, Ehud, Samson). Under good leaders the law was observed and the people prospered. Conversely, Israel suffered under bad leaders as the law was ignored.

Israel is presented as having been through repeated cycles of disobedience, oppression, and liberation. Under the rule of God-anointed liberators, the people unite and are victorious over their enemies. The law is observed

---

(cf. 24:2–15). In the end we discover that Israel is a people defined by decisions in the reciprocal choosing of YHWH and the nation." L. Daniel Hawk, *Berit Olam Studies in Hebrew Narrative and Poetry*, ed. David W. Cotter (Collegeville, MI: Liturgical Press, 2000), xxxi, xxxiii.
[18] Lucien Legrand, *The Bible on Culture: Belonging or Dissenting* (New York: Orbis Books, 2000), 6.
[19] Lori Rowlett, "Inclusion, Exclusion, and Marginality in the Book of Joshua," *JSOT* 55 (1992): 14–23.
[20] Hawk, *Berit Olam Studies in Hebrew Narrative and Poetry*, xxxii.
[21] David M. Gunn, "Joshua and Judges," in *The Literary Guide to the Bible*, ed. Robert Alter and Frank Kermode (Cambridge: Harvard University Press, 1987), 108.
[22] Gunn, "Joshua and Judges," 108.

when there is a leader. But the tribes go their own way in the absence of a leader and the nations around dominate them. Towards the end of the book, the tribes had to resort to war against their own—the tribe of Benjamin—when the tribe refused to comply with the norms. Judges is an argument for the need for good and strong prophetic leadership. It is not religious sins which are illustrated in Judges. Prominent stories such as the story of Abimelech (9:1–57) critiques royal presumptions. The story of Samson censures intermarriage (13:1–16:31). The story of Micah (17:1–18:31) illustrates folly in casting and adopting an idol. The last story (Judg 19–21) is a story of covenant violation and war among the tribes that undermined the twelve tribes' unity and strength.

Israel's subsequent history as narrated in the books of Samuel and Kings reinforce the themes in Joshua. Israel and Judah under bad leaders fail in their covenant obligations and eventually split. They suffer defeat and destruction in the hands of their enemies. United under prophet-leaders, Israel observes the law, occupies the land, and prospers. The EP teaches unity under the rule of Yahweh through observance of the law as a way of resisting foreign claims of power over Israel and over its land. In unity under the law, Israel stands strong. As idealized history, the book of Joshua gives a picture of unity and strength.

Textual Variants and Translation of Joshua 1:1–9

Textual studies of the Joshua manuscripts essentially affirm the integrity of the Masoretic texts that served as the basis for translations. The translation below notes the ranges of readings by the transmitters of the text. Some important manuscripts referred to are: the Septuagint (LXX; i.e., Old Greek, OG), which dates to 300–170 BCE;[23] Aquila (A), whose Greek translation of the Old Testament is dated around the time of the Council of Jamnia (90 CE);[24] Theodotion (Th), a revision of an earlier work dating from early first century BCE, done in the second half of the second century CE;[25] the Peshitta, the Syriac Old Testament which may have come from the latter half of

---

[23] Sidney Jellicoe, *The Septuagint and Modern Study* (Oxford: Clarendon, 1968), 49, 69. Nina Collins in an exhaustive study of the Greek translation argues that the translation was done much earlier in 281 BCE. See Nina Collins, "The Year of the Translation of the Pentateuch into Greek under Ptolemy II," in *LXX: Septuagint, Scrolls, and Cognate Writings*, ed. George J. Broke and Barnabas Lindars (Atlanta: Scholars Press, 1992), 403–503.

[24] Jellicoe, *Septuagint and Modern Study*, 82.

[25] Jellicoe, *Septuagint and Modern Study*, 83.

the first century CE;[26] Origen's *Hexapla* (OH; ca. 203-254 CE); and the Masoretic Texts (MT), the basis of the *Biblica Hebraica Stuttgartensia*.[27] Emanuel Tov states that textual evidence points to expansions that must be seen as additions in these manuscripts.[28] He traces some of the Masoretic additions in Josh 1:1-9 to Deuteronomic influence. A working translation of the text follows:

> 1. After the death of Moses the servant of the LORD, the LORD spoke to Joshua son of Nun,[29] Moses' assistant saying, 2. "Moses my servant is dead. [30] Now, Arise! Cross this Jordan.[31] You and all these people, to the land that

---

[26] Jellicoe, *Septuagint and Modern Study*, 247. See J. Cook, "Composition of the Peshitta Version of the Old Testament (Pentateuch)," in *The Peshitta: Its Early Text and History; Papers read at the Peshitta Symposium Held at Leiden 30-31 August 1985*, ed. P. B. Dirksen and M. J. Muller (Leiden: Brill, 1988), 152.

[27] See Page H. Kelly, Daniel S. Mynatt, and Timothy G. Crawford, *The Masorah of Biblia Hebraica Stuttgartensia* (Cambridge: Eerdmans, 1998). See Paul Sanders, "Missing Link in Hebrew Bible Formation," *BAR* 41.6 (2015): 46-52.

[28] Emanuel Tov, *Textual Criticism of the Hebrew Bible* (Minneapolis: Fortress, 1992), 328.

[29] According to Greenspoon, the clause ויאמר יהוה אל יהושע ("'[and] the Lord spoke to Joshua") occurs eleven times in Joshua. The presence and absence of the Hebrew *waw* and its equivalent *kai* ("and") in Greek is attested by almost the same number of texts. See Leonard Greenspoon, *Textual Studies in the Book of Joshua*, HSM 2 (Chico, CA: Scholars Press, 1983). It is also attested in the Peshitta and Vulgate. The reading with *waw* according to Erbes "softens the force of imperatives." See Johann E. Erbes, *The Peshitta and the Versions: A Study of the Peshitta Variants in Joshua 1-5 in Relation to Their Equivalents in the Ancient Versions* (Uppsala: Uppsala University, 1999), 63-64.

[30] Deuteronomic additions describe Moses as "the servant of the Lord" and adds "all teaching" in verse 7. The absence of the phrase "servant of the Lord" in verse 1 is observed by Erbes in some manuscripts in LXX. Indications point to the presence of shorter textual source(s) now lost. There are evident efforts to correct certain texts towards the longer version reflected in Bibles today. The phrase occurs eighteen times, of which fourteen are in Joshua. Textual variants from the Masoretic Texts use "my servant" or the majority "servant of God." Tov, *Textual Criticism of the Hebrew Bible*, 394. While Erbes cites Orlinsky and Greenspoon postulating that the phrase may not have been a part of the Hebrew manuscript (*Vorlage* or G*) used by the translators to Syriac or Greek, he proposes that the *Vorlage* text reflects the longer text as an explanatory in relation to Deut 34:5. Such explanation in his opinion was later integrated into the text. See Greenspoon, *Textual Studies in the Book of Joshua*, 89.

[31] The variant reading which omits "this" (הזה) before Jordan is found in OG and Coptic manuscripts. Erbes attributes the omission to the fact that the demonstrative is not absolutely necessary in the passage. הזה in MT is translated τουτον in Th, and לבני ישראל translated τοις υιοις ισραελ. In verse 3 MT לכם ("to you," masculine plural)

116 | A Filipino Resistance Reading

I am giving them, to the sons of Israel. 3. Every place which the sole of your feet tread,[32] I will give to you, as I have said to Moses. 4. From the wilderness and this Lebanon,[33] until the great river Euphrates, the whole land of the Hittites until the Great Sea where the sun goes down, shall be your borders. 5. No man will be able to stand against you all the days of your life, as I was with Moses, I will be with you, I will not fail you or forsake you. 6. Be strong, be courageous so that you will cause this people to inherit the land which I have sworn to give them.[34] 7. Only be strong and be very

---

is translated in Th as επ αυτου, which is observed in subsequent manuscripts as επ αυτον, επ αυτω, επ αυτην. This attests to Jewish collective reading—Israel as a collective attested both as masculine and feminine. Tov ascertains הזה as MT substantiation for the word Jordan in the OG. The same was also done in verse 4, so that the end product becomes "this Lebanon." He clarifies that these small supplementations were meant to elucidate. The Peshitta and MT has "arise!"; variant readings that do not have "arise" point to the fact that the word is presumed in the command to cross. Erbes, *Peshitta and the Versions*, 62–65; Greenspoon, *Textual Studies in the Book of Joshua*, 117; Tov, *Textual Criticism of the Hebrew Bible*, 391.

[32] The phrase כל-מקום in verse 3 is accordingly best translated "every place" as opposed to "the entire place," noting that every place is more encompassing than the entire place. The translation "your foot," as opposed to variant plural "your/their feet," is attested by the Peshitta and Masoretic texts. Erbes argues that the meaning of either the plural or singular form is the same. The LXX has the second person plural suffix "to you" as do the MT. Greenspoon states that it is common occurrence, though he believes that the singular second person suffix is more accurate as the text depicts God's instruction to Joshua. He attributes this to Deuteronomic influence. The plural rendering points to Israel as a collective. The same instance is observed in verses 4 and 8. Erbes, *Peshitta and the Versions*, 62–63, 66, 68, 123; Greenspoon, *Textual Studies in the Book of Joshua*, 70.

[33] Erbes comments that "this" in "this Lebanon" is redundant and can be removed. Shifts from second to third, singular to plural of the second person "your," and the plural form referring to the borders are accordingly to be expected. Erbes considered "for you" (plural) in some manuscripts as redundant. Erbes, *Peshitta and the Versions*, 81–85.

[34] The Hebrew תנחיל in MT (verse 6 translated "you will cause to inherit") is translated διελιες by Th., αποδιαστελεις in a group of manuscripts called N, while other manuscripts have διαστελεις and αποδιαστελεις διαμειρεις. Greenspoon notes that the most attested reading (αποδιαστέλλω) is found only in this verse and in 2 Macc 6:5, while διαιρω occurs forty times in LXX including three times in Joshua (18:4, 5; 22:8). He concludes that Th's διελιες reflect the OG. Αποδιαστέλλω expresses the forceful causative meaning of *hiphil* imperative. The translation of the instruction "be strong and be manly" (ανδριζου) (6, 7, 9) is in line with militaristic understanding of the passage. Ανδριζου connects חזק (be strong) with masculinity. Erbes, *Peshitta and the Versions*, 68, 70, 81, 83–85, 87–88; Greenspoon, *Textual Studies in the Book of Joshua*,

courageous by observing and doing according to all the law which you have been commanded by Moses my servant. Do not turn from it to the right or to the left so that you will be wise in all that you will do/in all your ways.³⁵ 8. This book of law³⁶ shall not depart from your mouth, and you shall recite it day and night so that you will keep doing according to all that is written in it in all your ways. Then your way will be prosperous and you will be wise. ³⁷ 9. Have I not commanded you be strong and be resolute do not be afraid nor be discouraged, for the LORD your God³⁸ is with you in all your endeavors.

The translation above establishes the integrity of Josh 1:1–9. Israel as a collective is prominent in the variant readings. The supplementation "the servant of the Lord" (v. 1) affirms the Deuteronomistic emphasis on obedience to the law and prophetic leadership. The Hebrew word הזה (this) anchors the reading of Joshua to concrete and present reality: this Jordan, this people, this book of law. The variant "your foot/feet"/"their feet" point to the interpretation of the pronominal suffixes to that of Joshua and the Israelite's feet. An attempt at gender inclusivity of the entity Israel has even

---

38, 123; 81; Tov, *Textual Criticism of the Hebrew Bible*, 390. See also A. Graeme Auld, *Joshua: Jesus Son of Naue in Codex Vaticanus* (Leiden: Brill, 2005).

³⁵ Speculating on the reason for the "incongruity" of ממנו meaning feminine singular ככל-התורה, Van der Meer suggests the shift from portraying Joshua as a military leader to a student and observer of the Torah. See Michäel van Deer Meer, "Textual Criticism and Literary Criticism in Joshua 1–7," in *X Congress of International Organization for Septuagint and Cognate Studies Oslo, 1998,* ed. Bernard A. Taylor (Atlanta: Society of Biblical Literature, 2001), 366–67. The shorter Septuagint and Peshitta differ from MT in verse 7: Peshitta and LXX: "Only be strong and be courageous, by observing and doing according to all the law which you have been commanded by Moses my servant. Do not turn from him to the right or to the left, so that you may prosper wherever you go." MT: "Only be strong and be very courageous, to keep and to do all the law which Moses my servant commanded you. Do not turn from them [law is feminine singular] to the right or to the left, so that you may prosper wherever you go."

³⁶ The nonagreement between הזה modifying התורה results in variant translations: Peshitta follows the MT ("this book of the law") whereas LXX translates "the book of this law" and other manuscripts smooth the translation from Hebrew with "the book of the law." In the same manner the ambiguous *waw* is reflected in the Greek translations. The Septuagint simply translates *waw* as conjunctive, but Erbes suggests a disjunctive reading following the Peshitta and Vulgate. Thus והגית is translated "but you shall recite it." See Erbes, *Peshitta and the Versions*, 89–91.

³⁷ Erbes, *Peshitta and the Versions*, 94. In verse 8, the persons vary from the first person ("I will make your way successful"; Syriac Hexapla), to second person ("you will prosper," and third "then he will prosper" or the mixed "I will make your way successful."

³⁸ Erbes, *Peshitta and the Versions*, 98. Some manuscripts omit "your God" אלהיך.

been attested in a variant reading (v. 3). The emphasis on the law and the land being feminine preclude an exclusively masculine reading of the text. The strength and courage enjoined in Josh 1:1–9 takes feminine forms of resistance. It requires cunning and thought (חישׂכיל) a result of study and meditation on the law (feminine) day and night. It is not dominating and does not capitalize on superior strength. But Greek translation of "be courageous" to Ανδριζου directs interpretation towards androcentricism that is being manly or masculine—a quality valued by imperial states. Yet the call to strength and courage emphasized in the text has been directed to the careful observance of the law. In this context the law is understood as covenant faithfulness in upholding Israel's communal aspirations for a just society under the rule of Yahweh.

Redaction, Literary, and Rhetorical Observations

Below is a proposed reconstruction of the editorial layering (three layers) of the passage:[39]

> An existing shorter conquest narrative (1:1–2, 9a);
> Preexilic Deuteronomistic composition (1:3–6) added to the existing material;
> Exilic/Secondary Deuteronomistic addition (1:7–9b) added to preexisting verses 1–6, 9a.

Rudolf Smend comments on the way the text has been redacted: "we have two distinct stages of interpretation of the original Deuteronomistic text before us, of which the second rested on the first and then carried it further." The secondary writer according to Smend recognized the inserts to the original text, but this did not deter that redactor from "repeating the words that had constituted the starting point of the additions once again at the end (v.9)."[40] The result is a strong emphasis on the book of law.[41]

The focus of Josh 1:1–6 is the land. Verse 5 stresses the military image of Joshua infusing the previous verses with the divine warrior theme.[42] It presupposes a Holy War concept. Verse 6 stands on its own and appears redundant after verses 1–5. Parallel ancient Near Eastern sources (cited

---

[39] This analysis follows Frank Moore Cross claim of a preexilic composition and exilic redaction presupposing preexisting sources.
[40] Smend, "Law and the Nations," 97–98.
[41] Smend, "Law and the Nations," 97–98.
[42] Sa-Moon Kang proposes that the concept of divine wars was formulated in Israel at the time of David and Solomon. See Sa-Moon Kang, *Divine War in the Old Testament and in the Ancient Near East* (Berlin: de Gruyter, 1989), 224.

below) are dated to the eighth century BCE onwards. Lohfink detects an installation formula composed of an encouragement (1:6a), a description of the task at hand (1:6b), and the promise of support (1:9b).[43] The phrase "be strong and be courageous" has elements of the "divine warrior" formula used to address a warrior leader in a battle. The warrior is to be "strong and be courageous" as a representative of the "divine warrior" who fights Israel's battle.[44]

Neo-Assyrian royal inscriptions trumpeted the ideology that Ashur secures Assyrian victory in battles. Conversely the defeat of Assyrian enemies is explained by divine abandonment. This connects with the ideology of expansion in the service of the deity. Such concept stands in continuity with the concept of the imperial god/gods in ancient Near East milieu. The deities are portrayed as having encouraged the invasion of other lands and peoples. The literary parallels point to a shared concept of God who is with his chosen king and secures his victory. Israel shared the tradition of divine war with the ancient Near Eastern nations.[45] Ancient Near Eastern societies waged their wars as holy endeavors in the service of the deity.[46] Perceived as a warrior, the deity goes to battle and defeats the enemy.[47] As Ashur and other deities sanction battles and encourage the king as agent of his will, Yahweh encourages Joshua and assures him of divine protection in his fight against the empire. Joshua thus appropriates the imperial conquest ideology.[48]

Roy G. Porter calls attention to the presence of a double installation formula in Josh 1:1-9: of Yahweh and of Moses. Behind the formula is the ideology that the king is divinely chosen, which is an important part of the installation ceremony.[49] Particular to Israelite ceremony, the king is bound to keep the law and is admonished that his success is dependent in doing so. Noting that Josh 1:7-9 parallels the injunctions to a king in Deut 17:18-20, and in royal succession narratives in the books of Kings and Chronicles, Porter concludes that the transfer of leadership from Moses to Joshua is to be understood in royal terms.[50] Hence he concludes that "Moses and Joshua

---

[43] Cited by Chapman, *Law and the Prophets*, 171.
[44] Conrad, *Fear Not Warrior*, 24, 25.
[45] Kang, *Divine War*, 224.
[46] Roland de Vaux, *Ancient Israel*, vol. 1 (Cambridge: Harvard University Press, 1961), 257.
[47] James B. Pritchard ed., *Ancient Near East Text Relating to the Old Testament* (Princeton: Princeton University Press, 1955), 267.
[48] George W. Coats, "An Exposition of the Conquest Theme," *CBQ* 47 (1985): 48.
[49] Porter, "Succession of Joshua," 160.
[50] Porter, "Succession of Joshua," 143-47. Porter takes the word *hazeh* as a hint in that an actual copy of the law book, which he presumes to be the Deuteronomic law, is handed over to the king.

are depicted as prototypes of Israelite King."⁵¹ Linking the tradition to ancient Near Eastern succession, Joshua is projected as the rightful successor to whom obedience is due. Yet Porter also notes that Joshua acted as covenant mediator in Josh 24 with Joshua's family as an example of being in covenant relationship with Yahweh. Further, the king as a warrior is not pivotal for success of Israel's war. Millard Lind says that the course of wars in the ancient Near East is determined by the state and military, but Israel rejected such in favor of the prophetic word, which was closely related to the office of Moses.⁵²

God as a warrior is prominent in many Hebrew Bible passages, for example, Exod 15:1–18, Ps 18, and Ps 24. However, verse 6 emphasizes the giving of the land theme in the use of the word נחל (*nachal*, hiphil) as opposed to the word ירש (*yaras*, to possess as in Josh 1:11, 15; 12:1;13:1; 23:5), which points to military conquest as the manner of possession.⁵³ The stress in verses 1–5 is on Yahweh's act of giving. The divine warrior theme in verses 1–5 is minimized in verse 6 in the use of *nachal* (נחל, to divide, allot, inherit).

The verses supplied by the Deuteronomic redactor (vv. 5, 6) assume the superiority of Yahweh's power. No one can withstand the divine warrior. Presupposing the source text (vvs. 1–2) as a production of the David or Solomon's court, Josh 1:1–5 speaks from a position of power. The moderation of military motif is seen in the following verses (vv. 6–9).

The law emphasis in verses 7–9a supersedes the military image in the preceding verses. This shift comes from a secondary redactor.⁵⁴ The motif of war connected with the encouragement (Deut 1:28; 31:17) was downplayed and replaced with law emphasis.⁵⁵ To the installation formula (1:1–6) was interjected emphasis on the law (vv. 7–9a) as a task of the leader.⁵⁶ In effect, military conquest was disconnected with the giving of land theme. Instead, land possession is made dependent on law observance. While verse 5 mentions that no one will be able to stand up against Joshua, no military

---

⁵¹ Porter, "Succession of Joshua," 158. See 1 Kgs 2:1ff; 1 Chr 22:6ff; 28:7ff.
⁵² Lind, *Yahweh Is a Warrior*, 167.
⁵³ Norbert Lohfink, "Yaras," *TDOT* 6:383–84.
⁵⁴ Noth attributes this to a later author. Noth, *Deuteronomistic History*, 36 n. 4.
⁵⁵ E. Axel Knauf, "Why Joshua," in Edelman, *Deuteronomy–Kings as Emerging Authoritative Books*, 80. Knauf states in a footnote, "In Exodus 17, Joshua enters the stage as a warrior, but at the end of the scene he is promoted to prophetic assistant (or apprentice) and given the word of God to commemorate."
⁵⁶ Rudolf Smend, "Das Gesetz und die Völker: Ein Beitrg zur deuteronomistischen Redakti-onsgeschichte," in *Probleme biblischer Theologie: Gerhard von Rad zum 70. Geburtstag*. Edited by Hans Walter Wolff (Munich: Kaiser, 1971), 494–509, as cited by Chapman, *Law and the Prophets*, 171–72.

term is used in the rest of the passage. Further, the feminine aspect of the passage referred to in the law and the wisdom that comes from meditating and studying it negates the employment of violence and sheer force in achieving an objective.

Divine encouragement and assurance of aid and presence in face of enemy attack is attested in Aramean documents:

> Be`elshamayn [spoke] to me through seers and through *diviners*. Be`elshamayn [said to me]: Do not fear, for I made you king, and I shall stand by you and deliver you from all [these kings who] set up a siege against you. [*Be`elshamayn*] said to me: [*I shall destroy*] all these kings who set up [a siege against you and *made this moat*] and this *wall* which [...] *charioteer* and *horseman* [...] its king in its midst [...]. I [*enlarged*] Hatarikka and added [to it] the entire district of [...] and *I made him ki[ng* ...] all these strongholds everywhere within the bor[ders].⁵⁷

The passage encourages and comforts the king promising him victory.⁵⁸ The annals of Sargon and Sennacherib's sanction conquest and reflect divine command and inspiration in wars:

> Upon a trust (-inspiring oracle given by) my lord Assur, I crushed the tribes of Tamud, Ibadidi, Marsimanu, and Haiapa, the Arabs who live, far away, in the desert (and) who know neither overseers nor official(s) and who had not (yet) brought their tribute to any king. I deported their survivors and settled (them) in Samaria.⁵⁹

Faced with the possibility of a larger army, we sense the anxiety of Sennacherib over the impending battle:

> Like the onset of locust swarms (many locust) of the springtime,
> They kept steadily coming on against me to offer battle.
> With the dust of their feet covering the wide heavens
> Like a mighty storm with (its) masses of dense (lit. pregnant) clouds,

---

⁵⁷ A document from the Aramean kingdoms: Zakir of Hamat and Lu`ath. See Pritchard, *Ancient Near Eastern Texts Relating to the Old Testament*, 655. The inscription of Zakir of Hamat is traditionally dated to the beginning of the eighth century BCE.
⁵⁸ Conrad, *Fear Not Warrior*, 148. See also James B. Pritchard, ed., *A New Anthology of Texts and Pictures by James Pritchard*, vol. 2 of *The Ancient Near East*, trans. Robert D. Biggs (Princeton: Princeton University Press, 1975), 398.
⁵⁹ Pritchard, *New Anthology of Texts and Pictures*, 296. See also Daniel David Luckenbill, *The Annals of Sennacherib* (Chicago: University of Chicago Press, 1924), 26–27, 34.

They drew up in battle array before me in the city of Halulê, and on the
   bank of Tigris.
They blocked my passage and offered battle.
As for me, to Assur,
Sin, Namashh, Bêl, Nabû, Nergal, Isthar of Neniveh,
Isthar of Arbela, the gods in whom I trust,
I prayed for victory over the mighty foe.
They speedily gave ear to my prayers and came.
To my aid. Like a lion rages I put on
(my) coat of mail. (My) helmet, emblem of victory (battle)[60]

In comparison to the first-person narration and the deity's direct address to the warrior king in the ancient Near Eastern literary parallels, the EP is narrated by a party that appears to be removed from the situation. The narrator assumes the all-knowing position of witnessing Yahweh speaking to Joshua after Moses' death. Joshua without a word obeys God's command to cross the Jordan (1:12). Unlike Moses in Exod 3:1–15, Joshua does not respond in anyway. He obeys and provides detailed instructions (1:11–15) for the crossing of the Jordan. The people in turn obediently comply. They echo the exhortation to be strong and be courageous (1:18) to Joshua.

The narrator(s) would have been educated and revered in Israelite society. He presumed authority. He may have been a religious leader. He probably belonged to the elite class. He presumed to counsel Joshua the national and God-anointed leader. For the narrator, faithfulness to the law gives strength to the people. It is the foundation that will bring well-being to the community. In the final text, the law, not the land became the central identity marker.

The people appear to be in the lowest rung in the hierarchy of speakers, under God and Joshua. They assure Joshua of their strict obedience. Detractors will be put to death. Though the least in the hierarchy of speakers, the people exhort Joshua to be strong and courageous (1:18). Hence, Joshua receives the exhortation to courage from God and the people. This collectivity called Israel stands strong under a leadership sanctioned by God and enjoys the support of all the people. Its life is sustained by study of the law and its practice. By their own accord and commitment, the tribes east of Jordan (1:12–15) are considered part of the congregation.

The passage presumes a location east of the Jordan river. It alludes to challenges facing Israel: the death of a revered leader (1:1, 2), the possession of the land (1:2, 3, 4, 6), and the making of important decisions for the continuing life of the people (1:2, 5, 7–9; 24:14–15, 19–18). Moses was con-

---

[60] Luckenbill, *Annals of Sennacherib*, 43–44.

sidered a revolutionary leader for he led the Israelites out of the bondage of slavery and gave them the law. The epithet "servant of the Lord" calls for emulation of Moses an ideal leader.

From the perspective of the early prophet's Hebrew readers, the mention of the death of Moses is a reminder that even the best of Israel's leaders died in hopeful expectation of the inheritance of the land. It brought consolation and hope to those who were gravely affected by the death of Josiah. The death of Moses signals a new era. But continuity is hinted by the assumption of leadership by Moses's assistant, whose training has prepared him for the job. Movement and change is hinted by the words "now," "arise," and "cross." What Moses has started, his assistant will continue. Possession of the land is projected as not only a past endeavor but an on-going process. God commands Joshua the leader to move forward. As Joshua advances the prophetic leadership and view of history, life in the land flourishes following God's word.

Land possession is depicted as actually treading the land. As the succeeding chapters and books (Judges, Samuel, Kings) narrate, they must be ready to fight for the land. The verb (נחל) points to incomplete action or an on-going process as well as a future hope. The allusion to the Amorites and Hittites establishes Israel's connection to these sociopolitical entities in the ancient Near East.[61]

The borders of the land given are at its most expansive. The borders in Josh 1:4 differ from the east west border mentioned in Josh 23:4. Indeed, there are differing maps in the book of Joshua. The first is the land west of Jordan (Josh 23:4). Second, the land that has still to be conquered (Josh 13:2-6), and the third is the land encompassed in the boundaries mentioned in Josh 1:4.[62] Furthermore, Josh 22:10-31 alludes to the peculiar situation of the tribes settled east of the Jordan. By their location, their being a part of the twelve tribes is held suspect. However, they themselves make it clear that they were a people of Yahweh (22:10-12, 22-27).

A scheme of ordering can be discerned in the mood shifts in Joshua. The introductory verse narrates the past, but the speech is constructed as a direct command for the present.[63] This points to a reading of the passage in its context, the obtaining situation in the time of writing. The Israelite lead-

---

[61] A. Haldar, "Amorites," *IDB* 1:115.
[62] Nelson, *Joshua*, 2.
[63] Victor Hamilton says of this shift, "This shift from indicative (what God promises to do) to imperative (what Joshua must do) parallels the same structural movement in the last chapter of Joshua 24:1-13, what God has done (verbs in the indicative mood, past tense); 24: 14-15, what the people must do (verbs in the imperative mood)." Victor Hamilton, *Handbook on the Historical Books: Joshua, Judges, Ruth, Samuel, Kings Chronicles, Ezra-Nehemiah, Esther* (Michigan: Baker Academic, 2001), 16.

er is commanded to act in concert with God's purpose and actions in the past. The phrase "Be strong and be courageous" in verse 6 presumes the task of land occupation (in verse 5), subsumed in the law emphasis in the succeeding verses.

Verse 7 exhorts strength and courage towards the observance of the law. The consequences are success and prosperity. From reassurance in verse 6 and command in verse 7, verse 9 forcefully commands strength and courage, to eliminate fear and discouragement premised in God's presence. The phrase "wherever you go" (ביכל עשר תלח) differs from "every place" (which the subject will trod given as gift 1:3 (כל מקמ). It is possible that the writer has deportation and dispersion in mind here which in Josiah's time had already been the fate of the Northern kingdom and a very real threat for Judah. The confident tone in verses 1–5 is gone. Verses 7-9 presume threatening situation.

The phrase be strong and be courageous (חזק אמצו, Deut 31:23; 1:6, 7, 9, 18) is mainly concerned with the appointment of Joshua as military leader of the people.[64] *Chazaq* (חזק) may have originated from the rituals of the Yahweh war.[65] The addressee is assured that he will accomplish the task of leading the Israelites into the land. But in comparison with the mention of campaigns, sieges, chariots, horses, and booty in ancient Near Eastern literature, Josh 1:1-9 makes no mention of warfare implements and instead stresses the law, a hint that the war Israel has to wage is not won by military capability. The conflict presented in Joshua is not armed conflict but cultural and ideological.[66] The law in Josiah's period is identified with the core of Deuteronomy, which codifies a social construction based on God's rule over Israel. God's speech in the passage points to important crises concerning leadership and the people.

Rhetorically, the passage projects Yahweh as speaker. Yet Josh 1:1–9 leads to hearing differing voices. A voice that emphasizes the task of allotting the land, another that commands strength and courage to the warrior leader (v. 5), and a third voice that emphasizes the observance of the law. The people in verse 17 express an assurance that God will be with Joshua as he was with Moses. It is Joshua to whom the exhortations to have strength and courage (6, 7, 9) is directed by God and the people (1:18). With the sanction of God and the support of the people, the leader instructs the people, and the people obey the leader. The passage gives a picture of unity.

The passage is profuse in exhorting courage not only in the explicit phrase "be strong and be courageous" in verses 6, 7, and 9a (and 18) and in

---

[64] Conrad, *Fear Not Warrior*, 27.
[65] Hesse, "חזק," *TDOT* 4:307.
[66] Legrand, *Bible on Culture*, 7.

negating fear in 9b. It also assures invincibility (5), God's presence (5, 9), and success (6, 8). The extravagance of the exhortation to courage stands out when compared with parallel ancient Near Eastern literature.

Joshua 1:1–9 expropriates imperial discourse towards subversive and liberative purposes. The words of encouragement are now Yahweh's to Joshua as prophet and warrior leader. The mention of Moses alludes to Egyptian liberation. Moses's prophetic image makes him a champion of the oppressed. Joshua 1:1–9 mimics the imperial ideology of the king as a warrior leader but infuses leadership with prophetic values. Restating imperial ideology as Yahweh's words transfers the power of the Assyrian God to Yahweh. But in contrast to the extensive claims of imperial Assyria, the land has limits in Joshua. Joshua carves out a part from what the empire claims for the imperial God. Joshua claims the land as having been conquered by Yahweh. The allusion to the warrior God's command to Joshua to appropriate the land as Israel's inheritance suggests militancy. The land is Yahweh's land. Yahweh is lord of the land. Assyria, Egypt, Babylon, or Persia cannot be allowed to have their way in the land. Granted to Israel, the continuing struggle to possess the land continues. The repeated phrase "be strong and be courageous" challenge the empire by its own ideology.

As cue for the understanding EP, Josh 1:1–9 underscores the need for strength and courage with regards to the land and people of Israel and for social justice enshrined in the law. Verses 1–5 stress the land, and verses 6–9 stress the law, but the law overrides a militaristic interpretation. It presupposes the covenant in Deuteronomy (29:1–30:20). It establishes social justice and care for the land. It underscores rigorous practice of cultural norms. Life and well-being in the land is made dependent on law observance (Josh 1:8; Deut 27:18–19, 24–25, 28:1–14). Joshua 1:1–9 thus speaks against colonialism as a form of land grabbing and cultural imperialism.

Following the redaction reconstruction that verses 7–9 comes from the hand of an exilic redactor, the struggle appears to have shifted from militant defense of the land to militant observance of the law. The toning down of militant and masculine rhetoric and the emphasis on the law is significant in the passage. Experiencing domination, Israel may have come to the critique and deconstruction of overly masculine view of power and reality. The story of Rahab in Josh 2 certainly calls attention to the feminine aspects of resistance.[67] In the Rahab story cunning, wisdom, family values, preser-

---

[67] Following Helene Cixious's idea, femininity stands for strategies of undermining domination that are life affirming and empowering. It does not impose its own ideas but allows a respectful distance for the other to be and flourish, thus opening a possibility for a two-sided conversation. It brings the female body into the discourse, it also aims to break new grounds for thinking, language, and representation for the

vation of life, and courage are underscored. A woman's wisdom saves the spies and leads to the conquest of Jericho. Domination is death dealing. By its very nature domination undermines itself; real power rests in resisting domination. Resistance shifts to more judicious means of undermining the power of oppressive systems. Joshua 1:1-9 underlines Israel's strength, which lies not in superior strength but in the knowledge of the vulnerability of the empire. The empire cannot endure; Israel in the end will prevail. The text points to certainty of victory. Certainly, the text exhibits the feminine aspects of society's strength and courage in standing up to domination: unity amidst differences, knowledge of the law, continuing life based on a people's way of life in the land.

As a literary composition, Josh 1:1-9 presumes a crisis concerning Israel as a people of God. Based on the emphases in Joshua, the crisis is connected with the threat of the loss of land, identity, and leadership. Jordan as body of water in ancient thought stands for the primeval chaos. It must be overcome. Order is established as Yahweh's will triumphs in the land.[68] Life on the land is tied up with a way of life based on the law.[69] In asserting its way of life, Israel affirmed the inseparable connection between land, its people, and the way of life that arose from the land itself. Joshua thereby constructs a nation. In stressing the entity called Israel or the twelve tribes of Israel, its territory and its law, Josh 1:1-9 affirms a people's aspiration for land, freedom, and self-government. Doing so in the context of ancient Near East is tantamount to a David challenging a Goliath. Israel stands behind Yahweh's standard against the empire. In the face of a superior army with chariots and javelins, and armors, Israel chooses to rely on Yahweh.

Joshua 1:1-9's insistence on the law linked with Deuteronomy stands for Israel's political, social, and economic aspirations.[70] It is a way of resist-

---

feminine; and engage the dominant thought through philosophy and political ethics. The main characteristic of femininity is grounded on matter, which for Cixous also stands for "mother": the substance of the world, our bodies, and the bodies of others. See Abigail Bray, *Helene Cixous: Writing and Sexual Difference* (New York: Palgrave, 2004).

[68] Bergman Ottosson, "ארץ," *TDOT* 1:388–405, particularly 401–5.

[69] McConville's reading accords with anthropological studies that affirm the importance of ritualized conquest of chaos and the establishment of ordered reality in ancient societies. See also Roy Rappaport, *Ritual and Religion in the Making of Humanity* (Cambridge: Cambridge University Press, 1999); Emile Durkheim, *The Elementary Forms of Religious Life*, trans. Joseph Ward Swain (New York: Free Press, 1947).

[70] Maria Aristodemou asserts that law like literature "constructs concepts, or abstractions like time or identity, aiming to create, and especially in law's case, to

ing imperial claim of sovereignty over Israel and its land, made operative in the exaction of surplus from the people by the elite (Deut 17:16–17). As far as the EP are concerned, Israel's kings are accountable (1 Kgs 21:21–22). The EP illustrate the consequences of oppressive local rule in the reign of Solomon and the consequent division of the Kingdom of Israel. Subsequently, Ahab's rule met a violent end in the hands of a people in revolt. The EP laud kings that resisted imperial rule. The first of the EP, Joshua institutionalizes the right of each family for a farm plot (Josh 1:6, *nachalah*). Deuteronomy, which Joshua upholds, commands social justice; "there must be no poor" in Israel (Deut 15:4). In no uncertain terms, land grabbing (1 Kgs 21:18–19) and land monopolization is condemned in Joshua and the EP.

---

impose, order out of chaos: to write on bodies and very souls of the subjects and fulfill as well as replace their unthinkable desires.... Both law and literature are social institutions situated in the culture that constitutes them as distinct discourses at the same time as it is constituted by them." See Maria Aristodemou, *Law and Literature: Journeys from Her to Eternity* (New York: Oxford University Press, 2000), 1, 7.

7.

JOSHUA 1:1-9: COLONIAL READINGS

Colonialism was a reality in Europe and the United States in the eighteenth and nineteenth centuries, but interpreters did not take into consideration the impact of coloniality on interpretations, on foreign missions, and more importantly on those at its receiving end. The interpretations appear to support colonizing "foreign" nations and thus reflect Western worldview, culture, and interests.

The location of religion to personal private sphere comes out in John Wesley's (1703-1791) short comment on Josh 1. In his reading, Josh 1:1-9 primarily addresses psychological concerns. Joshua feels inadequate as successor of Moses. Israel too was inadequate, in view of its failures. Thus the need for strength and courage.[1]

The commentary by C. F. Keil and F. Delitzsch has recently been republished.[2] As an online reviewer states: "a landmark of Biblical exposition a triumph of rigorous scholarship and sound theological judgment, Keil and Delitzsch remains one of the most popular Old Testament commentaries available."[3] The commentary presupposes the historical validity of the narrated events. It appears to have no problem with the violence attributed to the command of God. The moral superiority of Israel is presumed. Israel becomes the powerful center, and God is portrayed to be an imperial character who grants land, has the prerogative of taking it back, and exterminates the inhabitants if the gifts are abused. Extermination is justified on religious ground.

Western propensity towards personal piety is observed in Charles Spurgeon's (1834-1892) exposition of Josh 1 particularly verse 5. Spurgeon presupposes binaries in categorizing people as "us" and "the enemies." Quoted New Testament verses and Spurgeon's context point to the Christian West as the "us," and the "them" were non-Christians *qua* the enemies. Spurgeon alludes to male superiority over women. Men are the leaders:

---

[1] G. Roger Schoenhals, ed., *John Wesley's Commentary on the Bible* (Grand Rapids: Zondervan, 1990), 152.
[2] Keil and Delitzsch, *Joshua, Judges, Ruth*, 24-26.
[3] www.studylight.org/commentaries/kdo.

Moses, Joshua, and those to whom the message is directed. Women are connected with giving birth and the "weakest."[4]

Focusing on leadership themes, F. G. Marchant treads on the issue of land-giving from the point of view of the superiority of Israel's faith in relation to the Canaanites and the rest of the human race. He makes no reference to the text's context. The validity of the establishment of the Israelites in the land is equated with the publication and ascendancy of the gospel over the whole earth and people. Focus on the masculine gender is glaring in this commentary.[5]

The consequence of interpretation along historical understanding that does not take into account Israel's context is illustrated in the introduction of A. Plummer's volume on the books of Joshua to Nehemiah. Plummer makes the wide leap of putting Greece and Rome at par with ancient Israel. Thus he puts ancient Israel in the league of oppressive imperial powers. Plummer extolls the superiority of Western civilization, and sees very little that is worthwhile outside ancient Israel, Greece, and Rome. It is on this basis that the duty of Israel to execute justice is premised. Toward this end the suffering and deprivation of those supplanted by western civilization are considered just and deserved.[6]

Plummer instigates and justifies hate and violence against the undefined sin of the "Canaanites." The execution of God's vengeance against sinners is accordingly the temporary natural order of things through which "inequities that exist are ended." He clarifies that the executors of God's judgment were "simpler people." By this he considers the domination of certain empires as God's design comparable to what is narrated in the book of Joshua. His binary of barbarians and civilized is confusing. He calls on the West to avoid civilizational "decay" so as not to give chance for the "savages of Asia and Africa" to have mastery. For when that happens he believes punishment will fall upon the sins of luxury.

Plummer's interpretation makes sense if understood in the reverse—it is the Christian West which is "enervated by luxury—who should receive their just punishment." Plummer reasons that revelation available to us now was yet unknown in the Old Testament. He claims that what Joshua did against the Canaanites though severe was a punishment and not just "a mere outbursts of savage cruelty." From Plummer's imperial perspective,

---

[4] Charles Haddon Spurgeon, *Genesis to 2 Kings*, vol. 1 of *The Treasury of the Bible* (Grand Rapids: Baker, 1986), 493–94.

[5] F. G. Marchant, *The Preacher's Complete Homiletic Commentary*, vol. 5 (Grand Rapids: Baker, 1875), 4.

[6] A. Plummer, introduction to *The Pulpit Commentary*, ed. H. D. Spence and Joseph S. Exell, vol. 7 (Westchester, IL: Wilcox & Follett, n.d.), vii.

ancient Israel is the "godly" center that must be extended. As the ancient world could only gain from Jewish polity, the "world" will too through Western Christianity.[7]

In the expositions of Josh 1, *The Pulpit Commentary* dwells on historical reconstruction of the process of land occupation, geographical information, and the meaning of the words and phrases along historical grounds. But the homily contrasts the "morally and humanely" superior center with the "wicked" periphery. The land to be conquered is described as wicked and sinful.[8] The exposition appears to recruit carriers of the imperialistic project of expanding and establishing hegemonic Christian culture, justified by the "wickedness of the land and its people." Non-Christians are perceived as the evil to be "rooted out without compromise and without mercy."[9]

The problem of interpreting narratives as historical records that equates God's will with the literal reading of Joshua comes out in the introduction to the book of Joshua in *A Commentary on the Holy Bible*.[10] It is remarkable that the exposition dwells on relations between "so vicious and depraved" kingdoms and Israel. But the exposition runs mainly on religious and "spiritual sanitation." The construction of Canaanites as the evil other that deserves nothing but extermination and that such a vocation has a "good effect" for the Israelites must come from the untenable position that what is narrated in Joshua literally happened and must be justified. Such interpretation encourages racism and vigilantism from the West against the evil other.[11]

Spiritualization and personalization of the message of Joshua so that it has nothing to do with society or politics can be observed in the way J. Stalker expounds Josh 1:6.[12] The same tendency is demonstrated in the way A. Raleigh expounds verses 6 and 7 in "the Way to the City" of the Sermon Bible.[13]

Samuel Holmes demonstrates how historical criticism can serve as a parameter for interpretation. Holmes gives a comprehensive review of what biblical scholarship has uncovered about history and how it serves as check for understanding a text that neither narrates history nor gives instructions on how to treat the "Canaanites." Like most Western scholars, Holmes dwells on historical criticism, but he does not situate the narratives

---

[7] Plummer, introduction, xiv–v.
[8] J. J. Lias, "Exposition and Homiletics," in Spence and Exell, *Pulpit Commentary*, 5–6.
[9] Lias, "Exposition and Homiletics," 5–6.
[10] J. R. Dummelow, ed. *A Commentary on the Holy Bible by Various Writers* (New York: Macmillan, 1908), 141.
[11] Dummelow, *Commentary on the Holy Bible*, 142.
[12] J. Stalker, excerpt from *The New Song*, repr. in *The Sermon Bible: Genesis to Samuel*, vol. 1 (New York: Funk & Wagnalls, 1900), 358.
[13] A. Raleigh, excerpt from *The Way to the City*, repr. in *Sermon Bible*, 358.

in its sociocultural setting nor delve into how the text might have been understood in ancient Israel. His historical reconstruction faithfully represents the success and failure of historical criticism. Historical criticism is directed towards the historical reconstruction of the conquest. Holmes then concludes that the account is unscientific and has no moral value for today.[14] Of Josh 1:1-18, he says that the chapter "does not call for much comment."[15]

L. E. P. Erith's exposition also dwells on historical reconstruction. He applies the text to religion.[16] Erith describes the negative influences of the Canaanite religion upon the Israelites and concludes that Canaanite religion must necessarily be exterminated. Since he eschews sociopolitical meaning, he justifies Canaanite extermination. The stress on land, the law, and leadership of a people in the passage that he uncovers does not figure in the application.[17]

An exclusively religious point of view is the focus of Lindsay B. Longcare's commentary. He observes interest in national security and prosperity in the passage. But he glosses over politics in the application of meaning.[18]

John Garstang mainly dwells on the geography of the land of Canaan. He follows the theory that Israel evolved from the simple nomadic tribes but were contaminated by their contact with "town-life," stating in part that "in tents it was more possible to maintain the unity of their faith and their purity of race. Their Government was theocratic: their leader received his commands direct from Jehovah, and his powers in the execution of the divine law were absolute."[19] He understands military conquest as divinely sanctioned narrating in a matter of fact manner how Israel occupied the land following the account in the book of Joshua. Military outlook pervades his exposition of Josh 1:1-9.[20] He cites archeological findings to dispute the stated number of the Israelites attributing it to the error in interpreting the word "Alif" arriving at a considerably lesser number of Israelites—"six thousand souls, with fighting strength of some 1200-1500 men." He also cites "independent sources" that estimates the size of Canaanite cities to be

---

[14] Samuel Holmes, "Joshua," in *A Commentary on the Bible*, ed. Arthur S. Peake (New York: Nelson, 1919), 248–49.
[15] Holmes, "Joshua."
[16] L. E. P. Erith, "Joshua," in *A New Commentary on the Holy Scripture*, ed. Charles Gore, Henry Leighton Goudge, and Alfred Guillaume (London: SPCK, 1928), 189–91.
[17] Erith, "Joshua," 192.
[18] Lindsay B. Longcare, "Joshua," in *The Abingdon Bible Commentary*, ed. Frederick Carl Eiselen, Edwin Lewis, and David G. Downey (Nashville: Abingdon, 1929), 346–47.
[19] John Garstang, *The Foundations of Bible History* (London: Constable, 1931), 120.
[20] Garstang, *Foundations of Bible History*, 120.

about five to twelve acres.[21] Still he steers clear from political and social meaning. The same tendency is observed in Robert Jamieson's commentary.[22]

The problem of interpreting biblical narratives isolated from their lived reality is seen in E. J. Joyce's commentary. The text is read and assessed from the security of academic and ecclesiastical location. From such a vantage point, the strangeness of the text is perplexing. Such is the predicament of Joyce who subscribes to the idea that Israel's religion evolved from a primitive faith of which Joshua is considered a part.[23] Joyce contents himself with retelling along "deuteronomic thought and spirit" a story of "salvation through which God led Israel into the promised land fulfilling his promise." The relevance of such a story for today is left for the readers to ponder.[24]

In his introduction to the book of Joshua Hugh J. Blair deals with the "The Moral Problem of Israel's Warfare." He dismisses the idea that the accounts of Joshua were idealized picture of the past and states that the events narrated are contemporaneous with the time of writing. Dismissing the proposition that the revelation at this period were imperfect on account of the doctrine of inspiration, he upholds the validity of the command in Joshua to exterminate the Canaanites. He rationalizes the command on two grounds: its "religious service" and its "prophylactic function."[25] With this assumption as the premise of interpretation Blair's comment on Josh 1:1–9 gives emphasis on the continuity of the task entrusted to Joshua by Moses.[26] The literal understanding of what at first glance is a command to exterminate peoples is justified "as divine surgery of sin" and its preventive function for the world. Thus extermination of peoples is a legitimate action for the sake of Israel and the kingdom of God.

Matthew Henry introduces the book of Joshua as a part of the history of the Jews.[27] His exposition dwells on Joshua's call as a leader succeeding Moses, reassured by promises and solemn charges. The privileged position of Israel and the Christian West is evident in some parts of his commentary.[28]

---

[21] Garstang, *Foundations of Bible History*, 120.
[22] Robert Jamieson, *Genesis–Deuteronomy, Joshua–Esther*, vol. 1 of *A Commentary Critical, Experimental and Practical on the Old and New Testaments*, ed. Robert Jamieson, A. R. Fausset, David Brown (Grand Rapids: Eerdmans, 1945), 2.
[23] E. J. Joyce, C.P.P.S., "Joshua," in *A New Catholic Commentary on the Holy Scripture* (New Jersey: Nelson, 1953), 183, 283.
[24] Joyce, "Joshua," 284.
[25] Hugh J. Blair, "Joshua," in *The New Bible Commentary*, ed. F. Davidson (London: Inter-Varsity Press, 1953), 225.
[26] Blair, "Joshua," 226–27.
[27] Matthew Henry, *Commentary on the Whole Bible*, One vol. ed. (Grand Rapids: Zondervan, 1961), 210.
[28] Henry, *Commentary on the Whole Bible*, 211.

It may be inferred from his exposition that the dominance of Israel and the Christian West in the world is sanctioned and sustained by God. This is the reverse of the argument of this work. Joshua is part of the EP, which is a literature that resists dominating powers.

God's preferential treatment for Israel and the superiority of Judaism are presumed by E. Powers. The reading accords with ancient Israel's confession that God fought for and was with them. Power justifies the ban in Joshua on account of the superiority of Israel's religious values and the preservation of its purity. He extolls the singularity of Israelite faith.[29]

In his introduction to the book of Joshua, John Rea justifies the invasion of Canaan by the superiority of monotheism. He denigrates Canaanite religion. The categorization of Canaanite religion as immoral legitimizes the "ban" lest it contaminate what is pure.[30] He interprets Josh 1:1–9 as an exhortation to exterminate "wicked, god-rejecting peoples" as holy war indeed.[31]

Chester O. Mulder's interpretation follows the main topics: the person of Joshua, the task given to him after Moses's death, God's instructions for Joshua, God's promise of invincibility, "the importance of positive mindedness," the observance of the law as the key to success, and God was the one who initiated it all. The exposition dwells on personal piety. Yet he emphasized Zionist and imperialist reading of the passage: obedience which "meant victorious possession of the Promised Land."[32]

Mulder appears to equate the advance of righteousness to the expansion of modern Israel. There is no mention of sociocultural milieu or of the message of Joshua. But Mulder easily equates Joshua with Jesus and affirms the superiority of Christianity and the legitimacy of following the example in Joshua in establishing and propagating it.[33]

Charles R. Wilson's comments closely adhere to the themes of land and law. He insists on the historicity of the accounts like the conquest in Joshua. His exposition closely follows the narrator in elaborating how God spoke to Joshua, for example, through "intuition or conscience," or, who Joshua was, as portrayed in the Hebrew Bible. The commentary retells what the author

---

[29] Powers, *A Catholic Commentary on Holy Scripture*, 280–81.
[30] John Rea, "Joshua," in *The Wycliffe Bible Commentary*, ed. Charles F. Pfeiffer and Everett Harrison (London: Lowe & Brydone, 1963), 206.
[31] Rea, "Joshua," 208.
[32] Chester O. Mulder, *Joshua Beacon Bible Commentary*, vol. 2 (Missouri: Beacon Hill, 1965), 21–27.
[33] Mulder, *Joshua Beacon Bible Commentary*, 142.

insists was a historically rooted story. No attempt was made to bridge the hermeneutical gap on how this story relates to his readers.[34]

The limitations of historical interpretation come out still in the more recent commentary by John J. Davis and John C. Whitcomb, who treat the biblical narrative as plain historical account. Davis and Whitcomb ignore historical questions concerning the book.[35]

The militaristic theme of Joshua appears prominently in A. Graeme Auld's commentary. Presupposing Judeo-Christian tradition and the Christian West as bearers of the message, the commentary invites aggressive expansion and subjugation of non-Christian nations and the imposition of Western Christianity and culture.[36]

The isolation of the Bible from lived reality is also evident in Vernon McGee's reading of Joshua. Disregarding historical issues McGee attributes the writing of the book to Joshua himself.[37] McGee emphasizes Israel's "unconditional ownership" of the land as an "everlasting possession," thereby privileging modern Israel. He reiterates the spiritual message of Joshua in his comment on Josh 1:3 and even hints the gospel of health and prosperity for Israel and Jesus's followers.[38]

John Huffman uses the text as a springboard for addressing psychological issues among his readers.[39] Huffman interprets the text towards health and prosperity gospel based on a pietistic spirituality.[40] The presumption of historical contemporariness and emphasis on psychological/spiritual insight also comes out in Dale Ralph Davis's exposition.[41]

The problem of interpreting the book of Joshua along historical and spiritual lines apart from its context also surfaces in Madvig's exposition. Taken as a fact of history, Madvig is constrained to understand the violent conquest in Joshua as an act of God.[42] Yet while the direction of this interpretation is the socio-political sphere, Madvig reads it as a religious event. Hence Joshua's "spiritual leadership" is read as a central theme. But Madvig

---

[34] Charles R. Wilson, *Joshua–Esther*, vol. 1.2 of *The Wesleyan Bible Commentary* (Grand Rapids: Eerdmans, 1967), 11–16.
[35] John J. Davies and John C. Whitcomb, *Israel from Conquest to Exile: A Commentary on Joshua–2 Kings* (Grand Rapids: Baker, 1970), 31.
[36] A. Graeme Auld, *Joshua, Judges, and Ruth* (Philadelphia: Westminster, 1984), 8–11.
[37] J. Vernon McGee, *Joshua–Psalms*, vol. 2 of *Thru the Bible with J. Vernon McGee* (Nashville: Nelson, 1982), 1.
[38] McGee, *Joshua–Psalms*, 3.
[39] John Huffman, *Mastering the Old Testament: Joshua* (Dallas: Word, 1986), 28.
[40] Huffman, *Mastering the Old Testament*, 34.
[41] Dale Ralph Davis, *No Falling Swords: Expositions of the Book of Joshua* (Grand Rapids: Baker, 1988), 17.
[42] Donald H. Madvig, "Joshua," in *Deuteronomy to 2 Samuel*, vol. 3 of *The Expositor's Bible Commentary*, ed. Frank E. Gaebelein (Grand Rapids: Zondervan, 1992), 245.

vacillates from spiritual reading to militaristic reading.[43] As far as ancient Israel is concerned all things are religious and sacrosanct. But the use of its literature against dominant empires to assert what Israel understood to be God-given right on the land by its people is a far cry from advocating violence as a God sanctioned means to take possession of any land. Madwig starts with the awareness of the problem of violence in Joshua but justifies it for religious reasons captured in this quotation: "The most difficult thing to understand is the slaughter of innocent children. But we must remember that death is not the ultimate destiny of the human race, nor is it the greatest evil. Someday God will give a full explanation of his actions, which is something that only he can do."[44]

Gordon Harris basically reconstructs history as narrated in the book situating interpretation in the context of a "new era ... after the death of Moses." He states that the gift must be claimed with the assurance that God will grant the Israelites victory. Such assurance is especially needed as the people were "experiencing grief and loss at the death of Moses."[45]

Kenneth O. Gangel's exposition focuses on the desirable personality and characteristics of a leader.[46] The spiritual understanding of Joshua is evident in the application of the message that appropriates Jordan river to problems in life. The assurance of victory is taken as a guarantee of victorious "Christian life" if people will only have faith.[47]

Even though he wrote from Africa (previously colonized by Western nations), David Oginde did not address the problems in the interpretation of the book of Joshua. His exposition adheres to the Western mold that eschews sociocultural and political meanings in favor of marshaling biblical interpretation towards the cultivation of personal piety and gleaning religious insight. Oginde's introduction to the book of Joshua dwells on the fulfillment of God's promises to Abraham. On Josh 1:1–9, he lingers on the impact of death of a leader to a people. Thus he stresses the need for good leaders especially in Africa. In consonance with the introduction, he emphasizes the fulfillment of divine promises of land, victory, and God's continuing presence. He discusses the demands on leaders to advance the

---

[43] Madvig, "Joshua," 240.
[44] Donald H. Madwig, "Joshua," in *Old Testament*, vol. 1 of *Zondervan NIV Bible Commentary*, ed. Kenneth L. Barker and John R. Kohlenberger (Grand Rapids: Zondervan, 1994), 290.
[45] J. Gordon Harris, Cheryl A. Brown, and Michael S. Moore, *New International Biblical Commentary: Joshua, Judges, Ruth* (Peabody, MA: Hendrickson, 2000), 18.
[46] Kenneth O. Gangel, "Joshua," in *Holman Old Testament Commentary*, ed. Max Anders (Nashville: Broadman & Holman, 2002), 1–15.
[47] Gangel, "Joshua," 11, 14.

realization of God's promises. These include the unwavering commitment to the will of God revealed in the law. He does not elaborate on how the law of Israel applies to Christians today particularly for those in Africa. Instead he asks how the passage is to be understood particularly in the light of what is going on in Palestine.[48]

Surprisingly Oginde does not attempt to answer the questions raised in his comments in chapter 1 or in the succeeding chapters. In my opinion, adherence to the historical meaning of the text, that is, understanding the text as narration of actual events results in problematic reading. Hence Oginde's contextualization of the succeeding chapters of Joshua fall on gleaning "spiritual" insights or finding links between certain concepts alluded to in the narrated stories. A part of Oginde's comment on Josh 1:6-7 is in line with pietistic Western expositions of the passage.[49] Oginde proceeds by enumerating reasons why Joshua would have been afraid. He exhorts Christians today to be confident of the faith for "we are not those who shrink back and are destroyed, but ... those who believe and are saved (Heb 10:35-39)."[50]

Trent C. Butler entitled his comments on Josh 1:1-18 "Divine Marching Orders."[51] He identifies these themes in Josh 1: "warfare, land, leadership, the unity of the people, and the faithfulness of God," which he claims are also found throughout the book.[52] He observes that Josh 1:1-9 is Deuteronomic in vocabulary and literary connection, but he does not rule out use of earlier historical materials.[53] As to the meaning of the book, Butler emphasizes the land as a gift from God—a gift that is conditioned by obedience to God's law. He recognizes that the land was previously occupied by other nations. In order to fulfill the promise to Israel, other nations were "dispossessed" by God. Though Israel had to fight, it was God who dispossessed other nations in order to fulfill the promise to Israel. He proposes that God being sovereign over all nations has the power to give and take away land, though "he was bound to no nation, to no temple, and to no land."[54] Unable to detect the pervasive presence of the empire in the time of the EP, Butler thus comes to a contradictory statement.

---

[48] David Oginde, "Joshua," in *Africa Bible Commentary*, ed. Tokunboh Adeyemo (Grand Rapids: Zondervan, 2006), 258.
[49] Oginde, "Joshua," 258.
[50] Oginde, "Joshua," 259.
[51] Trent C. Butler, *Joshua 1-12*, WBC 7a, 2nd ed. (Michigan: Zondervan, 2014), 185.
[52] Butler, *Joshua 1-12*, 199.
[53] Butler, *Joshua 1-12*, 198.
[54] Butler, *Joshua 1-12*, 165-67.

Written in English by Western interpreters, the commentaries above echo Western context and concepts. Naturally and understandably, meaning-making arises from a subject's perspective. In a discipline like biblical studies that is dominated by Western thinkers, biblical interpreters from the margins must make a shift in perspective. A resistance interpreter must make a deliberate and conscious choice to give priority to the context of the Global South and use contextual lens. Though I write in English, I chose to use Filipino context and concepts to read and interpret Josh 1:1–9. The next chapter is a reading that aims to contribute to the reconstruction, healing, and reintegration of a society warped by colonialism.

8.
THE PHILIPPINES CONTEXT

The Philippine context, as the receptor context, is part of my interpretation triangle (see p. 7) that creates meaning with the text and the text's context. The context of the text establishes the meaning of the text and parameters of interpretation while the receptor's context provides the historical and cultural codes through which the meaning of the text is appropriated. Hence this chapter examines the Philippine sociocultural, political, and economic situation. Some of the Philippine literature in the nineteenth century will also be analyzed as the Filipino people's text.

Spanish and American Colonization/Christianization

There was no central government in the pre-Spanish Philippines. Land was owned communally. The person who cultivated the land reaped its produce. The villagers lived on the products of their labor and the abundance of the land. Bound by kinship and communal ties, community leadership was by consultation and consensus.[1] There was no ruling elite to support and for

---

[1] F. Landa Jocano, *The Filipino Prehistory Rediscovering Precolonial Heritage* (Manila: Punlad Research House, 1998), 199. Each barangay has an autonomous government governed by a body of custom handed down orally and through rituals. Most of these laws are part of the "religious prescriptions for good moral behavior" understood to maintain the well-being of the community. Known laws cover such aspects as "family relations, adoption, property rights, inheritance, divorce, partnership (political and trade alliances), crime and punishment, and loans." Crimes such as rape, incest, murder, trespass, sacrilege, lancery, and witchcraft are punished severely. Towards the end of the seventeenth century an Italian traveler by name of Gemelli Careri described the early Filipinos, "Their polity and laws, which, for barbarians, were not so very barbarous, consisted entirely of traditions and usages which they kept so strictly that they did not even admit to their possibility of being broken. They imposed, among other things, such reverence for parents and elders that among them one did not mention one's father by name, just as, among the Hebrews, one did not mention God by name; as also that private persons, even children must submit to the will of the community." See de la Costa, *Readings in Philippine History*, 5.

whom surplus goods must be produced.[2] Though social stratification was present in the pre-Spanish Philippine society, it was connected to social responsibility and did not depend on the person.[3] A person could regain his/her freedom and move up the social ladder through demonstration of ability and leadership.

From its very beginnings, Filipinos resisted Spanish colonialism. The famous explorer Ferdinand Magellan who first circumnavigated the earth met his death in the hands of Filipino warriors in 1521. Armed revolts marked the four centuries of imperial occupation of the islands.[4] These culminated in the 1896 Filipino Revolution against Spain. The peasant revolts that erupted throughout the Spanish occupation continued even after the surrender of Aguinaldo and the collaboration of the *ilustrados* with the Americans.[5] The 1896 revolution had popular support. Filipino masses saw imperial Spain, and later the United States, as enemies. Filipinos' struggle for liberation has been long and hard and continues to the present. Countless lives have been sacrificed.

Spain came first, "to make known to the natives of those parts our Holy Catholic faith and to determine (how) his patrimony and royal crown of Castile may be enhanced and the spices and other riches there obtainable be brought hither."[6] Thus, Miguel Lopez de Legazpi was sent by King Phillip of Spain to colonize the Philippines in November 1564. Cebu where he first landed was sacked. Legazpi's group proceeded to Panay island, where he was well received, and later to Luzon. There, he established a peace treaty sealed by a blood compact with Rajah Soliman.[7] But the blood compact did not allay fears on both sides, and hostilities precipitated by Legazpi's second in command, Goiti, soon commenced. In the absence of central government, the communities in Luzon were no match for Legazpi's force.

---

[2] Jocano, *Filipino Prehistory*. See also E. P. Petanñe, *The Philippines in the world of Southeast Asia: A Cultural History* (Quezon City: Enterprise, 1972), 329.
[3] Vicente elaborates, "Village society owed its apparent mobility to the displaceability of obligation. Status reflected indebtedness, not the person." See Vicente, *Contracting Colonialism*. See also Henry William Scott, *Slavery in the Philippines* (Manila: De La Salle University Press, 1991).
[4] Carlos Quirino lists fifty-five major battles engaged by Filipino rebels against Spain and the United States from 1521 to 1945, not including "scores of other armed encounters." See Carlos Quirino, *Filipinos at War* (Philippines: Vera-Reyes, 1981), 261.
[5] The *ilustrados* were the wealthy educated Filipinos.
[6] Fray Juan Francisco de San Antonio, *The Philippine Chronicles of Fray San Anotonio* trans. D. Pedro Picornel (Manila: Casalinda and Historical Conservation Society, 1977), 15–16.
[7] De San Antonio, *Philippine Chronicles*, 18–19.

Spain employed the strategy of divide and conquer. Visayan fighters were employed to establish Spanish settlements in Luzon.[8] They gained inroads in conversion by making use of tight kinship and communal ties of the natives. Converts and people of influence were used to win their families and communities.[9] The former rulers were given privileges including retention of the land they were tilling. They were enlisted as leaders who administered and marshaled the natives into the fold of the Catholic Church and the control of Spain.[10] Favored Spaniards were given the right to administer communal lands as *encomienda*.[11] This policy was the root cause of landlessness among the masses.[12] Catholic worship was imposed among subject communities. Resistance was subjugated by force.

But the over-all success of Christianity in the Philippines may be credited to the correspondences between Spanish Christianity and the folk religiosity in the Philippines.[13] Innately religious, the people were receptive to the introduction of a transcendent God presumed in the Christian religion. Fray San Antonio a Spanish chronicler writes of a supreme God known by a variety of names. Among the Tagalogs, God is called *Bathala Meycapal*, which means God the Author and Maker of Everything. Bathala's name is so sacred that it cannot be pronounced.[14] The Visayans use time as a point of reference in distinguishing God through the name *Lauon*, meaning the Ancient One.[15] Other names for God are *Akasi* for the Zambals, *Gugusang* for Bicolanos, *Apo-laqui* for Ilocanos, *Kamunian* for Igorots, and *Ama-kaoley* for the Pangasinenses.[16] The Filipino supreme God is believed to be benevolent

---

[8] De San Antonio, *Philippine Chronicles*, 18–19.

[9] To convert the natives, the priests persuaded the chiefs through their children who have been baptized, to embrace the new religion. The people soon submit to baptism following their chiefs. Generally followed as a manual of instructing the natives was the Doctrina of 1593, a Spanish Tagalog introduction to Christianity. See Petanñe, *Philippines in the World*, 210.

[10] The former *datus* (chiefs) continued to function and in addition were tasked to collect the tribute from their own people. They were called *principalia* (nobles). The principalias choose the *gobernadorcillo* (municipal judges) who were the leaders of the Pueblos.

[11] A royal grant to a deserving colonist of jurisdiction over a definite territory and its native inhabitants. See de la Costa, *Readings in Philippine History*, 21.

[12] Jesus S. Arcilla, S. J., *The Fine Print of Philippine* History (Makati, Philippines: St. Paul Publications, 1992), 69.

[13] Fabella, "Inculturating the Gospel," 122–23.

[14] Juana Jimenez Pelmoka, *Pre-Spanish Philippines* (Philippines: Self-published, 1990), 115.

[15] de San Antonio, *Philippine Chronicles of Fray San Aontonio*, 149

[16] Rosario Mendoza Cortes et al., *The Filipino Saga History as Social Change* (Quezon City, New Day, 2000), 21, Pelmoka, *Pre-Spanish Philippines*, 115.

142 | A Filipino Resistance Reading

and just, but in traditional religion he is thought to be remote and inaccessible. It was the Spaniards who introduced the concept of a loving God who gave his son for the sake of salvation. Nowadays, popular Christianity retain pre-Spanish folk beliefs and practices.

While the teaching of Spanish language to the natives was a law, the Spanish friars feared that the education of the natives would lead to resistance.[17] As a Spanish diplomat (1842) pointed out:

> Filipinos should not be taught Spanish, but should be taught to read and write in their own language. It is impossible to avoid the circulation in the provinces of papers and books which are dangerous for them to read, and experience has taught us that those who know our language are almost always the most headstrong in the pueblos, the ones who talk behind the back, criticize, and rebel against the curates and provincial governors.[18]

Fray Francisco Gainza, Vice-Rector of the University of Santo Tomas and member of the Crespo Educational Commission, vehemently opposed the teaching of Spanish to the Filipinos because doing so would give them a "common national language."[19]

Learning was by rote without attempt at understanding, following a curriculum centered on Catholic piety.[20] Learning materials mainly consisted of "monotonous litanies and exhortations to the Almighty, the endless stream of booklets and pamphlets about Christ and the miracles of the saints."[21]

Religious instruction was imposed on school children, and the town's people were required to attend mass and make confessions on pain of punishment. The town's *guardia civil* (civil guards) supported the Spanish friars. Life in the lowlands where *pueblos* had been established revolved around the church.[22] Religious fiestas were observed regularly. The year followed the Christian calendar, with Christmas and the long Lenten season,

---

[17] Cortes et al., *Filipino Saga History as Social Change*, 37.
[18] Carlos Botor, trans., *Informe Secreto de Sinabaldo De Mas*, rev. Alfonso Felix Jr. (Manila: Historical Society, 1963), 61.
[19] Encarnacion Alzona, *A History of Education in the Philippines* (Manila: University of the Philippines Press, 1932), 50.
[20] Alzona, *History of Education in the Philippines*, 50.
[21] Alzona, *History of Education in the Philippines*, 50. See also Teodoro Agoncillo, *Revolt of the Masses* (Quezon City: University of the Philippines Press, 1956), 9.
[22] Spanish resettlement of the native population in the lowlands for the purpose of pacification and Christian indoctrination.

which culminates in the Holy Week as the most important of the celebrations. Books had to be approved before they could be printed.[23]

The natives acceded to friars' impositions by applying themselves to the recitation and memorization of the *pasyons* (passion [of Christ]), the *awits* (romantic songs), and the *moro-moros* (stories about the Moros/Muslims). Steeped in oral tradition, the stories were passed by word of mouth in place of pre-Spanish epics. They became a vehicle for inculcating cultural and religious values. These stories and songs would have provided entertainment in community gatherings during funerals, *fiestas* (holidays), and family gatherings. They would have been shared and discussed among workers while going about their work. Teaching in school reinforced the popularity of such literature. The use of *Pasyons* in masses and rituals popularized it. In addition, the *Pasyons* were dramatized during the long Holy Week celebration as community activities in the nineteenth century towns revolved around the church.

Jovita Castro, an editor of a collection of early Filipino literature, proposes that this literature, either as songs or poetic verses, may have taken the place of the epics among the Christianized tribes.[24] Castro takes the translations of these writings in different Philippine languages as proof of the popularity and degree of dissemination of this literature.[25] While the general plot and character of these stories follow the Spanish originals, Filipino writers adapted the stories to Filipino language, concepts, and situations. Hence, the literature contained popular articulations of the people's understanding of Christianity. Naturally the Filipino translations reflect the context of oppression and articulations of the people's resistance against the dominant power.

Resistant Movements

The origins of the anticolonial and Filipino nationalist literature can be traced to folk Christianity.[26] Popular culture and literature played an important role in the awakening of revolutionary ideas among the masses. Progressive views were proliferated by newspapers in Manila towards the

---

[23] Printing presses were a monopoly of religious orders. See John J. Phelan, "Philippine Linguistics and Spanish Missionaries, 1565–1700," *Mid-America* 37 (1955): 158–59.

[24] Jovita Ventura Castro, ed., *Anthology of Asean Literature: Philippine Metrical Romances* (Quezon City: Published by the Editors, 1985), 4. See also Reynaldo Clemeña Ileto, *Pasyon and Revolution: Popular Movements in the Philippines, 1840–1910* (Quezon City, Ateneo de Manila University Press, 1979), 12.

[25] Ileto, *Pasyon and Revolution*, 5.

[26] Robert G. Woods, "Origin of the Colorum," *Philippine Magazine* 16 (1929): 428–29.

end of the nineteenth century.[27] This ushered in the propaganda period with the founding of *Diaryong Tagalog* (Tagalog newspaper), as well as other publications, most known of which were Rizal's novels.[28]

Revolutionary thinking developed from folk religious traditions that were vehemently suppressed by the Spaniards. Cultural values such as parental love, *damay* (solidarity, empathy), *utang na loob* (debt of gratitude), and *hiya* (sense of shame) served as basis for critique of Spanish rule. Deeply rooted in Filipino culture, these concepts usually promoted passivity but also had latent meaning that could be revolutionary. The *Pasyon* revolved around Christ, who was willing to suffer and die for the salvation of the many. The passion story provided a language for articulating the suffering of the masses that called for *damay* (solidarity and empathy), the ideal of *lingap* (nurture) that characterize parental relationship, particularly that of a mother, and hope of *kalayaan* (liberation).

Liwanag (light) was central in the ideals of the revolution. This is due to the influence of the *pasyon*.[29] The awakening of a commonality of race realized through a shared experience of oppression did not just come from the articulations of the *illustrados*. The masses saw through the lies of Spanish ideology, which demanded loyalty to "mother" Spain.[30] The peasants real-

---

[27] Agoncillo, *Revolt of the Masses*, 21–23. As early as 1814, a version of the pasyon was collected and burned by church authorities. For a time *pabasa* (oral recitation of the pasyon) was also stopped because "of secret fear that the indios would turn the religious gathering into a political forum." See Fred Sevilla, *Poet of the People Francisco Balatas and the Roots of Filipino Nationalism: Life and Times of the Great Filipino Poet and His Legacy of Literary Excellence and Political Activism* (Manila: Trademark, 1997), 497–98. See also Bernardita Reyes Churchill, ed., *Resistance and Revolution Philippine Archipelago in Arms* (Manila: National Commission for Culture and Arts, 2002).

[28] Agoncillo, *Revolt of the Masses*, 22.

[29] Reynaldo Ileto, Filipinos and their Revolt: Event, Discourse, and Historiography (Quezon City: Ateneo de Manila Unviersity,1998), 29ff. See also Muriel Montenegro, *The Jesus of Asian Women* (Maryknoll: Orbis, 2006), 130–31.

[30] Reynaldo Clemeña Ileto, *Filipinos and Their Revolt: Event, Discourse, and Historiography* (Quezon City: Ateneo De Manila University Press, 1998), 1. For instance, the Doctrina Cristiana says, "Ang dugong totoo nang atin panğinoon Jesuchristo, capara niun nabohos sa cruz nang na matai siya. T, ano caia ang gagauin nang mañga Christiano nang macaparoon sa lanğit? S, Ang susundin nila ang sangpo, uong otos nang dios, pati nang otos nang *sancta yglesia yna natin*" (relevant line highlighted, roughly translated "They must obey the ten commandments of God, including the commands of the holy church our mother." See Doctrina Cristiana. http://www.gutenberg.org/files/16119/16119-h/16119-h.htm.

ized that the harsh treatment by Spain necessitated action against the rulers represented by the friars who postured as their benefactors.

Florante at Laura is one of the most popular romantic poetry, evidenced by the translations and its twelve editions from 1838–1901.[31] The composer of this literary piece deliberately wove in a strong sociopolitical message.[32] In one of the episodes, for example, while Florante is chained to a tree, he decries the "subjugated and oppressed condition of the Filipinos in the colonial Philippines where, … the moral order is reversed and the *flag of the worst evils waves high.*"[33] In Teodoro Agoncillo's words, *Florante at Laura* "was a severe indictment of the ruling race, a voice raised in protest against Spanish iniquities and oppression, a fierce outcry of a sensitive and wounded soul asking for justice."[34]

Like other nationalist writers, Baltazar used the "parent-child" relationship to image colonial relationship. Castro notes Baltazar's innovation in introducing the need for human and not divine intervention in "saving the Christian hero from imminent death."[35] In the story, a Muslim whom Florante recognized as a brother rescues him. When at last Florante becomes king, peace, justice, and abundance are ushered in. Castro comments:

> Baltazar must have perceived that the colonizers used religion to gain control over the people—and so, to undermine its hold, he made his principal villain a Christian…. Baltazar intimates to his compatriots what they must do to liberate themselves, and right the reverse moral order. Considering that the only education available to most Filipinos then consisted of catechism and a little reading, writing, and counting, Baltazar advocates enlightenment as a means to personal and social liberation.[36]

Another popular *awit* titled *Juan Teñoso* explores the theme of child-rearing and the relationship of a son to his parent who ill-treated him. It concludes with the thought that severe punishment is not love but evil, "A path that leads to hell."[37]

---

[31] The popularity of the *Florante and Laura* is attested by its wide dissemination with the estimated total number of printed copies from its first appearance in 1838 to 1906 totaling 106,100 copies. It is presumed that each copy changed hands many times over. The nationalist Apolinario Mabini produced a hand-written copy of the 399 stanza poem from memory when challenged to "give a work of the most outstanding Filipino poet." See Sevilla, *Poet of the People*, 3,5.
[32] Castro, *Anthology of Asean Literature*, 328.
[33] Castro, *Anthology of Asean Literature*, 329.
[34] Agoncillo, *Revolt of the Masses*, 19.
[35] Agoncillo, *Revolt of the Masses*, 19.
[36] Castro, *Anthology of Asean Literature*, 329–30.
[37] Castro, *Anthology of Asean Literature*, 104.

Even the seemingly benign popular story of *Ibong Adarna* (a mythic bird) is not bereft of allusions to the situation of the *indios*.[38] The story points to the "treachery and betrayal of the highly born personages like kings and queens, princes and princesses, and dons, and doñas."[39] The main plot of the triumph of good over evil amidst tribulations and the eventual establishment of a just, peaceful, and prosperous kingdom must have stirred the imagination of Filipinos.

Another *awit* entitled *Bernardo Carpio* gave voice to the peasants' nationalist sentiments. The song articulated the travails of the main protagonist using symbols and values that speak to the masses. Through the Spanish hero, the people recaptured their past apart from Spanish impositions, and imagined a future liberated from Spanish oppression. Symbols and images meaningful to Filipinos were used in the song. Rooted in the Philippine experience, it appealed to Filipino values of being with the suffering people—*damay*, using the lament genre.[40]

Cultural resistance and appropriation of the colonialist discourses for the purpose of undermining colonial power is seen by Vicente Rafael in the ways the *Tagalogs* (lowlanders from Luzon speaking Tagalog) dealt with colonialism. The use of Tagalog and other local languages in preaching and teaching provided the avenue for the colonized to negotiate the forms of submission and resistance. Rafael notes the recurring complaints of the Spanish friars about the failure by the natives to fully grasp the deep things of the faith.[41] He proposes that the Filipinos outwardly acceded to the Spaniards' demands but withheld what was interiorly required, concluding that the people "submitted while at the same time hallowing out the Spanish call to submission."[42] Ultimately the people transformed the idea of submission so prominent in the *Pasyon*. It was not submission to the unrelenting Spanish demands that pushed people to death but submission to the call to die, even to desire a "beautiful death," exemplified by Jose Rizal.[43] The tie that bound the *indios* (Indians) to Mother Spain was a suffering piety that awaits a reward in heaven.[44] But the people reinterpreted the call to suffering and submission to Christ, to being with Christ and those who suffered and died—*damay*, and being willing to go through suffering and death for the sake of the many and their liberation, as Christ did.

---

[38] Meaning Indian, the Spaniards' term for the natives.
[39] Castro, *Anthology of Asean Literature*, 163.
[40] Reynaldo Clemeña Ileto, *Pasyon and Revolution Popular Movements*, 13.
[41] Rafael, *Contracting Colonialism*, 109.
[42] Rafael, *Contracting Colonialism*, 135.
[43] Rafael, *Contracting Colonialism*, 209.
[44] Ileto, *Filipinos and Their Revolt*, 245.

Unmasking the imperial projection of a caring mother, Filipino literature in the second half of the nineteenth century depicted Spain as a mother who was a fraud by her cruelty. The letter *K* in the flag of the Katipunan also means *kalayaan* (shared well-being and freedom).[45] This concept, harping on the problematic relationship between "parent and child," justifies separation and declares independence from an uncaring mother. It also captures the aspiration for shared well-being in a free society. The founders of the Katipunan coined the word, which does not appear in Sanlucar and Noceda's eighteenth-century dictionary. Reynaldo Ileto says of the word, "In '*kalayaan*', the revolutionists found an ideal term for independence that combined separation from a colonial ruler (i.e., a mother who showed cruelty instead of love) and the 'coming together' of people in the Katipunan (sacred society)."[46] Katipunan is *kalayaan* in that it is a recovery of the country's pre-Spanish condition that is experienced as *layaw* (cared for, free, and indulged) by the individual, who is able to embrace the national from familial.[47]

The name *Katipunan* comes from the word *tipon*, which means assemble. The prefix *ka-* and suffix *-an* affixed to a word denotes companionship, reciprocity, simultaneity, collectivity. Katipunan ideology is not only anticolonial. It aimed for national unity—katipunan (coming together of a collectivity). Father Evaristo Arias a Spanish Dominican priest says of the Katipunan:

> The identity of race is exploited in the Katipunan society by creating a veritable league of natives of the same blood, *kadugo*, as they say in Tagalog, proving they are all brothers (*kapatid*) and that they should band together against the Spaniard who are not *kadugo*, but rather who came to the islands to dominate and exploit them. The great strength of the Katipunan consists in turning the cause into question of race against race, dominated

---

[45] Ileto notes that *kalayaan* did not mean freedom or independence prior to the rise of separatist government. "In translating into Tagalog the ideas of 'liberty, fraternity, equality' learned from the West, propagandists like Bonifacio, Jacinto, and perhaps Marcelo H. del Pilar built upon the word *layaw* or *laya* which means 'satisfaction of one's needs', 'pampering by parents' or 'freedom from strict parental control'. Thus, *kalayaan* as a political term, is inseparable from its connotations of parent-child relationship, reflecting social values like the tendency of mothers in lowland Philippines to pamper their children and develop strong emotional ties with them. Childhood is fondly remembered as a kind of 'lost Eden', a time of *kaginhawahan* (contentment) and *kasaganaan* (prosperity)." Kalayan is also the name for the official paper of the *Katipuan*.

[46] The term *katipunan* has the same root as the term *tipon* (to assemble) and *tipan* (to agree). The Old Testament is, for example, translated to Pilipino as *Daan* (Old) *nga Katipan* (Testament).

[47] Ileto, *Filipinos and Their Revolt*, 86–87.

against dominators, convincing the natives that they can rule and govern themselves.[48]

The primer of the Katipunan (*kartilya*) stressed reason and enlightenment on the basis of Filipino values. It condemned racial discrimination, economic oppression, and abuses of those in power. It regarded women as partners and commanded advocacy of the cause of the poor and the oppressed.[49] Emilio Jacinto, Andres Bonifacio, and Apolinario Mabini each drafted and published their own Ten Commandments that stressed moral regeneration and service to fellow persons.[50] The law for Filipinos is based on the idea of inherent goodness.[51] Filipinos are motivated by one's sense of duty and not by external compulsion. The concept of *kagandahang loob* (inner goodness, inner beauty) is rooted in a worldview where there is a harmonious relationship among humans and with nature. A person sees the self as one who feels, thinks, wills and acts as a whole.[52] Such holistic concept is also demonstrated in decision-making that is made in consideration of one's community and not only as an individual. *Pagbabagong-loob* (moral regeneration) was an important component of the Filipino revolutionary aspirations. The revolution was founded on fraternity (*pagkakapatid*), equality (*pagkakapantaypantay*), shared well-being and prosperity (*kaginhawahan*), and shared abundance (*kasaganaan*).[53] Land redistribution and political democratization were some of the practical measures that have been identified to make this a reality.[54]

The coopted Filipino elites arrogated unto themselves the fruits of revolutionary struggle. The founder of the Katipunan was the first victim of

---

[48] The Notes on the Philippine Insurrection (Apuntes Sobre LaInsurrecion Filipina) written by father Evaristo F. Arias to a friend in Spain. See Fidel Villarroel, *The Dominicans and the Philippine Revolution 1896–1903* (Manila: University of Santo Tomas, 1999), 179.

[49] Andres Bonifacio's Decalogue and the *Katilya ng Katipunan* are availble on line at http://malacanang.gov.ph/7013-andres-bonifacios-decalogue-and-the-kartilya-ng-katipunan/. See also Jim Richardson, *The Light of Liberty Documents and Studies on the Katipunan, 1892–1897* (Quezon City: Ateneo de Manila University Press, 2013), 189–92.

[50] Gregorio F. Zaide, ed., *Documentary Sources of Philippine History*, vol. 9 (Metro Manila: National Bookstore, 1990), 269–72.

[51] Mercado, *Elements of Filipino Philosophy*, 151.

[52] Mercado, *Elements of Filipino Philosophy*, 70–71, 152–54.

[53] Ma. Teresa Sicat, "The Philippine Nation in Literary Discourse," in *Nationalist Literature: A Centennial Forum*, ed. Elemer A. Ordoñez (Quezon City: University of the Philippines and PANULAT, Philippine Writers Academy, 1996), 420.

[54] Woods, "Origin of the Colorum," 57.

class interest in the revolutionary government. Bonifacio, in the words of Jacinto, *"bearing on his shoulder all the burdens on the face of the earth*, at the age of thirty-three, did give his life in the struggle for *kalayaan*—a goal that one devoted his life to pursue—which involves hardship and shedding of blood."[55] Ileto said of Bonifacio, "Bonifacio's downfall can be traced to his preoccupation with 'sacred ideals' and moral transformation. He was led to this not so much by his personality ... as his familiarity with popular perceptions of change. Folk poetry and drama undoubtedly provided him with basic insights into the 'folk mind.'"[56]

Filipino religiosity played a role in arousing resistance. Many of the peasant group leaders were religious leaders. Furthermore, the movement's documents as well as those of other revolutionary millenarian peasant groups attest to the prominence of religious themes in the revolution.[57] "It was the vitality of the *pasyon* tradition that made it possible for ordinary folks to recognize the appearance of other Christ-like figures."[58] The cultural element of the revolution is seen in the use of vernacular language as its official language.[59]

Today, the aspiration for social justice and land by the revolutionaries remains a promise. The United States of America, a more powerful colonizer, replaced Spain. The local elites who were coopted by the Spaniards inherited the same privileged position under the Americans. When the *encomiendas* were abolished, the ruling elite had the means and influence to acquire ownership of lands through purchase and procurement of title.[60] Ideological propaganda and repressive policies later pacified the exhausted peasants who fought for the aspiration of land to till and freedom from colonial impositions. Interrupted, the social ideals of the revolution were not realized. With continuing clamor for social justice silenced and suppressed with the help of the Unites States armed forces, the remnants of Filipino revolutionary fighters and ideologues went underground. Disillusioned, many resorted to banditry and lawlessness. Peasant organizations such as the *Kalipunang Pambansa ng mga Magsasaka sa Pilipinas* (KPMP, roughly translated National Union of Farmers in the Philippines) and the *Aguman ding Malding Talapagobra* (General Workers Union) continued the peasants' struggle for land to till. The constituencies of these groups formed the

---

[55] Ileto, *Pasyon and Revolution*, 111.
[56] Ileto, *Pasyon and Revolution*, 109.
[57] Agoncillo, *Revolt of the Masses*, 87–101; Zaide, *Documentary Sources of Philippine History*, 194–229.
[58] Woods, "Origin of the Colorum," 57.
[59] Bienvenido Lumbera and Cynthia Nograles Lumbera, *Phillippine Literature: A History and Anthology*, English ed. (Pasig City: Anvil, 2005), 45.
[60] Dorothy Friessen, *Critical Choices: A Journey with the Filipino* People (Grand Rapids: Eerdmans, 1987), 35. See also Constantino, *Past Revisited*, 22.

armed group HUKBALAHAP (Hukbong Bayan Laban sa Hapon or People's Army against Japan). These groups and the Socialist Party of the Philippines coalesced in the founding of the Communist Party of the Philippines's in 1968.[61]

The economic and social causes of the Philippine revolution against Spain and the Americans persist to the present. Prejudice against non-Christians that has been sown by Spanish and American colonizers continues. Lives continue to be sacrificed both on the side of the government and rebel groups in wars fed by appalling economic inequality and abuse of power. Propped up by the dominant West, the Philippine postcolonial governments appear secure in its legitimacy. Complacency and patronage politics perpetuate the status quo. Nationalist rhetoric fails to touch chord among the masses as it served the purposes of those in power. Genuine love and pride of country do not develop as it is identified with an unjust state. Renato Constantino describes interrupted development of the nation in these words:

> the process of making a nation was interrupted and later tragically redirected to produce what is now a confused people who in their pathetic search for identity look to an idealized indigenous past and to the Hispanized culture of their colonial forebears and who in their desire to solve the problems of the present, dream of a future anchored on western concepts and values.
>
> ... the Filipino must now discover himself in the realm of consciousness—that is, a consciousness that articulates its own economic, political and cultural aspirations and contraposes itself to an all-pervading consciousness that seeks to keep the Filipino people permanently integrated in a worldwide system that produces poverty, wars and degradation for the underdeveloped nations of the world.[62]

Independent yet Colonialist

Seventy years after the Philippines was "granted" independence by the United States underdevelopment continues to plague the nation. Measured with an unrealistic poverty threshold of Php 9,140 for a family of five,[63] which translates to a total food and nonfood expenditure of Php 61.00 per

---

[61] William Chapman, *Inside the Philippine Revolution* (Quezon City: Rex, 1987), 54, 58, 74.
[62] Chapman, *Inside the Philippine Revolution*, 54.
[63] Poverty incidence among Filipinos registered at 26.3 percent, according to the Philippine Statistics Authority, "2015 Census of Population," psa.gov.ph/statistics/census/2015-census-of-population.

person per day (1.33 US dollars), 26.3 percent of the population come out poor.[64] Most of the poor (53 percent) live in the rural area compared with 23 percent in urban areas.[65]

Significant to this study is the widely accepted assertion that traces the continuing underdevelopment to the failure to harness the cultural resources of the Filipino society towards national development.[66] Colonial dominance and miseducation produced a negative self-image among Filipinos who esteem the white race and culture above its own. Consequently, the general populace remains subservient to Western economic and political interests as Filipinos are vulnerable to foreign cultural influence. Cultural subjugation and economic dependence, combined with the failure to develop land and harness human resources, are the reasons why the Philippines, still an agricultural country, remains poor. A legacy of colonial governments, agricultural production is monopolized by the richest 5 percent of the population who controls 45 percent of the country's arable lands.[67] Filipino farmers are consigned to being farm laborers, workers, and tenant farmers. Beholden to and in collusion with their foreign counterparts, the Filipino elite maintain the dominance of the Western companies' interests in the Philippines.[68] The Philippines' crony-capitalism index, the wealth controlled by crony sector, is very high at 11.3 percent of the Gross National Product.[69] Better educated and skilled Filipinos seek to migrate to the United States and other developed countries. Lack of opportunities and employment push people to seek those in other countries.

---

[64] Countrymeters, "Population of the Philippines 2015 Philippines Population 2016 | Current Population," http://countrymeters.info/en/Philippines. Philippine population numbered 101, 498, 763 people on January 2016.

[65] The World Bank, "The Phillipines: A Strategy to Fight Poverty," http://web.worldbank.org/WBSITE/EXTERNAL/TOPICS/EXTPOVERTY/EXTPA/0,,contentMDK:20204974~menuPK:435735~pagePK:148956~piPK:216618~theSitePK:430367,00.html.

[66] Felipe M. De Leon Jr., "In Focus: Beyond the Dona Victorina Syndrome," Office of the President, National Commission for Culture and Arts, 25 February 2015, ncca.gov.ph/about-culture-and-arts/in-focus/beyond-the dona-victorina-syndrome. See also Ma Melegrito, et al., eds., "Philippine National Situation," *Palaso* 1.1 (2013): 45. See also Fabella, "Inculturating the Gospel."

[67] *IBON Facts and Figures*, 18.23–24 (1995): 11.

[68] Temario C. Revira, *Landlords and Capitalists* (Quezon City: University of the Philippines Press, 1994), 73, 127–28.

[69] Ben O. de Vera, "PH Rises to Third Place in Crony-Capitalism Index," *Philippine Daily Inquirer* 31.152 (2016): A2. De Vera quotes the *Economist*: "Crony capitalism—or 'rent-seeking,' as economist call it—shades from string-pulling to bribery. Much of it is legal, but all of it is unfair. It undermines trust in the state, misallocates resources and stops countries and true entrepreneurs from getting rich."

Resistance and opposition to the established government is very much alive in the postcolonial Philippines. Widely perceived as power hungry and corrupt, demonstrations, protest marches, and civil disobedience against the government are common occurrences in the country. A people's movement toppled the more than two decades of dictatorial leadership by Ferdinand Marcos. Fifteen years later in 2001, another president was removed by popular call. The armed resistance movements, the Moro national Liberation Front, its split movement the Moro Islamic National Liberation front, and the longest revolutionary movement in Asia—the Communist Party of Philippines and its armed wing the New People's Army—continue to thrive because of socioeconomic grievances against the government. The present situation of the Philippines is a stalemated status quo: on the one side is the established ruling elite who maintain the status quo, and on the other side are those who undermine the programs of the government and fight it, draining its resources and making development in the countryside and areas of conflicts problematic.

The Filipino intellectual E. San Juan Jr. analyzes the Filipino situation in a postcolonial perspective and concludes:

> the Philippines today exemplifies a disintegrated socioeconomic formation in which the major contradictions of our time—antagonistic forces embodying the pressures and impulses of class, ethnicity, gender, nationality, religion, sexuality, and so on—converge into fissured and disjunctive panorama open for misinterpretation, critique, and ecumenical exchanges. The challenge is posed and made more urgent by the suffering of at least 70 million people. But can U.S. knowledge production of the traditional kind ..., whose performance and achievement cannot be disassociated from its complicity with imperial capital, ever succeed in confronting what it has produced or comprehend the dialectic of material forces that is its condition of possibility, its raison d'etre?[70]

Recent government statistics project positive gains in the economy and in land redistribution. But much of the economic benefits of progress are confined to those who are coopted by the liberal economic system.[71] Progress is trumpeted as achievable only by accommodating the interest and ways of powerful nations. There appears to be no alternative to economic dependency on more advanced nations that facilitate out flow of surplus wealth through multinational corporations. The powerful center of the

---

[70] San Juan, *After Postcolonialism*, 93.
[71] In Cielito F. Habito's term the economy's growth has been "narrow, shallow, and hallow." Cielito F. Habito, "Towards More Dispersed Growth," *The Philippine Daily Inquirer* 31.147 (2016): A13.

globalizing world is as dominant as ever. In the Philippines, the people and the country's natural resources are drained as the tentacles of the greedy center sap the land of life and resources.

But the weak is not without weapons of resistance. The majority of the Philippine population—the poor—have the numbers. Distilled by the wisdom of the ages, rich and varied cultures and subcultures are resources that can define distinct identities and will empower peoples to stand up for their way of life and land. Peoples and communities who are grounded in their land realize the wisdom of symbiotic relationship with nature that has been cornerstone of indigenous worldview. It is in upholding equality, fraternity, and mutual help that good life can be achieved as opposed to accumulation and domination. The dominant mass media's promotion of consumerist lifestyle can be exposed for what it is—a propaganda that ensures the exploitation and hold of multinational companies on the resources of those in the peripheries.

For development to benefit the more than one hundred million *Juanas and Juans*, it must be attuned to the capacities and creativities arising from the Filipino material and cultural resources. Environmental and developmental policy must accord with the Filipino worldview of the land as *Inang Bayan* who gives life and nourishes its people. In turn it must be regarded as sacred deserving respect, gratitude, and care. The *loob* (interiority) of society must reflect inherent goodness that is the source of the Filipino morality. Philippine education must be geared towards developing our God-given material and human capacities first for the benefit of the Filipino. Economic production must foster interdependence where the gifts and resources of different groups and regions are valued and utilized for the good of the whole.

The construction of a society that brings healing and dignity to a nation shattered by colonialism and at present at the mercy of the world's powerful few is a responsibility that theology must not abscond. This way Christianity's complicit role in the colonization and Westernization of the country can be arrested and redressed. It is Christianity that is in the position to constitute a broad coalition of reform minded people. Theological and hermeneutical constructions toward sociopolitical dimension can pave the way for the deconstruction of systemic imperial culture that has dominated the nation for almost five centuries.

Presently, uncertainty grips the nation as a new set of national leaders took office in 2016. The threat of Chinese annexation of Philippine territorial waters, despite the ruling of the International Court of Arbitration that upheld the integrity of Philippine territorial claims and its dominance in its economy, are very real threats. Philippine market remains dominated by foreign companies. Propelled by globalization, materialist and consumerist culture pave the way for the influx of imported goods. Western dominance in practically every aspect of life, and especially in technology and communications ensures the perpetuation of hegemonic knowledge.[72] Western companies continue to profit as new local industries fail to compete with the technologically advanced and well-financed foreign counterparts. The tight hold on power by the colonially entrenched ruling elite is as strong as ever.

Christianity was used as the legitimating narrative for the Spanish and American colonization. But Christianity has taken root in the Philippine context and has been used to empower resistance and revolt against Spain. Since then, Filipino identity has been tied up with religiosity—indeed both Muslims and Christians are people of the book who regard the Bible as authoritative.

Given the problematic role of Christianity in the colonization of the Philippines, by the Spaniards and the United States, and its complicit role in the westernization of our culture at present, the call of contextualized hermeneutics is more urgent.

Biblical Interpretation in the Philippines

A serious engagement with context of interpretation prioritizes concrete historical and social engagement. It paves the way for a dialogue between the Bible's context and the recipient context mediated by the text. Trium-

---

[72] Edward Said for example summarizes what the few books on literary criticism from the point of view of imperialism say of Western culture, "All these books point out the centrality of imperialist thought in modern Western culture." Said quotes William Appleman Williams, "imperial outreach made it necessary to develop an appropriate ideology" in alliance with military, economic, and political methods. These made it possible to "preserve and extend the empire without wasting its psychic or cultural substance." There are hints in these scholars work that, again to quote Williams, imperialism produces troubling self-images, for example, that of "a benevolent progressive policeman." Said further notes that literature produced from the Age of imperialism builds on underlying earlier ideologies such as, "To think about distant places, to colonize them, to populate or depopulate: all of this occurs on, about, or because of land…. As conclusions of the novel confirm and highlight an underlying hierarchy of family, property, nation, there is also a very strong spatial *hereness* imparted to the hierarchy…. In all these areas—gender, class, race—criticism has correctly focused upon the institutional forces in modern Western societies that shape and set limits on the representation of what are considered essentially subordinate beings, thus representations itself has been characterized as keeping the subordinate, the inferior." In general, the relationship imperialism and culture is largely overlooked in literary criticism. See Said, *Culture and Imperialism*, 64–65, 78–80.

phalism is precluded as sociocultural and political location are assumed. The approach that gives due recognition to the importance of a particular context is naturally critical of the biblical text and context. It is premised in a dialogue between the receptor's context and the Bible's historical context and text. The text is analyzed using local concepts and reality, and vice versa. While most historical and textual studies are set in hegemonic language, reading and articulating meaning in categories and cultural symbols (from a receiving community) necessitates deconstruction of imperializing and triumphalist ideologies (from other cultures).

The articulation of meaning in vernacular language empowers local meaning construction. Interpretation of a text in local context makes theology and hermeneutics accessible, participative, and people oriented. A contextual reading will naturally be resistant to cultural homogenization as it gives priority to the thought and social construction of particular communities.[73] Contextualization integrated into meaning construction gives serious attention to the lived experiences of particular communities as a hermeneutical resource. Contextual reality has the capacity to unmask the exploitative nature of hegemonic language and worldview. Expressed in language and codes familiar to a local community, contextualized interpretation can empower local communities to contribute to the process. With the land and its people as significant aspect, the development of a powerful knowledge production center is foiled. This way, hermeneutics is a means in creating authentic identity. An acknowledged theological location and community of accountability will make theological and hermeneutical endeavor responsible. Contextualization will give way to life-giving social structures and contribute to the construction of a just world order versus globalization and hegemonic theologizing.

Resistance and the Bible

Poverty and oppression of Filipino peasants did not end when the Filipino-American war ceased. American colonial policies such as the sedition law—which made advocacy of independence a serious crime—provoked continuing resistance. Yet colonial education and propaganda portrayed America as a vanguard of freedom and democracy.

Filipino priests who identified with the aspirations of the revolution carried on resistance against the Americans.[74] Folk religion continued to

---

[73] It is widely recognized, for example, that Western monocropping, which worked in the West, had destructive effects to the land and the people in Africa whose terrain, weather, and needs are more conducive to diversified cropping.
[74] John N. Schumacher, SJ, *Revolutionary Clergy: the Filipino Clergy and the Nationalist Movement 1850–1903* (Quezon City: Ateneo De Manila University, 1981), 193–94.

inspire further struggle,[75] and millenarian peasant groups such as the *Santa Iglesia* led by charismatic leaders were formed.[76]

Being in a precarious situation having been identified with Spain, the Catholic Church could not be a voice of critique. Neither could the protestant churches established by missionaries who came with the new colonizers. Protestant converts were naturally sympathetic with the Americans. But the religious zeal for resistance continued in the nationalist church that emerged during the revolution—the *Iglesia Filipina Independiente* or *IFI* (Philippine Independent Church).[77]

At the coming of the Japanese, the resistance groups formed the *Hukbo ng Bayan Laban sa Hapon* (HUKBALAHAP or People's Army Against Japan). After the Japanese American war, when America recognized the Philippine's independence in 1946, the peasant organizations' demand for socio-economic reforms was directed towards post-American governments. These peasant organizations later came under the leadership of PKP (Partido Komunista ng Pilipinas or Communist Party of the Philippines) formed by radical student activists. Thus the peasant movements gained a secular nonreligious identity. The peasant organizations and PKP became the core members and fighters when the Communist Party of the Philippines—New People's Army—was established in 1968.

In the 1960's Vatican II and the World Council of Churches encouraged social activism. Christians felt called to be with the struggling poor. Solidarity with the poor led many to join political marches and rallies. Identification with the oppressed sector, and the experience of persecution both from the established churches and the government, compelled many activist Christians to go underground and join CPP-NPA as fighters or educators, or simply as supporters. In 1972, the organization Christians for National Liberation (CNL) was formed. (This organization became a part of the National Democratic Front—NDF—the umbrella organization led by the Communist Party [CPP] of the Philippines.) The theology identified with those taking part in the political and ideological struggle against the Philippine government came to be known as the "theology of struggle." Using class analysis and discerning the effects of American imperial interests in the Philippines, theology of struggle served the cause of the oppressed sectors in the Philippines by critiquing the collusion of the elitist government with the imperial West.

Most Protestant missionaries brought Bibles and encouraged Bible reading. Bible Schools were established. The Union Theological Seminary

---

[75] Ileto, *Pasyon and Revolution*, 186–94; Constantino, *Past Revisited*, 270–86.
[76] Ileto, *Filipinos and Their Revolution*, 139–45, 151–53.
[77] Constantino, *Past Revisited*, 252–55.

(Manila, 1907), Central Philippine University College of Theology and Silliman Bible Training Institute (Visayas, 1905 and 1914), and the Asian Theological Seminary (Manila, 1969) were established to train pastors and church workers. The early teachers in these seminaries were from the West, particularly from North America. Critical analysis of biblical texts employed in the European and North American Protestant seminaries spilled over to missionary established seminaries in the Philippines.

Contextualizing the Bible was advanced with the establishment of the ATSSEA, now Association of Theological Education in South East Asia (ATESEA), in 1957. The above-mentioned seminaries became the founding members. This was a big push towards the development of quality and contextualized theological education in the Philippines among Protestants. In 1971 the consortium adapted the Critical Asian Principle (CAP) as a framework for Theological Education. CAP emphasizes the context of South East Asia as an important source in the theologizing and interpreting processes. CAP emphasized Asia's diverse cultures and religions among which Christianity is a minority. It also underscored South East Asia's colonial experience and search for authentic identity in the process of nation building.

Four facets of CAP were stressed in theological education: "the situational, the hermeneutical, the educational, and missiological."[78] Applied to biblical studies, CAP gave emphasis to Asian orientation and contextualization in the interpretation of the Bible. The CAP was later enriched specifying the Asian situation: the prevalence of poverty, the marginalization of certain groups of people such as women and the indigenous peoples, the need to foster life-sustaining theologies, and the theological task of empowering resistance against economic and cultural imperialism. Today, many professors in Protestant theological schools in South East Asia are graduates of the consortium of South East Asian Theological Schools, the South East Asia Graduate School of Theology (SEAGST) and ATU (ATESEA Theological Union), and thus espouse a contextualized methodology and Bible reading.

Among the Roman Catholics in the Philippines, Vatican II encouraged the use and reading of the Bible and its contextualization.[79] More courses in biblical studies were incorporated in theological studies. Catechetical teaching in the Catholic Church subscribes to two hermeneutical principles: the

---

[78] The World Bank, "The Critical Asian Principle," https://web.archive.org/web/20070222131109/http://www.atesea.org:80/CAPrev.htm.

[79] See Patricia Panganiban, "Inculturation and the Second Vatican Council," *Landas* 18 (2004): 59–93. Roman Catholic theologians appear to prefer the term inculturation defined as the process by which the gospel becomes a part of the culture of a people. See Sabino A. Vengco, "Another Look at Inculturation," *Philippine Studies* 32 (1984): 181–96, particularly 188.

use of historical-critical and other exegetical methods to discover authorial intention, and the discernment of the spiritual meaning of the text.

Significant to the development of biblical studies among Philippine Catholics is the establishment of the Catholic Biblical Association of the Philippines (CBAP), an association of biblical scholars and professors established in 1999. Current journals from Catholic schools point to intentional contextualization such *Landas* (way), and *Diwa* (soul or essence).[80]

Thus Filipino theologians and Bible interpreters became more engaged with Philippine sociopolitical reality. Filipino reality, thought, and language became important sources in theologizing. Two diverging tendencies can be observed in Filipino Bible interpretations. On the one hand are those who largely follow Western readings that emphasized personal spiritual meanings mainly observed but not exclusive among the evangelical wing. On the other are those who equate God's actions with the actualization of God's justice in the lives of the people, particularly among groups connected with the National Council of Churches in the Philippines and among many Roman Catholic theologians and Bible interpreters.

Filipino biblical reading and theology use Filipino sources and elements in the hermeneutical process and theological articulation.[81] Many books have been published along this line. The titles of these books bear this out: *God's Liberating Acts*,[82] *God's Kingdom and Human Liberation*,[83] *The Path to Liberation*,[84] *Ang Kristiano ay Rebolusyonaryo* (roughly translated *A Christian Is a Revolutionary*),[85] *Revolutionary Spirituality*,[86] *Radical and Evangelical: Portrait of a Filipino Christian*,[87] *Introduction to the Old Testa-*

---

[80] *Landas*: Journal of the Loyola School of Theology; *Diwa*, Journal published by the Graduate Schools of the Divine Word Seminary, Tagaytay City and Christ the King Mission Seminary, Quezon City, Philippines.

[81] The name *Filipino* first referred to the group that professed loyalty to the Philippine nation and people. Everett Mendoza elaborates, "Filipino ... is fundamentally a political, rather than a racial, term." Everett Mendoza, *Radical and Evangelical: Portrait of a Filipino Christian* (Quezon City: New Day, 1999), 9.

[82] Melanio L. Aoanan, *God's Liberating Acts* (Quezon City: New Day, 1985).

[83] Antonio M. Pernia, *God's Kingdom and Human Liberation* (Manila: Divine Word Publications, 1990.

[84] James R. Whelchel, *The Path to Liberation: The Theology of Struggle in the Philippines* (Quezon City: New Day, 1995).

[85] Perdo V. Salgado, *Ang Kristiano ay Rebolusyonaryo* (Manila: Lucky, 1995).

[86] Mariano C. Apilado, *Revolutionary Spirituality: A Study of the Protestant Role in the American Colonial Rule of the Philippines 1898–1928* (Quezon City: New Publishers, 1999).

[87] Mendoza, *Radical and Evangelical.*

ment: Liberation Perspective,[88] and *Reading and Hearing the Old Testament in Philippine Context*. Few women have ventured into biblical studies.[89] Filipina Bible interpreters and theologians tap into the common revolutionary roots and in addition bring in the Filipina feminist perspective that critique dominating masculinity of texts and interpretations.[90]

Rodrigo D. Tano in his study of contextualization in the writings of four Filipino theologians identifies three themes: liberation and development, modernization and social change, and the church mission. He explains in part:

> The economic and social inequalities which separate the rich and the poor underscore the need to redress the situation and the theologians address themselves to this problem. Under the name of "total salvation," Abesamis lays down the basis for a theology of liberation and development and defines the mission of the church in the Philippines today. The meaning of salvation for the Filipino involves not only the liberation of the soul from personal sin and guilt. It includes liberation of the total person from all forms of human ills: oppression, exploitation, disease, hunger, despair.... Arevalo addresses the problem of political and economic violence institutionalized in the form of oppression by the local elite, imperialism by developed nations, and the preservation of the status-quo by the local governments.... De la Torre moves beyond mere theorizing or theologizing. His radical commitment to the case of the oppressed masses has led him not only to develop a political theology but also to align himself with the oppressed in their sufferings and strivings.... De la Torre's radical stance is clear from his revolutionary practice of politicizing the people and organizing them as potent force for social change. For his part Nacpil deals with the theme of liberation at the level of worldview and attitude.[91]

Recent works by Revelation E. Velunta (biblical studies, Old Testament)[92] and Ely Fernandez (theology) follow the mold of Robert Warrior's Bible reading.[93] They read the Bible from the perspective of the receiving

---

[88] Ceresko, *Introduction to the Old Testament*.
[89] I only know one other woman who specialized in biblical studies (Hebrew Bible): Arche Ligo. Unfortunately, I have no access her work.
[90] See Lily Fetalsana-Apura, "Reclaiming Biblical and Cultural Heritages: Femininity and Masculinity in Creation," in *Asian Feminist Biblical Studies*, ed. Maggie Low (Hong Kong: The Chinese University Press, forthcoming).
[91] Rodrigo D. Tano, *Theology in the Philippine Setting: A Case of Contextualization of Theology* (Quezon City: New Day, 1985), 143.
[92] See Revelation E. Velunta, "Onesimus and Today's OFW's: Reading Philemon Inside a Jeepney," *The Union Seminary Bulletin* 4 (2007): 11.
[93] Robert Warrior, "Canaanites, Cowboys, Indians: Deliverance, Conquest, and Liberation Theology Today," *Christianity and Crisis* 49.19 (1989): 261–65.

community. The methodology used in this book treads on path forged by Filipino biblical interpreters and theologians. What Everett Mendoza says of theology can also be observed in Filipino Bible interpretation—it is engaged not in the abstract and theoretical biblical issues but with the "life-and-death issues that Christians face today"—the Filipinos' struggle for liberation.[94]

This book incorporates critique of the biblical context, the text, and the context of interpretation, thus imbedding resistance in the hermeneutical process. The concrete reality of varying people presents valid categories that determine meaning. At the same time, I take the Bible as a resistance text that can critique culture and the receiving context. Doing so, I assert and ensure that hermeneutics serve the cause of the weak and oppressed.

Resistant Reading

This study affirms that the context of the text is the text's co-text. Its importance for an informed interpretation of a text cannot be overemphasized. Similarly, a text can only be meaningful as it is contextualized in the receptor's context. An interpretation that takes the text seriously must give equal importance to the text's context, the text itself, and the receptor's context. A thorough study of the scripture and the receptor contexts provide an informative dialogue facilitated by the text. As the text is always mediated by a carrier culture, the construction presented in the text is culture specific. But the dialogic process presumes the validity of concrete reality in determining interpretation. It therefore opens both contexts as well as the text to critique. This method opens up the hermeneutical process towards the recognition of positive values in the other cultures and in lived reality. The irrelevant aspects of the co-text and the text come out as these encounter a particular living reality. The material and sociocultural achievements of a society is specific to the location and characteristics of its land and challenges presumed meanings. Communication rests on commonality of symbols; hence, the text can only be fully apprehended in the language and symbols meaningful and practicable in a particular society. Contextual interpretation gives space for the other to be what it is. It is not dominating. The process of translation paves the way for the deconstruction of the carrier culture. Further, the translation of a text will give space for colonial redress in recognizing cultural imperialism and allow reconstruction following the receptor's context.

The contextual methodology used in this work focuses on the following points:

---

[94] Mendoza, *Radical and Evangelical*, 13.

1. The context of the text
   - The world and worldview of ancient Israel. What are the dominant powers and worldviews that undergirded established norms and social construction?
   - The impact of hegemonic culture and politics on ancient Israel. What are cultural and historical impacts of the international situation on Israel and how are these related to the literature being interpreted?

2. The Text
   - The larger literature of which the text is a part. How is the text understood in view of the larger cultural and literary milieu (synchronic meaning)?
   - Issues regarding reading and interpretation of the early prophetic corpus, in view of its context and content.

3. The Receptor's Context
   - A historical and cultural description of the receptor context.
   - A critical study of Western interpretational location and related texts.
   - A study of the historical and sociocultural symbols relevant to the text.
   - A translation of the text using sociocultural codes and language of the receptor community.

Employing the methodology above led to the recovery of the resistance meaning of Josh 1:1–9 and its translation to the Philippine context. Resistance is a reaction to dominance. Where power asymmetry is present, resistance is to be expected. The discernment of resistance therefore involves analysis of ideological and power structures.

The resistance function of the Hebrew Bible comes out as biblical interpretation takes notice of hegemonic culture that determine biblical interpretation. Trade liberalization and globalization trumpets the gospel that prioritizes individualistic outlook and gratification. The promotion of unhealthy and environmentally unsustainable consumption of the products of transnational corporations reaches the furthest communities. Dominant corporations dictate the way of life disseminated and advertised by the powerful center and their local counterparts. Hegemony is inscribed in the values and lifestyle of dominated people as they have become internalized.

Resistance develops sensitivity against hegemony. It is attuned to concrete human and environmental reality. It is life enhancing as it seeks to construct community well-being and dignity.

9.
JOSHUA 1:1–9: A FILIPINO READING

The Hebrew Bible remains an important authority for the majority population of the Philippines. As a product of its time, the Hebrew Bible particularly the EP and Josh 1:1–9 are resistance texts, which are relevant to the challenges facing the Filipino people and nation, and Asia in general. The dominating and pervasive presence of the empire is the context of the Bible's production. Employing contextual hermeneutics, the function of Josh 1:1–9 as a text that resists the empire comes out.

Reconstructing a People Shattered by Colonialism

As a part of a national narrative, Joshua must be read in its international context. A small and weak nation, dominated by the great empires of the ancient Near East, Israel expropriated the divine warrior concept against its colonial proponents. While Israel adapted the monarchy as a political structure, it circumscribed the monarchs of power for self-aggrandizement. Instead, the king was presented as a teacher and vanguard of the law. He was a brother of the people, responsible for the well-being of the whole nation. He was to be obeyed and supported by the people in as much as he upholds the law (1:18). The legitimacy of a monarch's rule was made dependent on observing the law. The law in Israel protected the poor and the marginalized from victimization. Customs and traditions such as the Sabbath, the festivals, and the Sabbath years instilled normative community ideals. The taboos and case laws preserved a community's way of life and wisdom. In defiance of the empire, Israel claimed to be a people of Yahweh and none other. Leaning on its faith in Yahweh, tiny Israel dared to resist the ancient superpowers. In alluding to war waged and fought by Yahweh, Israel declared war against colonialism.

Israel's covenant with God stood at the core of its identity. The rule of a just God was the center of the community characterized by well-being. Israel did not just dream of a free and just society. Out of the foundational values that characterized its social aspirations—fraternity, liberty, prosperity for all, faith in God, social justice—Israel constructed a national social program and ideology. Rooted in the land that served as the melting pot of civilizations, indigenous and foreign concepts made its way into Israel's idea of God and nation. Israel bound its law on its land and legitimized this claim by claiming a divine suzerain of its own. Standing up for a way of life that is firmly grounded and nourished by life in the land, Israel resisted and withstood assimilationist drive.

Joshua 1:1-9 underscores the importance of national unity. Ruling by God's direction, a leader upholds the law and defends the patrimony of a nation. He secures the well-being of the people. To be able to achieve this a leader must study and observe the law. He must listen to the people. For the sake of this responsibility he must be strong and courageous. In Josh 1:1-9, God and the people stress the need for strong leadership particularly in relation to colonialism, against which Israel has to contend for most of its history as a people.

Joshua 1:1-9 calls a people to courageously defend their land. Resistance against imperialism is a fight for the land. In the text, the practice of a people's social values and cultural norms are decisive for national success not military capability. Narratives define nations.[1] A national narrative such as Joshua would have stirred Israelites to stand up for their land and people. Alluding to Moses, the leader who was instrumental in the formation of Israel as nation, Josh 1:1-9 taps into the revolutionary origins of Israel. Likeminded leaders are called to continue what Moses have started. God's expressed will of having granted the land to Israel must be brought to realization. Joshua (meaning "Yahweh is your salvation") affirms Yahweh as the only God of Israel. Joshua the warrior leader is assured of Yahweh's presence and aid. The essence of resistance following the militant tradition of Moses and Joshua is exhorted. It asserts that the might of an empire cannot subjugate such spirit. Yahweh's presence abides with such leaders.

The law surpasses the importance of the land as rallying point of resistance. Like Israel's narratives, laws are constructs that create order. Both are products of historical and sociocultural forces at work in the society. Joshua makes the study and practice of Israel's cultural heritage imperative. The cultural fabric that binds Israel is strengthened. As the depository of the achievements of a society, a people's culture ensures the perpetuation of wisdom gleaned from Israel's material and social environment. Joshua affirms that Israel's way towards prosperity and success is to stand and fight for what Israel as a people has achieved.

Joshua 1:1-9 stresses the inseparable bond between the land, its people, and their way of life.[2] Land is an important aspect of nationhood.[3] For

---

[1] Said, *Culture and Imperialism*, xiii.
[2] Knauf, "Why Joshua," 80–82.
[3] Grosby, *Biblical Ideas of Nationality*, 27.

Israel it is an indispensable part of being a people of Yahweh. The acquisition and continuing possession of the land is a consequence of law observance. Towards this end, strength and courage against colonial pretensions are exhorted. Joshua 1:1–9 begs to be interpreted as a program of nation-building. Such purpose fits the colonial context of Joshua. Joshua's emphasis on leadership, land, and people bear this out. This interpretation affirms the relationship between a people's literature, their land, and their people, further reinforced by the claim of covenant with Yahweh. Bound to a territory Israel claims God's sanction of nationhood.[4] As a nation lives in the land, the land personifies its people. The law as an embodiment of a people's culture is the rallying point in resisting foreign influence.[5] Doing so, Israel encodes resistance in the heart of the Israelite culture. In other words, Israel in insisting on its way of life, in its land, constructs a culture of imperial resistance.[6] There can only be ancient Israel in the land of Israel. Joshua as literature affirms love of the land, the unity of its people, and the validity of its way of life. Punctuated by the exhortations—Arise! Now, Be strong! Be Courageous! Be brave! Do not lose hope—the passage presents a purposeful resistance against domination. The passage affirms the importance of the here and now and ensured the survival of Israel.

Mentioned only in verse 2, the existence and importance of the people is always presupposed in the passage. The people are the recipients of Yahweh's actions. It is for their sake that land must be acquired. The people observe the law to live in the land. It is for their prosperity and well-being that the law is given. In Josh 1:1–9, the twelve tribes stand united. At the beginning of the book (Josh 1:1–18), the themes of land and the law are stressed, and the book concludes with the same themes in Josh 24.

Deuteronomy and Josh 1:1–9 are located east of the Jordan. This location projects a situation of landlessness. Former slaves are suspended in a "no man's land" though they had been granted land by Yahweh. Israel projects a situation where colonialism had consigned them to being slaves, wanderers, refugees in a state of landlessness. In Deuteronomy, they claim identity (a people of Yahweh), with its own way of life (law and culture), and political structure (polity). The EP as Israel's national narrative elaborates the possible actualization of these themes. As a sovereign people Israel is portrayed to be autonomous and self-governing. They have fought for the sake of their land. They have a right to live according to their socio-cultural construction apart from imperial impositions. In this context, the

---

[4] Rose, "Deuteronomistic Ideology and Theology," 444. See also Zimmerli, *Old Testament Theology*, 65.
[5] Frankel, *Land of Canaan*, 38–39.
[6] Israel, in insisting on living by the law, stood firm on its identity like a badge of protest.

prohibition of treaty is a way of precluding assimilation, since treaties as illustrated in the reign of Solomon undermine a nation's social and moral integrity. Joshua anchors this social construction in a bounded territory. This claim is grounded to the settlement of the land five hundred years prior, claiming it as land grant from Yahweh their God. The allusion to the place where the sole of their feet have trod may be read as a code for the place where they actually stand. Israel lays stake on the land her people occupies. Joshua 1:1-9 affirms actual occupation, not a theoretical claim for the legitimation of conquest. This can be read as a taunt to colonial ambition of claiming distant lands. On their land Israel through Joshua is assured "no one will be able to stand against them." A confident assertion coming from a people whose ties with the land is unimpeachable. This assertion is borne by historical basis—the mighty Assyria failed to defeat Jerusalem.

Alas, the Babylonians dealt the blow to the backbone of Israel's national ideology. Israel was defeated. Yahweh did not fight for Israel in defense of the land. A humbled nation, Israel had to justify "abandonment" by Yahweh—an Assyrian imperial ideology. Expelled from the land, Israel held out the law as resistance rallying point. Israel's covenant relationship with God is her main identifying mark. Israel courageously stands for the law. This covenant relationship made effective by law observance is not dependent on land occupation. Yahweh will always be with Israel, as long as that covenant relationship survives; the covenant promises remain; the promise of land still anticipates fulfillment.

But the land remains an important aspect of the Hebrew faith. Though overshadowed in importance by the law, the occupation of the land is an important command for ancient Israel.

Having identified the central message of Josh 1:1-9, the common context between ancient Israel and the Filipino people is most remarkable. The function of vernacular literature in articulating shared experience of oppression stands out. Contextualizing Assyria's imperial ideology and treaty, Israel formulated a resistance text. In the same way, contextualized Christian concepts exposed Spain's claim as a farce. "Motherland" stands for life-giving relationship. Spain had not been a mother to the Philippines. The real motherland had been abused and subjected to the worst of evils. Contextualization paved the way for the critique of the dominant religious teaching that emphasized after life to justify oppression. It nullified the claim of '*utang na loob*' (debt of gratitude). Spain had been identified as an oppressive empire. Contextual understanding of the *pasyon* exposed the pretensions of a religious leadership that talks of truth but is unjust. Spain, not Christianity, was the enemy. Contextualized imperial proclamation inspired a national revolution and would have successfully expelled colonial Spain were it not for the intervention of another powerful colonizer—the Americans.

The Filipinos Are Not Israel

The Filipinos are not Israelites. Israel's polity and identity cannot be the polity and identity of Filipinos. To be fair it was never intended to be so. As mentioned it is a resistance literature of ancient Israel. In this regard, Bruce Malina's insight into the context of message receptor can be helpful.

> Meanings in fact are rooted in people's enculturation, socialization, interrelationships and interactions. The reason for this is that human beings are essentially social. They do not construct reality, not even socially. Rather they interpret all of their experiences by means of socially shared conceptions. These socially shared conceptions and the behaviors consequent upon them constitute what I am calling "the social system" (See Kilby 1993).[7]

William Larkin advances the same principle in interpretation by proposing the recasting of biblical message to culturally specific mediums:

> Culture specific commands communicate the value of a specific cultural action, but the shared understanding of the meaning of such an action is assumed, not expressed. In order for such a command to be carried out with the same meaning in another culture, it must be recast in a culture-specific form appropriate to that people's understanding. Because forms change in meaning from culture to culture, the same form or type of behavior will not necessarily express the same biblically intended function. And so, whether the biblical content is a human-universal, a general-principle, or a culture specific command, all can and should be expressed in a contemporary culture, in a dynamically equivalent way so that the effect on and in the response of the receptor will be as close as possible to that of the original audience.[8]

Joshua 1:1–9 is culturally and historically specific. It speaks of Israel to Israel. To communicate the message of resistance against imperialism to Filipinos the message must be recast in cultural and historical codes that are meaningful to Filipinos. This way the meaning which Joshua intended for ancient Israel is faithfully communicated to Filipinos today. Otherwise, Joshua will remain a document of ancient Israel and would have very little connection to the Philippine situation. As Paula McNutt elucidates: "Meaning is the only category which grasps the full relation of the past to the

---

[7] Bruce J. Malina, "Rhetorical Criticism and Social-Scientific Criticism: Why Won't Romanticism Leave Us Alone," in *The Social World of the New Testament*, ed. Jerome H. Neyrey and Eric C. Stewart (Peabody, MA: Hendrickson, 2008), 5–21.
[8] William J. Larkin Jr., *Culture and Biblical Hermeneutics: Interpreting and Applying the Authoritative Word in a Relativistic Age* (Grand Rapids: Baker, 1988), 149.

whole in life, for value, being dominantly effective, belongs essentially to an experience in a conscious present."[9]

The cited thinkers suggest encapsulating the message in a medium that speaks to Filipinos and connects with its social and cultural context. Having stated thus, an analysis of the Philippine context as a postcolonial and neocolonial nation affirms the common context between the two societies. To a degree the common context serves to further elucidate each other's contexts. For instance, present analysis of the Philippine situation affirms the importance of indigenous way of life as a potent force in resisting hegemonic knowledge. A sense of national identity is important in the formation of national consciousness and unity. Land is also an important theme in the Philippine revolution. Arising from its relationship with the land is a people's way of life. A people's way of life reflects a people's intimate knowledge of the land. It encodes ethical practices that work for the perpetuation of a way of life that enhances life. Land, the ground of material and cultural life of a people, is an indispensable part of a national life.

The early Filipinos were coerced to be Christians. But, the Judeo-Christian faith used as a tool of exploitation and oppression by the Spaniards took root in the native's soil. Folk Christianity it was called—the natives' appropriation of Christian faith in their own concepts, experience, and aspirations. Despite the inculcation of a passive faith and its isolation from reality in the service of the status-quo, the basic narrative of the Bible contained in the *Pasyon*, juxtaposed with the reality of unjust suffering, led to the realization of its authentic meaning—the affirmation of God's will for the liberation of the oppressed.

In the same way, the subjugated people apprehended the subversive meaning of literature used by the empire. Contextualization paved the way for the people to make their own interpretation, and construct their own meaning based on local values and concepts. The friars used *utang na loob* to bind the masses to Spanish loyalty, but for the people *utang na loob* (debt of gratitude) works in a particular social relationship, the violation of which, nullifies it. Contradiction in the life and practices of the friars allowed the peasants to see the reality of the *loob* (inner motivations) of the colonizers. They do not have *damay* (empathy); they are without shame; they are not real mothers; they did not give *layao* (freedom and care). The onerous relationship has violated the people's understanding of what is good and just. The Filipinos realized that their obligation is to the *Inang Bayan* (Motherland) and *Anak ng Bayan* (children of the land) who suffer, not to Spain.

---

[9] McNutt, *Forging of Israel*, 266.

It is to be noted that the popular teaching that emerged was characteristically a feminine theology that empathizes with the suffering *Inang Bayan* expressed in the worship of the Virgin Mother and the adoration of the child Jesus. A similar trend was observed by Rosemary Radford Ruether among various Christian communities throughout the history of Christianity—the apprehension and appreciation of the feminine aspect of the divine. This can be a reaction to the abusive friars, *guardia civils* (civil guards), Spanish officials, all imaged by males, drunken with power, devoid of nurturing, merciful, caring qualities that are valued in Filipino society.[10] Corpus has noted the fact that the Hispanic Christianity that was propagated in the Philippines was in a "most militant and narrow form" preached by colonizers "who held attitudes of sovereignty, power, and even overweening arrogance."[11] The people have made a break between Spain and the Christian God, because they believed in a merciful, loving, and forgiving supreme God, imaged by a mother towards her child.[12]

A juxtaposition of ancient Israel's context and the Philippine context expose the weaknesses of the post-Spanish Philippine revolutionary society, which persist to the present. The leaders of the *Katipunan* who came from the more comfortable class easily capitulated to the Americans.[13] They were coopted through colonial education and political patronage.[14] The

---

[10] Ruether concludes of the inclination to represent the divine as feminine, "its roots lie in the processes by which we are all responding to similar challenges and coming up with similar solutions in the context of a twenty-first-century world threatened by military violence, economic exploitation, and ecological collapse. It is based on a shared recognition that a male hierarchical concept of the divine is a major ideological reinforcement of these patterns of social domination. This recognition is creating views of the divine and of humanity and the earth in relation to the divine that, if not exactly the same, have a great deal of similarity. See Rosemary Radford Ruether, *Goddesses and the Divine Feminine: A Western Religious History* (Berkley: San Francisco University Press, 2005), 320.

[11] Onofre D. Corpuz, *The Roots of the Filipino Nation* (Quezon City: Aklahi Foundation, 1970), 40.

[12] Isabelo De Los Reyes, "The Religion of the Katipunan," in *Views on Philippine Revolution*, ed. Felina G. Mapa, vol. 1 (Quezon City: University of the Philippines and Toyota Foundation, 2002), 216, 218.

[13] Michael Cullinae, *Illustrado Politics: Filipino Elite Responses to American Rule, 1898–1908* (Quezon City: Ateneo De Manila University, 2003), 40, 43–6. In Cullinae's words, "Between 1899 and 1901, the success or failure of the resistance forces in most provinces was linked to the degree of commitment to the cause demonstrated by segment of the municipal elites. By 1901, most municipal elites had abandoned the struggle, not simply as a result of American military might but also with the realization that the American had no intention to rule over the casa tribunal (the administrative centers of local affairs, the domain of the local elites)."

[14] Cullinae, *Illustrado Politics*, 38; Lumbera, *Philippine Literature*, 85.

wealthy educated Filipino elite determined the course of the Philippine society in collaboration with the Americans.[15] In deciding important policies, class, and economic interests prevailed. The communal and historical ties that bound the villagers and their leaders have been severed completely. The development of cultural values and themes significant in the revolution were disrupted. In its place, American hegemonic discourse was promoted.

Anti-colonialist ideology united the disparate groups and regions in the uprising against Spain. But the grand narrative that fostered common identity against colonial interest was not established. Nor did it translate to polity. Consequently, the aspirations of the people as a whole, especially those of the vulnerable sectors did not find realization in the postcolonial governments. Philippine colonial and postcolonial governments accommodated policies inimical to Filipinos. American colonial policies made sure it would be so. Most known of these laws is the Sedition law which criminalized advocacy for independence. This law undermined resistance against US colonization and occupation.[16] The use of English as a medium of instruction paved the way for the influx of dominant Western culture and ideology. Colonial values promoted in education, print and broadcast instilled positive image of America and the West.[17] Coopted by the colonialist government, educated Filipinos failed to use Filipino literary productions in the service of the Filipino people.[18] Colonial education and propaganda have suppressed the development of vernacular language, indigenous knowledge, literature, and art. The symbiotic relationship with the environment cherished in indigenous culture was replaced by an anthropocentric utilitarian worldview. The development of literature in English presupposed Western worldview. Individualism, materialism, and modernism made headway into the folk mind.[19] It is remarkable that US colonialism ended at a time when Philippine literature had regained the character of nationalist literature patterned after the patriotic and resistance writings in the early years of American occupation.[20]

It is to Israel's traditionists' credit that Israel's grand narrative gained widespread acceptance. It must have represented and united the interests of a broad spectrum of ancient Israelite society. Israel's scriptures and Philippine history attest to the potency of literature as a means of resistance. Literature keenly represents society's realities that in turn impacts social

---

[15] Cullinae, *Illustrado Politics*, 47–48.
[16] Cullinae, *Illustrado Politics*, 74.
[17] Lumbera, *Philippine Literature*, 94–95.
[18] Lumbera, *Philippine Literature*, 94–95.
[19] Lumbera, *Philippine Literature*, 97.
[20] Lumbera, *Philippine Literature*, 103.

movements. Literature, a depository of society's thoughts, reflects the pressures upon society internally and externally.[21] It has the capacity to undermine hegemonic knowledge, shape public opinion, and shake the political establishment. For the Jews the development of common identity is a product of a widely disseminated national literature. The survival of Jewish communities in diaspora attests to the resiliency of culture as a resource of resistance against homogenization. Culture is a "society's life support system."[22] It is "the sum total of original solutions that a group of human beings invent to adapt to their natural and social environment."[23] Assimilation and foreign influence corrode national identity and unity. A community's development has always been linked with its culture.

Particular to the Philippine situation, the importance of a national narrative as a means of resistance is important. Mendoza states:

> What is anomalous in the Philippine case is that owing to the historic displacements of colonialism, what has prevailed so far is a form of reverse ethnocentrism, i.e., the adoption of new view from the outside as the normative Filipino worldview. Discourse (particularly of the state) is one carried on in a wide-open circuit of communication penetrated freely by dominant discourses emanating from the outside (of the national community) without any clear controlling reference point from within. Here, it is often the case that others are allowed to monopolize the initiative, determine the agenda, and dictate the terms and trajectory of engagement. Whether in actuality or psychically—via the internalized gaze of the other/s—what is seen to prevail in this order of things is an alien platform dictating the national agenda and making mockery of the term "national interest," which, historically, has not been in actuality clearly articulated, if at all. Again, while such a normative ethno-centered worldview is simply a default position for other nations for whom the call may even be to transcend such if its singularity is not to become internally oppressive, for the historically disenfranchised, it may rightfully, precisely, be the call of the day. This is all the more crucial in the face of an impending post-national

---

[21] Lumbera, *Philippine Literature*, 96–97, 104.
[22] De Leon, "In Focus."
[23] Steven Grosby's insight on the importance of national identity sheds light on the Philippine situation, "When attachment to the conceptual center of a nation is shaken by military defeat and especially territorial conquest, the nation may face death because those beliefs constitutive of the center are on the verge of ceasing to be accepted. It faces death inasmuch as the collective self-consciousness faces extinction, because the belief in the power of their nation and its institutions to safeguard the processes of the propagation and maintenance of life, its vitality, has been shown to be insufficient." Grosby, *Biblical Ideas of Nationality*, 110.

global scenario where survival calls for a clearly defined platform from which to assert one's collective interest.[24]

Ancient Israel's national narrative is clearly rooted in the interests of the constituents of Israelite community. Similarly, a Filipino national narrative must be in the service of Filipinos. Historical verity is important, where ambivalences exist the aspects of the narrative which contribute to the cause of nation building are preferred.[25] Mendoza cites a personal communication of Z. A. Salazar, whom she quotes in her call to situate the construction of national narrative in the Filipino community's lived experience:

> Lahat ng kapookan ay may kontradiksyon; lahat ng pagpopook ay nagdaranas ng kontradiksyon bahagya at pansamantala man. (No grounding is ever free from contradiction; all grounding [or platform-construction] is accompanied by the experience of ambivalence, no matter how slightly or momentarily).... Ang importante, sa palagay ko, ay ang paninindigan—dito, sa kahulugang nakatindig ka sa iyong napiling pook at tingnan and lahat ng implikasyon sa paninindigang ito. (What matters ultimately, in my opinion, is conviction—here, in the sense of your standing on your chosen ground and being able to have a clear-sighted view of all the implications that that particular grounding or conviction entails).[26]

Historical objectivity is a Western myth. Philippine historiography must contend with social location. E. San Juan comments on the necessity of "ethno-centered" national discourse:

> To speak then to Filipino of the productivity of postcolonial "hybrid" identities, "ambivalences," and the moment or state of "in-betweeness," is on one level, merely to speak of the commonplace and to miss out on the point entirely. For in the case of the majority of Filipinos, such invocations are merely uninteresting default positions, already the doxa of their reverse ethnocentric worldview, often conceived in terms of a kind of *halo-halo* (lit. "mix-mix") identity. I submit then that rather than expanding the space of agency, such postcolonial invocations, crassly appropriated, are bound merely to reinforce the prevailing neocolonial status quo.[27]

---

[24] Lily S. Mendoza, *Between the Homeland and the Diaspora: The Politics of Theorizing Filipino and Filipino American identities* (Manila: University of Santo Tomas Press, 2006), 220.
[25] A ready example is Glenn Mays's book, *Inventing A Hero: The Posthumous Re-Creation of Andres Bonifacio* (Quezon City: New Day, 1997).
[26] See Mendoza, *Between Homeland and the Diaspora*, 218.
[27] San Juan, *After Postcolonialism*, 93.

The function of literature, historical or otherwise, as resistance text against imperialism is affirmed by similar function in Africa. African fiction literature focused on culture.[28] The same function is gleaned from reading African-American literature as it stressed the aspirations of African American community.[29] But like Israel, literature must reflect structural reflections and cultural construction. This is necessary so that political structures and material life become an integral part of postcolonial reconfiguration. This shortcoming is also observed in theology and hermeneutics: failure to find an alternative allows the perpetuation of the status quo.[30]

Historical and literary production can be powerful tools in shaping a people's worldview particularly when written in the community's language.[31] Language prescribes a way of constructing reality. The English language presupposes Western worldview. The use of English has been a means through which the values and techniques of the West are internalized. It is in this aspect that knowledge of biblical language and receptor language is most valuable. Contextualized translation demands a critical analysis of a receptor culture as it presupposes deconstruction of carrier culture and language. In the process, it rules out moral absolutism and cultural superiority.

Joshua 1:1–9 is a nationalist text. It is a part of a national narrative. Building on Deuteronomy as a polity, the EP tapped on Israel's historical and cultural roots as resource of national identity, cultural heritage, and land claim, to constitute an ideology that will resist assimilation and sustain its sociopolitical reconstruction. This is necessary for the translation of the aspirations of the oppressed into a viable social program and political struc-

---

[28] Phillip Darby, *The Fiction of Imperialism: Reading between International Relations and Postcolonialism* (London Cassell, 1998), 180.

[29] Demetrice A. Worley and Jesse Perry Jr., eds., *African American Literature: An Anthology of Nonfiction, Fiction, Poetry, and Drama* (Lincolnwood, IL: National Textbook, 1993), xviii.

[30] Charles Villa-Vicencio, *A Theology of Reconstruction: Nation Building and Human Rights* (Cambridge: Cambridge University Press, 1992), 23.

[31] Torres-Yu says of literature: "literature as a social form of consciousness which is inextricably linked with the complex relationship to economic and political structures. As social consciousness, it reflects objective social processes. At the same time, it also serves as an instrument for mediating an understanding of such society, either by affirming existing social relationships or by questioning such relationships in order to change them." See Rosario Torres-Yu, "The State of Philippine Literature," in *Nationalist Literature: A Centennial Forum*, ed. Elemer A. Ordoñez, trans. Cheree Quizon (Quezon City: University of the Philippines Press and PANULAT, Philippine Writers Academy, 1996), 317.

ture.³² Biblical hermeneutics must play a part in the construction of local theologies that is liberating so as not to be a party to the ascendancy of dominating forces that sap surplus towards the center. What Gelacio Guillermo says of the role of national art and literature in nation building is true for Israel:

> A truly national art and literature unite the broadest segment of our population against US imperialism and its local agents from the big landlord and big comprador bourgeois classes. They combat ideas and values of the dominant colonial, feudal and fascist culture which, among others, affirms that the interest of the ruling classes and the people are one and the same, at the same time abetting divisiveness along regional, linguistic, and religious lines. In contrast to colonial, feudal and elitist art and literature, a national art and literature assert the right of the people for national sovereignty, unite them on the basis of this right, and cultivate everything that can enhance this unity and national dignity.³³

In the case of Josh 1:1–9, the original text is in Biblical Hebrew. The language anchors the text in a particular setting and culture. But the meaning of the text changes as it is translated into another language and context. For instance, English translations of Joshua presuppose Western worldview and uproot the text from its culture and historical mooring. Meaning is anchored on lived reality. This aspect of the text cannot just be ignored. The context gives rise to the text and establishes its meaning. In this connection, Israel's context begs for an interpretation of its history and/or literature as resistance text. It came out of Israel's valiant efforts to resist and survive massive forces of oppression and internationalization. The literature itself taken out of context can be a tool of domination. But the context powerfully establishes the resistance and liberating intent of Josh 1:1–9.

In the same way, the oppressed can subvert and mimic the dominant ideology. But it cannot be taken as affirmation of imperial ideology. The context significantly changes the function of such ideology. Directed against the powerful the same ideology becomes a means of self-defense. While a literature may originate from the exploitative class, the intent and meaning of the same changes as the context changes. Extravagantly violent words in the mouth of the weak become rhetoric, or satire as it is literally implausible. It can be a way of exposing the brutality of those who practice it. But as an ideology of the powerful, backed by structural power, texts can be a tool

---

³² See Aristodemou, *Law and Literature*, 1.
³³ Gelacio Guillermo, "The New Mass Art and Literature," in *Nationalist Literature: A Centennial Forum*, 358.

of oppression. It inscribes domination on the very soul, bodies, political structure, and land of subjects.

Yet the resistance of the weak as opposed to the propaganda of the powerful is more potent. It is based in concrete reality. It is life-affirming as it arises from the land and its people. Conversely, power abuse that feeds greed is death dealing. The claim for legitimacy of wealth accumulation by the world's privileged few loses moral basis when weighed against the reality of more than 10 percent of the world's population suffering from severe undernourishment.[34] Insatiable greed surfaces at the root cause of hunger and suffering, as the wealthiest 20 percent of the world accounts for 76.6 percent of total private consumption. While the poorest 20 percent or the fifth of the world's population account for just 1.5 percent total private consumption.[35] Present consumption level of an average person from high-consumption country is estimated by William Rees, an urban planner at the University of British Columbia, to require four to 6 hectares of land. But there were only 1.7 hectares ecologically productive land available for each person. He concluded that the deficit is made up in core countries by drawing from the natural resources of their own countries and expropriating the resources, through trade, of peripheral countries.[36] Capitalist market system continues to accumulate capital and profit. This system cannot be allowed to continue to dominate the world. It is morally evil and is not environmentally sustainable. Furthermore, this system feeds on exploitation of labor and thrives on wasteful consumption. The hegemonic consumerist and materialistic worldview is propped up by dominant ideologies promoted by the telecommunication media corporations. Empowering resistance against corporate greed is a function that biblical critics cannot ignore.

Resistance reading gives priority to dominated communities. In the case above, Filipino reading parallels the context of the text. The marginal position of ancient Israel and the Filipino nation in relation to the Christian West is significant in meaning appropriation. Though a marginal society, the Filipino Christian community can be in a position of power compared to another community such as the Muslim community in Mindanao, hence this reading cannot be applied in relation to Christian settlement in Mindanao. In relation to the dominant power, resistance reading is a form of critique. Resistance hermeneutics gives special emphasis on cultural and historical

---

[34] Hunger Notes, "2018 World Hunger and Poverty Facts and Statistics," https://www.worldhunger.org/world-hunger-and-poverty-facts-and-statistics/.
[35] Available statistic comes from 2005 (site waslast updated in 2014). See Anup Shah, "Consumption and Consumerism," Global Issues, 5 January 2014, http://www.globalissues.org/issue/235/consumption-and-consumerism.
[36] Based on 1990 statistics. See Anup Shah, "Effects of Consumerism in Global Issues," Global Issues, http://www.globalissues.org/article/238/effects-of-consumerism.

heritages as tools or lenses in exposing and deconstructing the myth of superiority by the dominant worldview. In resistance hermeneutics the sacred bond between a land, the way of life arising from it, and the people are the core of a community's stand against triumphalist ideology. Resistance hermeneutics is always contextual.

Bibliography

Aberback, David. *Imperialism and Biblical Prophecy 750–500 BCE*. New York: Routledge, 1993.

Ackroyd, Peter. "The Biblical Interpretation of the Reigns of Ahaz and Hezekiah." Pages 247–59 in *the Shelter of Elyon: Essays on Ancient Palestinian Life and Literature in Honor of G.W. Ahlström*. Edited by W. B. Barrick and J. R. Spencer. JSOTSup 31. Sheffield: JSOT Press, 1984.

Adam, A. K. M., ed. *Handbook of Postmodern Biblical Interpretation*. Saint Louis: Chalice, 2000.

Adam, Klaus-Peter. "What Made the Books of Samuel Authoritative in the Discourses of the Persian Period? Reflection on the Legal Discourse in 2 Samuel 14." Pages 170–82 in *Deuteronomy–Kings as Emerging Authoritative Books: A Conversation*. Edited by Diana V. Edelman. Atlanta: Society of Biblical Literature, 2014.

Agoncillo, Teodoro. *Revolt of the Masses*. Quezon City: University of the Philippines Press, 1956.

Albert, Rosita, Edina Schenieveis, and Iva Knobbe. "Strengthening, Hiding or Relinquishing Ethnic Identity in Response to Threat: Implications for Intercultural Relations." *Intercultural Communications Studies* 14 (2005): 107–18.

Albertz, Rainer. *From the Beginning to the End of the Monarchy*. Vol. 1 of *A History of Israelite Religion in the Old Testament Period*. Louisville: Westminster John Knox, 1992.

———. *Israel in Exile: The History and Literature of the Sixth Century B.C.E*. Atlanta: Society of Biblical Literature, 2003.

———. "Social History of Ancient Israel." Pages 347–67 in *Understanding the History of Ancient Israel*. Edited by H. G. M. Williamson. Oxford: Oxford University Press, 2007.

Alter, Robert. *The Art of Biblical Narrative*. New York: Basic Books, 2011.

Altieri, Charles. *Canons and Consequences Reflections of the Ethical Force of Imaginative Ideals*. Evanston, IL: Northwestern University Press, 1990.

———. "The Idea and Ideal of a Literary Canon." *Critical Inquiry* 10 (1983–1984): 41–64.

Altmann, Peter. *Festive Meals in Ancient Israel: Deuteronomy's Identity Politics in Their Ancient Near Eastern Context*. Berlin: de Gruyter, 2011.

Alzona, Encarnacion. *A History of Education in the Philippines*. Manila: University of the Philippines Press, 1932.
Amit, Yairah "Who Was Interested in the Book of Judges in the Persian-Hellenistic Period." Pages 103–14 in *Deuteronomy–Kings as Emerging Authoritative Books: A Conversation*. Edited by Diana V. Edelman. Atlanta: Society of Biblical Literature, 2014.
Andaya, Leonard Y. "Ethnicity in the Philippine Revolution." Pages 49–82 in *The Philippine Revolution of 1896: Ordinary Lives in Extraordinary Times*. Edited by Florentino Rodao and Felice Noelle Rodriguez. Quezon City: Ateneo de Manila University Press, 2001.
Anderson, Benedict. *Imagined Communities*. New ed. London: Verso: 1983.
Anderson, Bernhard. *Understanding the Old Testament*. Quezon City: Claretian, 1986.
Aoanan, Melanio L. *God's Liberating Acts*. Quezon City: New Day, 1985.
Apilado, Digna B. "Andres Bonifacio as Nationalist and Revolutionary." Pages 74–98 in *Determining the Truth: The Story of Andres Bonifacio*. Edited by Bernadita Reyes Churchill. Quezon City: Manila Studies Association, 1997.
Apilado, Mariano C. *Revolutionary Spirituality: A Study of the Protestant Role in the American Colonial Rule of the Philippines 1898–1928*. Quezon City: New Publishers, 1999.
Arcilla, Jesus S., S. J. *The Fine Print of Philippine History*. Makati: St. Paul Publications, 1992.
Aristodemou, Maria. *Law and Literature: Journeys from Her to Eternity*. New York: Oxford University Press, 2000.
Armstrong, John. *Nations before Nationalism*. Chapel Hill: University of North Carolina Press, 1982.
Aster, Shawn Zelig. "Transmission of Neo-Assyrian Texts in Judah in the Late Eighth Century B.C.E." *HUCA* 78 (2007): 1–44.
Astour, M. C. "Hittites." Pages 111–12 in *The Interpreter's Dictionary of the Bible*. Edited by Keith Crim. Nashville: Abingdon, 1976.
Ateek, Naim Stefan. *Justice, and Only Justice: A Palestinian Theology of Liberation*. New York: Orbis Books, 1997.
Auld, A. Graeme. *Joshua, Judges, and Ruth*. Philadelphia: Westminster, 1984.
———. *Joshua: Jesus Son of Nun in Codex Vaticanus*. Leiden: Brill, 2005.
Baines, John. "Kingship, Definition of Culture, and Legitimacy." Pages 3–47 in *Ancient Egyptian Kingship*. Edited by David Bourke, David O'Connor, and P. Silverman. Leiden: Brill, 1994.
Barbalet, Jack M. "Power and Resistance." *British Journal of Sociology* 36 (1985): 521–48.
Bartkowski, Maciej J. *Recovering Non-violent History: Civil Resistance in Liberation Struggles*. Denver: Lynne Rienner, 2013.

Baron, Salo Wittmayer. *A Social and Religious History of the Jews*. 2nd ed. Vol. 1. New York: Columbia University Press, 1952.
Barth, Fredrick, ed. Introduction to *Ethnic Groups and Boundaries: The Social Organization of Culture Difference*. London: Allen & Unwin, 1969.
Baumgarten, Albert. *The Flourishing of Jewish Sects in the Maccabean Era: An Interpretation*. Leiden: Brill, 1997.
Beaulieu, Aul-Alain. "King Nabonidus and the Neo Babylonian Empire." Pages 969–79 in vol. 2 of *Civilizations of the Ancient Near East*. Edited by Jack Sasson. 4 vols. New York: Scribner's, 1995.
Ben Zvi, Ehud. "Total Exile, Empty Land and the General Intellectual Discourse of Yehud." Pages 155–68 in *The Concept of Exile in Ancient Israel and Its Historical Contexts*. Edited by Ehud Ben Zvi and Christoph Levin. BZAW 404. Berlin: de Gruyter, 2010.
Berger, Peter L. *The Sacred Canopy: Elements of a Sociological Theory of Religion*. New York: Doubleday, 1967.
Berquist, Jon L. "Identities and Empire: Historiographic Questions for the Deuteronomistic History in the Persian Period." Pages 3–14 in *Historiography and Identity (Re)formulation in the Second Temple Historiographical Literature*. Edited by Louis Jonker. New York: T&T Clark, 2010.
———. *Judaism in Persia's Shadow: A Social and Historical Approach*. Minneapolis: Fortress, 1995.
Bewer, Julius A. *The Literature of the Old Testament*. New York: Columbia University Press, 1962.
Bhabha, Homi. *The Location of Culture*. London: Routledge, 1994.
Black, Matthew. "The Biblical Languages." Pages 1–11 in *The Cambridge History of the Bible from the Beginnings to Jerome*. Edited by P. R. Ackroyd and C. E. Evans. Cambridge: Cambridge University Press, 1970.
Blair, Hugh J. "Joshua." Pages 223–26 in *The New Bible Commentary*. Edited by F. Davidson. London: Inter-Varsity Press, 1953.
Blanton, Richard E. "Theories of Ethnicity and the Dynamics of Ethnic Change in Multiethnic Societies." *Proceedings of the National Academy of Sciences of the United States of America* 112.30 (2015): 9176–81.
Blenkinsopp, Joseph. *Ezra-Nehemiah Old Testament Library*. London: SCM, 1988.
———. *Prophecy and Canon: A Contribution to the Study of Jewish Origins*. Notre Dame: University of Notre Dame Press, 1986.
Block, Daniel I. "The Role of Language in Ancient Israelite Perception of National Identity." *JBL* 103 (1984): 321–40.
Boer, Roland. "Marx, Postcolonialism, and the Bible." Pages 166–83 in *Postcolonial Biblical Criticism*. New York: T&T Clark International, 2005.
Bolin, Thomas O. "1–2 Samuel and Jewish Paideia in the Persian and Hellenistic Periods." Pages 133–58 in *Deuteronomy–Kings as Emerging*

Authoritative Books: A Conversation. Edited by Diana Edelman. Atlanta: Society of Biblical Literature, 2014.

Boling, Robert G. *Joshua: A New Translation with Notes and Commentary.* AB 6. New York: Doubleday, 1982.

Bonifacio, Andres. "Decalogue and the Katilya ng Katipunan." Malacañan Palace Presidential Museum and Library. http://malacanang.gov.ph/7013-andres-bonifacios-decalogue-and-the-kartilya-ng-katipunan/.

Borowski, Obed. "Hezekiah's Reforms and the Revolt Against Assyria." *BA* 58.3 (1995): 148–55.

Botor, Carlos, trans. *Informe Secreto de Sinabaldo De Mas.* Revised by Alfonso Felix Jr. Manila: Historical Society, 1963.

Bowman, Barrie. "Future Imagination: Utopianism in the Book of Jeremiah." Pages 243–49 in *Jeremiah (Dis)placed: New Directions in Writing/Reading Jeremiah,* Edited by A. R. Pete Diamond and Louis Stulman. New York: T&T Clark International, 2011.

Boyd, Robert, and Peter J. Richerson. *The Origin and Evolution of Culture.* New York: Oxford University Press, 2005.

Bray, Abigail. *Helene Cixous: Writing and Sexual Difference.* New York: Palgrave, 2004.

Brett, Mark. "National Identity as Commentary and as Metacommentary." Pages 28–40 in *Historiography and Identity (Re)formulation in Second Temple Historiographical Literature.* Edited by Louis Jonker. New York: T&T Clark International, 2010.

———. "Literacy and Domination: G. A. Herion's Sociology of History Writing." Pages 109–34 in *Social-Scientific Old Testament Criticism: A Sheffield Reader.* Edited by David J. Chalcraft. Sheffield: Sheffield Academic, 1997.

———. "Reading as A Canaanite: Paradoxes in Joshua." Pages 231–46 in *Interested Readers: Essays on the Hebrew Bible in Honor of David J. A. Clines.* Edited by James K. Aitken, Jeremy M. S. Clines, and Christl M. Maier. Atlanta: Society of Biblical Literature, 2013.

Bright, John. *The History of Israel.* 3rd ed. Philadelphia: Westminster, 1981.

Brueggemann, Walter. *The Creative Word.* Philadelphia: Fortress, 1982.

———. "Faith in the Empire." Pages 25–40 in *In the Shadow of the Empire.* Edited by. Richard Horsely. Louisville: Westminster John Knox, 2008.

———. *Redescribing Reality: What We Do When We Read the Bible.* London: SCM, 2009.

———. *Sabbath as Resistance: Saying No to the Culture of Now.* Louisville: Westminster John Knox, 2014.

———. "Theodicy in a Social Dimension," Pages 260–80 in *Social-Scientific Old Testament Criticism: A Sheffield Reader.* Edited by David Chalcraft. Sheffield: Sheffield Academic, 1997.

———. *The Prophetic Imagination*. Minneapolis: Fortress, 2001.
Bunimovitz, Shlomo. "On the Edge of Empires—Late Bronze Age (1500–1200)." Pages 320-31 in *The Archeology of Society in the Holy Land*. Edited by Thomas E. Levy. Virginia: Leicester University Press, 1995.
Butler, Trent C. *Joshua 1–12*. WBC 7a. 2nd ed. Michigan: Zondervan, 2014.
Callahan, Allen Dwight. "The Arts of Resistance in an Age of Revolt." Pages 21-40 in *Hidden Transcripts and the Arts of Resistance: Applying the Work of James C. Scott to Jesus and Paul*. Edited by Richard A. Horsley. Atlanta: Society of Biblical Literature, 2004.
Capulong, Noriel C. *Reading and Hearing the Old Testament in Philippine Context*. Vols. 1 and 2. Quezon City: New Day, 2002, 2009.
Carroll, Robert P. "Removing an Ancient Landmark: Reading the Bible as Cultural Production." Pages 6-14 in *Borders, Boundaries and the Bible*. Edited by Martin O'Kane. JSOTSup 313. Sheffield: Sheffield Academic Press, 2002.
Castro, Jovita Ventura, ed. *Anthology of Asean Literature: Philippine Metrical Romances*. Quezon City: Published by the Editors, 1985.
Ceresko, Anthony R. *Introduction to the Old Testament: A Liberation Perspective*. Quezon City: Claretian, 1992.
Cetina, Edesio. "Joshua." Pages 525-47 in *The International Bible Commentary*. Edited by William R. Farmer. Quezon City Philippines: Claretian, 2001.
Chan, Michael. "Isaiah 10:5-34 and the Use of Neo-Assyrian Royal Idiom in the Construction of an Anti-Assyrian Theology." *JBL* 128 (2009): 717-33.
Chan, Tina, "National Identity Formation in a Postcolonial Society: Comparative Case Studies on Hong Kong and Taiwan." http://www.tisr.com.tw/wp-content/uploads/2012/05/National-Identity-Formation-in-a-Post-colonial-Society.pdf.
Chapman, Stephen B. *The Law and the Prophets: A Study in Old Testament Canon Formation*. Tübingen: Mohr Siebeck, 2000.
Chapman, William. *Inside the Philippine Revolution*. Quezon City: Rex Incorporated, 1987.
Chase-Dunn, Christopher, and Peter Grimes. "World-Systems Analysis." *Annual Review of Sociology* 21 (1995): 387-417.
Childs, Brevard. *Introduction to the Old Testament as Scripture*. Philadelphia: Fortress, 1979.
Christensen, Duane L. *Transformations of the War Oracles in Old Testament Prophecy Studies in the Oracles against the Nations*. Montana: Scholars Press, 1975.
Churchill, Bernardita Reyes, ed. *Resistance and Revolution Philippine Archipelago in Arms*. Manila: National Commission for Culture and Arts, 2002.

Clay, Albert T. *The Origin of Biblical Tradition Hebrew Legends in Babylonia and Israel*. New Haven: Yale University Press, 1923.
Clements, Ronald E. "The Book of Deuteronomy: Introduction, Commentary, and Reflections." Pages 269–538 in vol. 2 of *The New Interpreter's Bible*. Edited by Leander E. Keck. Nashville: Abingdon, 1998.
Coats, George W. "An Exposition of the Conquest Theme." *CBQ* 47 (1985): 47–54.
Cogan, Mordecai. "Judah under Assyrian Hegemony: A Reexamination of Imperialism and Religion." *JBL* 112 (1993): 403–14.
———. "Literary-Critical Issues in the Hebrew Bible from an Assyriological Perspective: Additions and Omissions." Pages 401–13 in *Mishneh Todah Studies in Deuteronomy and Its Cultural Environment in Honor of Jeffrey H. Tiga*. Edited by Nili Sacher Fox, David A. Glatt-Gilad, and Michael J. Williams. Winona Lake: Eisenbrauns, 2009.
Cogan, Morton. *Imperialism and Religion: Assyria, Judah and Israel in the Eighth and Seventh Centuries B.C.E.* SBLMS 19. Atlanta: Scholars Press, 1974.
Collins, Nina. "The Year of the Translation of the Pentateuch into Greek under Ptolemy II." Pages 403–503 in *LXX: Septuagint, Scrolls, and Cognate Writings*. Edited by George J. Broke and Barnabas Lindars. Atlanta: Scholars Press, 1992.
Conrad, Edgar W. "Changing Context: The Bible and the Study of Religion." *Perspectives on Language and Text*. Edited by Edgar W. Conrad and Edward G. Newing. Winona Lake: Eisenbrauns, 1987.
———. *Fear Not Warrior: A Study of 'al tîra Pericopes in the Hebrew Scriptures*. Chico, CA: Scholars Press, 1985.
Constantino, Renato. *The Philippines: The Past Revisited*. Vol. 1. Quezon City: Renato Constantino, 1975.
Coogan, Michael David. "Joshua." Pages 110–31 in *The New Jerome Bible Commentary*. Edited by Raymond E. Brown. New Jersey: Prentice Hall, 1968.
———. *The Old Testament: A Historical and Literary Introduction to the Hebrew Scriptures*. Oxford: Oxford University Press, 2006.
Cook, J. "Composition of the Peshitta Version of the Old Testament (Pentateuch)." Pages 147–68 in *The Peshitta: Its Early Text and History; Papers read at the Peshitta Symposium Held at Leiden 30–31 August 1985*. Edited by P. B. Dirksen and M. J. Muller. Leiden: Brill, 1988.
Coote, Robert B. "The Book of Joshua: Introduction, Commentary, and Reflections." Pages 555–719 in vol. 2 of *The New Interpreter's Bible*. Nashville: Abingdon, 1998.
Coote, Robert B., and Keith W. Whitelam. "The Emergence of Israel: Social Transformation and State Formation following the Decline in the Late

Bronze Age Trade." Pages 107–47 in *Community, Identity, and Ideology: Social Science Approaches to the Hebrew Bible*. Edited by Charles E. Carter and Carol L. Meyers. Winona Lake: Eisenbrauns, 1996.

Coote, Robert B., and Mary P. Coote. *Power, Politics, and the Making of the Bible: An Introduction*. Minneapolis: Fortress: 1990.

Corpuz, Onofre D. *The Roots of the Filipino Nation*. Quezon City: Aklahi Foundation, 1970.

Cortes, Rosario Mendoza, Celestina Puyal Boncan, and Ricardo Trota Jose. *The Filipino Saga History as Social Change*. Quezon City: New Day, 2000.

Countrymeters. "Population of the Philippines 2015 Philippines Population 2016 | Current Population." http://countrymeters.info/en/Philippines.

Creach, Jerome F. D. *Joshua*. Interpretation: A Bible Commentary for Teaching and Preaching. Louisville: John Knox, 1989.

Crenshaw, James. *Education in Ancient Israel: Across the Deafening Silence*. New York: Bantam Doubleday, 1998.

Cryer, Frederick H. "Chronology: Issues and Problems." Pages 659–62 in vol. 2 of *Civilizations of the Ancient Near East*. Edited by Jack M. Sasson. Peabody, MA: Hendrickson, 1995.

Cross, Frank Moore. *Canaanite Myth and Hebrew Epic*. Cambridge: Harvard University Press, 1973.

———. *From Epic to Canon: History and Literature in Ancient Israel*. Baltimore: John Hopkins University Press, 1998.

———. "The Themes of the Book of Kings and the Structure of Deuteronomistic History." Pages 174–89 in *Canaanite Myth and Hebrew Epic*. Cambridge: Harvard University Press, 1973.

Crüsemann, F. *The Torah: Theology and Social History of the Old Testament Law*. Translated by A. W. Mahnke. Minneapolis: Fortress, 1996.

Cullinae, Michael. *Illustrado Politics: Filipino Elite Responses to American Rule, 1898–1908*. Quezon City: Ateneo de Manila University Press, 2003.

Dalley, Stephanie. "Ancient Mesopotamian Military Organization." Pages 413–22 in vol. 1 of *Civilizations of the Ancient Near East*. Edited by Jack M. Sasson. Peabody, MA: Hendrickson, 1995.

Damrosch, David. *The Narrative Covenant: Transformations of Genre in the Growth of Biblical Literature*. San Francisco: Harper & Row, 1987.

Darby, Phillip. *The Fiction of Imperialism: Reading between International Relations and Postcolonialism*. London Cassell, 1998.

Davenport, Frances Gardiner, ed. *European Treaties bearing on the History of the United States and Its Dependencies to 1648*. Washington, DC: Carnegie Institution of Washington, 1917.

Davidson, Basil. *Africa in Modern History: The Search for a New Society*. London: Allen Lane, 1978.

Davies, John J., and John C. Whitcomb. *Israel from Conquest to Exile: A Commentary on Joshua–2 Kings*. Michigan: Baker, 1989.

Davies, Philip R. *In Search of Ancient Israel*. JSOTSup 148. Sheffield: Sheffield Academic, 1992.
———. *Scribes and Schools: The Canonization of the Hebrew Scriptures*. Louisville: Westminster John Knox, 1998.
Davis, John J., and John C. Whitcomb. *Israel from Conquest to Exile: A Commentary on Joshua–2 Kings*. Grand Rapids: Baker, 1970.
Davis, Dale Ralph. *No Falling Swords: Expositions of the Book of Joshua*. Grand Rapids: Baker, 1988.
Dearman, J. Andrew. *Religion and Culture in Ancient Israel*. Peabody: Hendrickson, 1992.
Deist, Ferdinand E. *The Material Culture of the Bible: An Introduction*. Sheffield: Sheffield Academic, 2000.
De la Costa, Horacio. *Readings in Philippine History*. Manila: Bookmark, 1992.
De Leon, Felipe M., Jr. "In Focus: Beyond the Dona Victorian Syndrome." Office of the President, National Commission for Culture and Arts. 25 February 2015. ncca.gov.ph/about-culture-and-arts/in-focus/beyond-the dona-victorina-syndrome.
De Los Reyes, Isabelo. "The Religion of the Katipunan." Pages 197–299 in vol. 1 of *Views on Philippine Revolution*. Edited by Felina G. Mapa. Quezon City: University of the Philippines and Toyota Foundation, 2002.
De Mieroop, Marc Van. *The Ancient Mesopotamian City*. New York: Oxford University Press, 1999.
De San Antonio, Fray Juan Francisco. *The Philippine Chronicles of Fray San Antonio*. Translated by D. Pedro Picornel. Manila: Casalinda and Historical Conservation Society, 1977.
De Vaux, Roland. *Ancient Israel*. Vol. 1. Cambridge: Harvard University Press, 1961.
———. *The Early History of Israel*. Philadelphia: Westminster, 1978.
De Vera, Ben O. "PH Rises to Third Place in Crony-Capitalism Index." *Philippine Daily Inquirer* 31.152 (2016): A2.
Dever, William G. "How to Tell a Canaanite from an Israelite." Pages 26–56 in *The Rise of Ancient Israel*. Edited by Herschel Shanks. Washington, DC: Biblical Archeology Society, 1992.
Dietrich, Walter. "Martin Noth and the Future of the Deuteronomistic History." Pages 153–75 in *The History of Israel's Traditions: The Heritage of Martin Noth*. Edited by Steven McKenzie and M. Patrick Graham. JSOTSup 182. Sheffield: Sheffield Academic, 1994.
Dion, Paul E. "Deuteronomy 13: The Suppression of the Alien Religious Propaganda in Israel during the Late Monarchical Era." Pages 147–216 in *Law and Ideology in Monarchic Israel*. Edited by Baruch Halpern and Deborah W. Hobson. Sheffield: Sheffield Academic, 1991.

Donner, Herbert. "The Separate States of Israel and Judah." Pages 381–434 in *Israelite and Judean History Israelite and Judean History*. Edited by John H. Hayes and J. Maxwell Miller. Philadelphia: Westminster, 1977.

Driver, S. R. *An Introduction to the Literature of the Old Testament*. New York: Scribner's, 1910.

———. *Introduction to the Old Testament as Scripture*. New York: Scribner's, 1913.

Duiker, William J., and Jackson J. Spielvogel. *World History*. 2nd ed. New York: West & Wadsworth, 1998.

Dummelow, J. R., ed. *A Commentary on the Holy Bible by Various Writers*. New York: Macmillan, 1908.

Durant, Will. *Our Oriental Heritage: The Story of Civilization*. New York: Simon & Schuster, 1954.

Durkheim, Emile. *The Elementary Forms of Religious Life*. Translated by Joseph Ward Swain. New York: Free Press, 1947.

Dutcher-Walls, Patricia. "The Circumscription of the King: Deuteronomy 17:16–17 in Its Ancient Social Context." *JBL* 121 (2002): 601–16.

———. "The Social Location of the Deuteronomists: A Sociological Study of Factional Politics in Late Pre-exilic Judah." Pages 341–57 in *Social-Scientific Old Testament Criticism*. Edited by David J. Chalcraft. Sheffield: Sheffield Academic, 1997.

Düttmann, Alexander García. "The Art of Resistance." Paper delivered in the context of the Literaturfestival Berlin on the 18th of September 2015. http://www.fourbythreemagazine.com/the-art-of-resistance.html.

Dyck, Jonathan E. "A Map of Ideology for Biblical Critics." Pages 108–28 in *Rethinking Contexts, Rereading Texts: Contributions from the Social Sciences to Biblical Interpretation*. Edited by Daniel M. Carroll. JSOTSup 299. Sheffield: Sheffield Academic, 2000.

Edelman, Diana ed. Introduction to *Deuteronomy–Kings as Emerging Authoritative Books: A Conversation*. Atlanta: Society of Biblical Literature, 2014.

Eiselen, Frederick Carl, ed. *The Abingdon Bible Commentary*. New York: Cokesbury, 1929.

Eliade, Mircea. *The Sacred and Profane: The Nature of Religion*. Translated by Willard R. Trask. London: Harcourt, 1987.

Eliot, "T. S. Tradition and the Individual Talent." Pages 2–11 in *Selected Essays*. New ed. New York: Hardcourt, Brace & World.

Erbes, Johann E. *The Peshita and the Versions: A Study of the Pershitta Variants in Joshua 1–5 in Relation to Their Equivalents in the Ancient Version*. Uppsala: Uppsala University, 1999.

Erith, L. E. P. "Joshua." Pages 189–98 in *A New Commentary on the Holy Scripture*. Edited by Charles Gore, Henry Leighton Goudge, and Alfred Guillaume. London: SPCK, 1928.

Esler, Anthony. *The Western World: A Narrative History Prehistory to the Present.* Upper Saddle River, NJ: Prentice Hall, 1997.

Evans, Carl D. "Judah's Foreign Policy from Hezekiah to Josiah." Pages 157–78 in *Scripture in Context: Essays on the Comparative Method.* Edited by Carl D. Evans, William W. Hallo, and John B. White. Pennsylvania: Pickwick, 1980.

Evans, Carl D., William W. Hallo, and John B. White, eds. *Scripture in Context: Essays on the Comparative Method.* Pennsylvania: Pickwick, 1980.

Eynikel, Erik. *The Reform of King Josiah and the Composition of the Deuteronomistic History.* Leiden: Brill, 1996.

Fabella, Virginia. "Inculturating the Gospel: The Philippine Experience." www.theway.org.uk/back/39Fabella.pdf.

Fenigan, Jack. *Light from the Ancient Past: The Archeological Background of the Hebrew-Christian Religion.* Vol. 1. Princeton: Princeton University Press, 1976.

Fernandez, Eleazar S. "(Home)land, Diaspora, Identity, and the Bible in Imperial Geopolitics: What Does the Asia-Pacific Region Have to Do with Israel-Palestine?" Paper for the Fourth International Conference in Bethlehem. August 8–12, 2011.

Fewell, Danna Nolan. "Joshua." Pages 69–72 in *Women's Bible Commentary.* Edited by Carol A. Newsom and Sharon H. Ringe. Louisville: Westminster John Knox, 1998.

Finkelstein, Israel. "Archeology and Text in the Third Millennium: A View from the Center." Pages 323–42 in *International Organization for the Study of the Old Testament Congress Volume Basel 2001.* Edited by A. Lemaire. Leiden: Brill, 2002.

———. "The Great Transformation: The 'Conquest' of the Highland Frontiers and the Rise of Territorial Israel." Pages 349-65 in *The Archeology of Society in the Holy Land.* Edited by Thomas E. Levy. London: Leicester University Press, 1998.

Flanders, Henry Jackson, Robert W. Crapps, and David A. Smith. *People of the Covenant: An Introduction to the Hebrew Bible.* 4th ed. New York: Oxford University Press, 1996.

Fleming, James. *Personalities of the Old Testament.* London: Scribner's, 1951.

Fohrer, Georg. *Introduction to the Old Testament.* Translated by David E. Green. London: SPCK, 1968.

Foucault, Michael. *Discipline and Punish: The Birth of the Prison.* Translated by Alan Sheridan-Smith. London: Penguin, 1977.

———. *The History of Sexuality: An Introduction.* Vol. 1. Harmondsworth: Penguin, 1990.

Frankel, David. *The Land of Canaan and the Destiny of Israel: Theologies of Territory in the Hebrew Bible.* Winona Lake: Eisenbrauns, 2011.

Frankfort, Henri. *Kingship and the Gods: A Study of Ancient Near Eastern Religions as the Integration of Society and Nature.* Chicago: University of Chicago Press, 1978.

Frick, Frank S. *A Journey through the Hebrew Scriptures.* New York: Harcourt Brace College, 1995.

———. "*Cui Bono?*–History in the Service of Political Nationalism: The Deuteronomic History as Political Propaganda." *Semeia* 66 (1995): 79–92.

Friedman, Richard Elliott. "From Egypt to Egypt: Dtr¹ Dtr²." Pages 167–81 in *Traditions in Transition Turning Points in Biblical Faith.* Edited by Baruch Hapern and Jon D. Levenson. Winona Lake: Eisenbrauns, 1981.

Friessen, Dorothy. *Critical Choices: A Journey with the Filipino People.* Grand Rapids: Eerdmans, 1987.

Frolov, Serge. "The Case of Joshua." Pages 85–101 in *Deuteronomy–Kings as Emerging Authoritative Books: A Conversation.* Edited by Diana Edelman. Atlanta: Society of Biblical Literature, 2014.

Fukuyama, Francis. "The State of Nature." Pages 26–46 in *The Origins of Political Order: From Pre-human Times to French Revolution.* New York: Farras, Straus & Geroux, 2011.

Gangel, Kenneth O. "Joshua." Pages 1–15 in *Holman Old Testament Commentary.* Edited by Max Anders. Nashville: Broadman & Holman, 2002.

Garstang, John. *The Foundations of Bible History.* London: Constable, 1931.

Geertz, Clifford. *The Interpretation of Cultures.* New York: Basic Books, 1973.

Geoghegan, Jeffrey C. *The Time, Place, and Purpose of the Deuteronomistic History.* Providence, RI: Brown Judaic Studies, 2006.

Gerbrandt, Gerrald Eddie. *Kingship according to the Deuteronomistic History.* Atlanta: Scholars Press, 1979.

Gillmayr-Bucher, Susanne. "Memories Laid to Rest: The Book of Judges in the Persian Period." Pages 115–32 in *Deuteronomy–Kings as Emerging Authoritative Books: A Conversation.* Edited by Diana Edelman. Atlanta: Society of Biblical Literature, 2014.

Gorringe, Tim. "Political Readings of Scripture." Pages 67–80 in *The Cambridge Companion to Biblical Interpretation.* Cambridge: Cambridge University Press, 1998.

Gottwald, Norman K. *The Hebrew Bible: A Socio-literary Introduction.* Philadelphia: Fortress, 1985.

———. *The Hebrew Bible in Its Social World and Ours.* SemeiaSt 25. Atlanta: Scholar's Press, 1993.

Grant, Robert. *A Short History of the Interpretation of the Bible.* 2nd ed. Louisville: Fortress, 1973.

———. *The Politics of Ancient Israel.* Louisville: Westminster John Knox, 2001.

Grabbe, Lester L. "The History of Israel: The Persian and Hellenistic Period." Pages 403–27 in *Text in Context: Essays by Member of the Society of Old*

Testament Study. Edited by A. D. H. Mayes. Oxford: Oxford University Press, 2000.

Grayson, A. K. "Assyrian Rule of Conquered Territories." Page 960 in vol. 2 of *Civilizations of the Ancient Near East*. Edited by Jack M. Sasson. Peabody, MA: Hendrickson, 1995 2:960.

Greengus, Samuel. "Legal and Social Institutions of Ancient Mesopotamia." Pages 469–84 in vol. 1 of *Civilizations of the Ancient Near East*. Edited by Jack M. Sasson. Peabody, MA: Hendrickson, 1995.

Greenspoon, Leonard J. *Textual Studies in the Book of Joshua*. HSM 2. Chico, CA: Scholars Press, 1983.

Grosby, Steven. *Biblical Ideas of Nationality Ancient and Modern*. Winona Lake: Eisenbrauns, 2002.

Guillermo, Gelacio. "The New Mass Art and Literature." Pages 358–78 in *Nationalist Literature: A Centennial Forum*. Edited by Elmer A. Ordoñez. Quezon City: University of the Philippines Press and PANULAT, Philippine Writers Academy, 1996.

Gunn, David M. "Joshua and Judges." Pages 102–21 in *The Literary Guide to the Bible*. Edited by Robert Alter and Frank Kermode. Cambridge: Harvard University Press, 1987.

Habito, Cielito F. "Towards More Dispersed Growth." *The Philippine Daily Inquirer* 31.147 (2016): A13.

Haddon Spurgeon, Charles. *Genesis to 2 Kings*. Vol. 1 of *The Treasury of the Bible*. Grand Rapids: Baker, 1986.

Halligan, John. "Unsolved Mysteries: The Second Temple." Pages 142–58 in *Sense and Sensitivity: Essays on the Reading of the Bible in Memory of Robert Caroll*. Edited by Alastrair G. Hunter and Phillip R. Davies. JSOTSup 348. Sheffield: Sheffield Academic, 2002.

Hallo, William. "Biblical History in Its Near Eastern Setting: The Contextual Approach." Pages 1–26 in *Scripture in Context Essays on the Comparative Method*. Edited by Carl D. Evans, William W. Hallo, and John B. White. Pennsylvania: Pickwick, 1980.

Halpern, Baruch. "Sociological Comparativism and the Theological Imagination: The Case of the Conquest." Pages 53–67 in *"Sha'rei Talmon," Studies in the Bible, Qumran, and the Ancient Near East Presented to Shermayahu Talmon*. Edited by M. Fishbane and E. Tov. Winona Lake: Eisenbrauns, 1992.

———. *The First Historians: The Hebrew Bible and History*. San Francisco: Harper & Row, 1996.

Hamilton, Victor. *Handbook on the Historical Books: Joshua, Judges, Ruth, Samuel, Kings Chronicles, Ezra-Nehemiah, Esther*. Michigan: Baker Academic, 2001.

Hamlin, John E. *Inheriting the Land: A Commentary on the Book of Joshua*. Grand Rapids: Eerdmans, 1983.

Harlow, Barbara. *Resistance Literature*. New York: Menthuen, 1987.

Harris, J. Gordon, Cheryl A. Brown, and Michael S. Moore. *New International Biblical Commentary: Joshua, Judges, Ruth*. Peabody, MA: Hendrickson, 2000.

Harvey, John E. *Retelling the Torah: The Deuteronomistic Historian's Use of Tetrateuch*. London: T&T Clark International, 2004.

Hastings, Adrian. *The Construction of Nationhood: Ethnicity Religion and Nationalism*. Cambridge: Cambridge University Press, 1997.

Hawk, L. Daniel. *Berit Olam Studies in Hebrew Narrative and Poetry*. Edited by David W. Cotter. Collegeville, MI: Liturgical, 2000.

Hawkes, Jacquetta, and Leonard Woolley. *Prehistory and the Beginnings of Civilization*. New York: Harper & Row, 1963.

Hayes, John H., and J. Maxwell Miller, eds. *Israelite and Judean History*. Philadelphia: Westminster, 1977.

Healy, Marl. *The Ancient Assyrians*. London: Osprey Publishing, 1991.

Heaton, E. W. *The School Tradition of the Old Testament: The Hampton Lectures for 1994*. Oxford: Clarendon, 1940.

Heinz, Marlies. "Sargon of Akaad: Rebel and Usurper in Kish." Pages 67–87 in *Presentation of Political Power: Case Histories from the Times of Change and Dissolving Order in the Ancient Near East*. Edited by Marlies Heinz and Maria H. Feldman. Winona Lake: Eisenbrauns: 2007.

Henry, Matthew. *Commentary on the Whole Bible*. One vol. ed. Grand Rapids: Zondervan, 1961.

Herrera, Rene, Ralph Garcia Bertrand, and Francisco M. Salazano. *Genomes, Evolution, and Culture: Past Present, and Future of Humankind*. New Jersey: John Wiley, 2016.

Herion, Gary. "The Role of Biblical Historiography in Biblical Thought: The Tendencies Underlying Old Testament Historiography." *JOST* 21 (1981): 25-57.

Hertzberg, Arthur. "Zionism." Pages 783–84 in *Collier's Encyclopedia*. Vol. 23. New York: Collier, 1994.

Herzog, Chaim, and Mordecai Gichon. *Battles of the Bible*. Pennsylvania: Stackpole, 1997.

Hill, Christopher. *The Intellectual Origins of the English Revolution*. Oxford: University, 1965.

Hitchcock, Louise. "One Cannot Export a Palace on Board a Ship." *Backdirt* (Fall/Winter 2000): 6–7.

Hobbs, T. R. *A Time for War: A Study of Warfare in the Old Testament*. Delaware: Glazier, 1935, 1989.

Hobsbawm, E. T. Ranger. *Invention of Tradition*. Cambridge: Cambridge University Press, 1984.

Hoffman, Yair. "The Deuteronomist and the Exile." Pages 659–76 in *Pomegranates and Golden Bells: Studies in Biblical, Jewish, and Near Eastern Ritual, Law, and Literature in Honor of Jacob Milgrom*. Edited by David P. Wright, David Noel Freedman, and Avi Hurvits. Winona Lake: Eisenbrauns, 1995.

Holmes, Samuel. "Joshua." Pages 248–56 in *A Commentary on the Bible*. Edited by Arthur S. Peake. New York: Nelson, 1919.

Horsley Richard, ed. "Early Israel as an Anti-Imperial Community" Pages 9–24 in *In the Shadow of the Empire*. Louisville: Westminster John Knox, 2008.

———. *Hidden Transcripts and the Arts of Resistance: Applying the Work of James C. Scott to Jesus and Paul*. Atlanta: Society of Biblical Literature, 2004.

Huffman, John. *Mastering the Old Testament: Joshua*. Dallas: Word, 1986.

Hultkrantz, Åke. "Religion before History." In *Introduction to World Religions*. Edited by Christopher Patridge. Minneapolis: Fortress, 2005.

Hunger Notes. "2018 World Hunger and Poverty Facts and Statistics." https://www.worldhunger.org/world-hunger-and-poverty-facts-and-statistics/.

IBON Facts and Figures 18.23–24 (1995).

Ileto, Reynaldo Clemeña. *Filipinos and Their Revolution: Event, Discourse, and Historiography*. Quezon City: Ateneo De Manila University Press, 1998.

———. *Pasyon and Revolution Popular Movements in the Philippines, 1840–1910*. Quezon City: Ateneo de Manila University Press, 1979.

Ishida, Tomoo. *History and Historical Writing in Ancient Israel*. Studies in Biblical Historiography. Leiden: Brill, 1999.

Jacobsen, Thorkild. "Primitive Democracy in Ancient Mesopotamia." *Journal of Eastern Studies* 2 (1983): 159–72.

James, E. O. *Prehistoric Religion: A Study in Prehistoric Archeology*. London: Thames & Hudson, 1957.

James, Leo. "Makabayan." Page 182 in *Tagalog—English Dictionary*. Quezon City: Capitol Publishing House, 1986.

Jamieson, Robert. *Genesis–Deuteronomy, Joshua–Esther*. Volume 1 of *A Commentary Critical, Experimental and Practical on the Old and New Testament*. Edited by Robert Jamieson, A. R. Fausset, and David Brown. Grand Rapids: Eerdmans, 1945.

Jamieson-Drake, David W. *Scribes and Schools in Monarchic Judah: A Socio-archeological Approach*. The Social World of Biblical Antiquity 9. Sheffield: Almond, 1991.

Janzen, David. *The Social Meaning of Sacrifice in the Hebrew Bible: A Study of Four Writings*. Berlin: de Gruyter, 2004.

Jellicoe, Sidney. *The Septuagint and Modern Study*. Oxford: Clarendon, 1968.
Jocano, F. Landa. *The Filipino Prehistory Rediscovering Precolonial Heritage*. Manila: Punlad Research House, 1998.
Johnson, Willa Mathis. "Ethnicity in Persian Yehud: Between Anthropological Analysis and Ideological Criticism." Pages 177–86 in *Society of Biblical Literature 1995 Seminar Papers*. Edited by Eugene H. Lowering, Jr. Atlanta: Scholar's Press, 1995.
Jonker, Luis. Introduction to *Historiography and Identity (Re)formulation in the Second Temple Historiographical Literature*. Edited by Louis Jonker. New York: T&T Clark, 2010.
Joyce, E. J., C.P.P.S. "Joshua." Pages 282–93 in *A New Catholic Commentary on the Holy Scripture*. Edited by Reginald C. Fuller. New Jersey: Nelson, 1953.
Kagan, Donald. *Problems in Ancient History: The Ancient Near East and Greece*. 2nd ed. New York: Prentice Hall, 1975.
Kaiser, Otto. *Introduction to the Old Testament*. Minneapolis: Augsburg, 1975.
———. "The Law as the Center of the Hebrew Bible." Pages 93–103 in *"Sha'arei Talmom": Studies in the Bible, Qumran and the Ancient Near East Presented to Shemaryahu Talmon*. Edited by Michael Fishbane and Emanuel Tov. Winona Lake: Eisenbrauns, 1993.
Kanafani, Ghassan. *Literature of Resistance in Occupied Palestine: 1948–1968*. Beirut: Institute for Arab Research, 1981.
Kang, Sa-Moon. *Divine War in the Old Testament and in the Ancient Near East*. Berlin: de Gruyter, 1989.
Kaufman, Stephen A. "A Reconstruction of the Social Welfare Systems of Ancient Israel." Pages 277–86 in *In the Shelter of Elyon: Essays on Ancient Palestinian Life and Literature in Honor of G. W. Ahlström*. Edited by W. Boyd Barrick and John R. Spencer. Sheffield: Sheffield Academic, 1984.
Keil, C. F., and F. Delitzsch. *Joshua, Judges, Ruth*. Vol. 4 of *Biblical Commentary on the Old Testament*. Grand Rapids: Eerdmans, 1950.
Kelle, Brad. "What's in a Name? Neo-Assyrian Designations for the Northern Kingdom and Their Implications for Israelite History and Biblical Interpretation." *JBL* 121 (2002): 639–66.
Keller, W. Phillip. *Joshua Man of Fearless Faith*. Waco, TX: Word, 1983.
Kelly, Page H., and Daniel S. Mynatt, and Timothy G. Crawford. *The Masorah of Biblia Hebraica Stuttgartensia*. Cambridge: Eerdmans, 1998.
Kern, Paul Bentley. *Ancient Siege Warfare*. Bloomington: Indiana University Press, 1999.
Kidd, Jose Ramirez E. *Alterity and Identity in Israel: The גר in the Old Testament*. Berlin: de Gruyter, 1999.

King, Phillip J. *Jeremiah: An Archeological Companion*. Louisville: Westminster John Knox, 1993.

Kipling, Rudyard. *Verse Inclusive Edition 1885–1918*. New York: Hodder & Stoughton, 1930.

Knauf, E. Axel. "Does "Deuteronomistic Historiography (DH) Exists?" Pages 388–98 in *Israel Constructs Its History: Deuteronomistic Historiography in Recent Research*. Edited by Albert de Pury, Thomas Römer, and Jean-Daniel Macchi. Sheffield: JSOT, 2000

———. "Why Joshua?" Pages 73–84 in *Deuteronomy–Kings as Emerging Authoritative Books: A Conversation*. Edited by Diana V. Edelman. Atlanta: Society of Biblical Literature, 2014.

Kofoed, Jens Bruun. *Text and History: Historiography and the Study of the Biblical Text*. Winona Lake: Eisenbrauns, 2005.

Kramer, Samuel Noah. "Sumerian Literature in the Bible." Pages 272–84 in *The Bible in Its Literary Millieu*. Edited by John Maier and Vincent Tollers. Grand Rapids: Eerdmans, 1979.

Laato, Antti. *Josiah and David Redivivus*: *The Historical Josiah and the Messianic Expectations of Exilic and Postexilic Times*. Sweden: Almqvist and Wikell International, 1992.

Lamsa, George M. *Old Testament Light*: *The Indispensable Guide to the Customs, Manners, and Idioms of Biblical Times*. Cambridge: Harper & Row, 1964.

Larkin, William J., Jr. *Culture and Biblical Hermeneutics: Interpreting and Applying the Authoritative Word in a Relativistic Age*. Grand Rapids: Baker, 1988.

Lasine, Stuart. "Manasseh as Villain and Scapegoat," Pages 163–83 in *The New Literary Criticism of the Hebrew Bible*. Edited by J. Cheryl Exum and David J. A. Clines. JSOTSup 143. Sheffield: Sheffield Academic, 1993.

Legrand, Lucien. *The Bible on Culture: Belonging or Dissenting*. New York: Orbis Books, 2000.

Leichty, Erle. "Esarhaddon, King of Assyria." Page 952 in vol. 2 of *Civilizations of the Ancient Near East*. Edited by Jack M. Sasson. New York: Scribner's, 1995.

Lemche, Niels Peter. *The Old Testament between Theology and History*. Louisville: Westminster John Knox, 2008.

Lemos, T. M. "Forging a Twenty-First Century Approach to the Study of Israelite." Pages 271–86 in *Warfare Ritual, and Symbol in Biblical and Modern Context*. Edited by Brad E. Kelle, Frank Ritchel Ames, and Jacob L. Wright. Atlanta: Society of Biblical Literature, 2014.

Leprohon, Ronald J. "Royal Ideology and State Administration in Pharaonic Egypt." Page 274 in vol. 1 of *Civilizations of the Ancient Near East*. Edited by Jack M. Sasson. New York: Scribner's, 1995.

Levinson, Bernard M. "You Must Not Add Anything to What I Command You: Paradoxes of Canon and Authorship in Ancient Israel." *Numen* 50.1 (2003): 1–51.

———. *Deuteronomy and the Hermeneutics of Legal Innovation*. Oxford: Oxford University Press, 1997.

Levirani, Mario. *The Ancient Near East: History, Society and Economy*. Translated by Soraia Tabatabai. London: Routledge, 1988.

Levy, Thomas E., ed. *The Archeology of Society in the Holy Land*. London: Leicester University Press: 1998.

Lias, J. J. "Exposition and Homiletics." Pages 5–6 in to *The Pulpit Commentary*. Edited by H. D. Spence and Joseph S. Exell. Vol. 7. Westchester, IL: Wilcox & Follett, n.d.

Lind, Millard C. *Yahweh Is a Warrior: The Theology of Warfare in Ancient Israel*. Telford, PA: Herald, 1980.

Linville, James R. "On the Authority of Dead Kings." Pages 203–22 in *Deuteronomy–Kings as Emerging Authoritative Books: A Conversation*. Edited by Diana Edelman. Atlanta: Society of Biblical Literature, 2014.

Liverani, Mario. *The Ancient Near East: History, Society and Economy*. Translated by Soraia Tabatabai. New York: Routledge, 1988.

Lohfink, Norbert. "Distribution of the Functions of Power: The Laws Concerning Public Office in Deuteronomy 16:18–18:22." Pages 336–52 in *A Song of Power and the Power of Song: Essays on the Book of Deuteronomy*. Edited by Duane L. Christensen. Winona Lake: Eisenbrauns, 1993.

———. "Was There a Deuteronomistic Movement?" Pages 36–67 in *Those Illusive Deuteronomists the Phenomenon of Pan-Deuteronomism*. JSOTSup 268. Sheffield: Sheffield Academic Press, 1999.

———. "Which Oracle Granted Perdurability to the Davidides." Pages 421–44 in *Reconsidering Israel and Judah: Recent Studies on the Deuteronomistic History*. Edited by Gary N. Knoppers and J. Gordon McConville. Winona Lake: Eisenbrauns, 2000.

Long, Burke O. "Social Dimension of Prophetic Conflict." *Semeia* 21 (1981): 30–53.

Longcare, Lindsay B. "Joshua." Pages 343–56 in *The Abingdon Bible Commentary*. Edited by Frederick Carl Eiselen, Edwin Lewis, David G. Downey. Nashville: Abingdon, 1929.

Loomba, Ania. *Colonialism/Postcolonialism* 2nd ed. New York: Routledge, 1998.

Lowery, R. H. *The Reforming Kings: Cults and Society in First Temple Judah* JSOTSup 120. Sheffield: Sheffield Academic, 1991.

Lucas, Henry. *A Short History of Civilization* 2nd ed. New York: McGraw-Hill, 1953.

Luckenbill, Daniel David. *The Annals of Sennacherib*. Chicago: The University of Chicago Press, 1924.

Lumbera, Bienvenido, and Cynthia Nograles Lumbera. *Philippine Literature: A History and Anthology*. English ed. Pasig City, Philippines: Anvil, 2005.
Machinist, Peter. "Literature as Politics: The Tikulti-Ninurta Epic and the Bible." *CBQ* 38 (1976): 455–82.
Madvig, Donald H. "Joshua." Pages 237–371 in *Deuteronomy to 2 Samuel*. Vol. 3 of *The Expositor's Bible Commentary*. Edited by Frank E. Gaebelein. Grand Rapids: Zondervan, 1992.
———. *Old Testament*. Vol. 1 of *Zondervan NIV Bible Commentary*. Edited by Kenneth L. Barker and John R. Kohlenberger. Grand Rapids: Zondervan, 1994.
Malamat, Abraham. "The Historical Background of the Assassination of Amon, King of Judah." *IEJ* 3 (1953): 26–29.
———. "The Kingdom of Judah between Egypt and Babylon: A Small State within A Great Power Confrontation." Pages 117–29 in *Text and Context: Old Testament and Semitic Studies for F. C. Fensham*. Edited by W. Claassen. JSOTSup 48. Sheffield: JSOT, 1988.
Malina, Bruce J. "Rhetorical Criticism and Social-Scientific Criticism: Why Won't Romanticism Leave Us Alone." Pages 5–21 in *The Social World of the New Testament*. Edited by Jerome H. Neyrey and Eric C. Stewart. Peabody, MA: Hendrickson, 2008.
Marchant, F. G. *The Preacher's Complete Homiletic Commentary*. Vol. 5. Grand Rapids: Baker, 1875.
Mason, Rex. *Propaganda and Subversion in the Old Testament*. London: SPCK, 1997.
Matthews, Victor H., and Don Benjamin. *The Old Testament Parallels: Laws and Stories from the Ancient Near East*. New York: Paulist, 2006.
———. *Social World of Ancient Israel 1250–587 BCE*. Grand Rapids: Baker, 2011.
Mays, Glenn. *Inventing A Hero: The Posthumous Re-Creation of Andres Bonifacio*. Quezon City Philippines: New Day, 1997.
Mays, James L. "Justice: Perspectives from the Prophetic Tradition." Pages 57–71 in *Constituting the Community: Studies on the Polity of Ancient Israel in Honor of S. Dean McBride Jr.* Edited by John T. Strong and Steven S. Tuell. Winona Lake: Eisenbrauns, 2005.
Mayes, Andrew D. H. "Deuteronomistic Ideology and the Theology of the Old Testament." Pages 456–80 in *Israel Constructs Its History: Deuteronomistic Historiography in Recent Research*. Edited by Albert de Pury, Thomas Römer, and Jean-Daniel Macchi. Sheffield: JSOT, 2000.
Mbuwayesango, Dora. "Joshua." Pages 64–73 in *Global Bible Commentary*. Nashville: Abingdon, 2004.
McBride, Dean S., Jr. "Polity of the Covenant People." Pages 17–34 in *Constituting the Community: Studies on the Polity of Ancient Israel in Honor of*

S. Dean McBride Jr. Edited by John T. Strong and Steven S. Tuell. Winona Lake: Eisenbrauns, 2005.

McConville, J. G. *Deuteronomy*. Appollos Old Testament Commentary 5. Leicester, England: Intervarsity, 2002.

———. *God and Earthly Powers*. New York: T&T Clark, 2006.

McNeil, William H. *The Rise of the West: A History of Human Community*. New York: University of Chicago Press, 1990.

McNutt, Paula. *The Forging of Israel: Iron Technology, Symbolism and Tradition in Ancient Society*. JSOTSup 108. Sheffield: Sheffield Academic, 1990.

McTernan, Oliver. *Violence in God's Name*. MaryKnoll, NY: Orbis Books, 2003.

Meer, Michäel van der. "Textual Criticism and Literary Criticism in Joshua 1:7." Pages 355–71 in *X Congress of the International Organization for Septuagint and Cognate Studies Oslo, 1998*. Edited by Bernard A. Taylor. Atlanta: Society of Biblical Literature, 2001.

Quilaton, Gregorio L. *Philippine National Situation*. Palaso 1.1 (2013): 45.

Mendoza, Everett. *Radical and Evangelical: Portrait of a Filipino Christian*. Quezon City: New Day, 1999.

Mendoza, Lily S. *Between the Homeland and the Diaspora: The Politics of Theorizing Filipino and Filipino American identities*. Manila: University of Santo Tomas Press, 2006.

Mercado, Leonardo N. *Elements of Filipino Philosophy*. Tacloban City, Philippines: Divine Word University Publications, 1993.

Midlarsky, Manus I. *The Evolution of Inequality: War, State Survival, and Democracy in Comparative Perspective*. Stanford: Stanford University Press, 1999.

Mitchell, Gordon. *Together in the Land: A Reading of the Book of Joshua*. Sheffield: JSOT, 1993.

Mitchell, Timothy. "Everyday Metaphors of Power." *Theory and Society* 19 (1990): 545–77.

Monroe, Christopher. "Money and Trade." Pages 155–68 in *A Companion to Ancient Near East*. Edited by Daniel Snell. Oxford: Blackwell, 2005.

Montenegro, Muriel. *The Jesus of Asian Women*. Maryknoll: Orbis Books, 2006.

Mulder, Chester O. *Joshua Beacon Bible Commentary*. Vol. 2. Missouri: Beacon Hill Press of Kansas City, 1965.

Mullen, Theodore, Jr. *Ethnic Myths and Pentateuchal Foundations: A New Approach to the Formation of the Pentateuch*. Atlanta: Scholars Press, 1997.

———. *Narrative History and Ethnic Boundaries: The Deuteronomistic Historian and the Creation of Israelite National Identity*. Atlanta: Scholars Press, 1993.

Murnane, William J. "The History of Ancient Egypt: An Overview." Pages 1086–1108 in vol. 2 of *Civilizations of the Ancient Near East*. Edited by Jack M. Sasson. New York: Scribner's, 1995.

Na'aman, Nadav. "The Deuteronomist and Voluntary Servitude to Foreign Powers." Pages 259–72 in vol. 3 of *Ancient Israel's History and Historiography: The first Temple Period Collected Essays*. Winona Lake: Eisenbrauns, 2006.

Nelson, Richard D. *Deuteronomy: A Commentary*. Louisville: John Knox, 2002.

———. *Joshua: A Commentary Old Testament Library*. Louisville: Westminster John Knox, 1997.

———. "Josiah in the Book of Joshua." *JBL* 100 (1981): 531–40.

Nemet-Nejat, Karen Rhea. *Daily Life in Ancient Mesopotamia*. Boston: Hendrickson, 1998.

Newsom, Carol. "Reflections on Ideological Criticism and Postcritical Perspectives." Pages 541–59 in *Method Matters*. Edited by Joel LeMon and Kent Harold Richards. Atlanta: Society of Biblical Literature, 2009.

Nicholson, Ernest W. *Deuteronomy and Tradition*. Oxford: Basel Blackwell, 1967.

Niditch, Susan. *Oral World and the Written World*. Louisville: Westminster John Knox, 1996.

Noort, E. "Joshua of Reception and Hermeneutics." Pages 199–215 in *Past, Present, Future: The Deuteronomistic History and the Prophets*. Leiden: Brill, 2000.

Noth, Martin. "The Central Theological Themes." Pages 20–30 in *Reconsidering Israel and Judah: Recent Studies on the Deuteronomistic History*. Edited by Gary N. Knoppers and J. Gordon McConville. Winona Lake: Eisenbrauns, 2000, .

———. *The Deuteronomistic History*. 2nd ed. JSOTSup 15. Sheffield: Sheffield Academic, 1981.

———. *The History of Israel*. New York: Harper, 1958.

Oesterly, W. O. E., and Theodore H. Robinson. *Hebrew Religion Its Origin and Development*. London: SPCK, 1952.

Oginde, David. "Joshua." Pages 255–94 in *Africa Bible Commentary*. Edited by Tokunboh Adeyemo. Grand Rapids: Zondervan, 2006.

Orlin, Louis Lawrence. *Life and Thought in Ancient Near East*. Ann Arbor: University of Michigan, 2007.

Otto, Eckart. "Political Theology in Judah and Assyria: The Beginning of the Hebrew Bible as Literature." *SEÅ* 65 (2000): 59–76.

Padilla, Estela P. "Theologizing in the Philippines INScCT REPORT." https://insecttheology.files.wordpress.com/2013/11/regional-report-philippines-theologizingphilippines.pdf.

Panganiban, Patricia. "Inculturation and the Second Vatican Council." *Landas* 18 (2004): 59–93.
Pareti, Luigi, Paolo Brezzi, and Luciano Petech, eds. *The Ancient World, 1200 B.C. to A.D. 500*. Vol. 2 of *The History of Mankind, Cultural and Scientific Development*. Translated by Guy E. F. and Sylvia Chilver. New York: Harper & Row, 1965.
Parker, Bradley J. *The Mechanics of Empire*. Neo-Assyrian Text Corpus Project. Helsinki: University of Helsinki Press, 2001.
Parker, Simon B. *Stories in Scripture and Inscriptions: Comparative Studies in Northwest Semitic Inscriptions and the Hebrew Bible*. New York: Oxford University Press, 1997.
Parpola, Simo. "Asssyria's Expnasion in the Late Eighth and Seventh Centuries and Its Long-Term Repercussions in the West." Pages 99–111 in *Symbiosis, Symbolism, and the Power of the Past*: *Canaan, Israel, and Their Neighbors in the Late Bronze Age to the Romans*; *Proceedings of the Centennial Symposium W.F. Albright Institute of Archeological Research and American Schools of Oriental Research, Jerusalem, May 29–31, 2000*. Edited by William Dever and Seymour Gitin. Winona Lake: Eisenbrauns, 2003.
Peckam, Brian. *The Composition of the Deuteronomistic History*. Atlanta: Scholars Press, 1985.
Pedersen, Johs. *Israel Its Life and Culture*. Vols. 3 and 4. London: Oxford University Press, 1953.
Pelmoka, Juana Jimenez. *Pre-Spanish Philippines*. Philippines: Self-published, 1990.
Pernia, Antonio M. *God's Kingdom and Human Liberation*. Manila: Divine Word, 1990.
Person, Raymond F, Jr. *The Deuteronomic School: History, Social Setting, and Literature*. Atlanta: Society of Biblical Literature, 2002.
Petaññe, E. P. *The Philippines in the World of Southeast Asia: A Cultural History*. Quezon City: Enterprise Publication, 1972.
Petersen, David L. *The Prophetic Literature: An Introduction*. Louisville: John Knox, 2002.
Phelan, John J. "Philippine Linguistics and Spanish Missionaries, 1565–1700." *Mid-America* 37 (1955): 158–70.
Philippine Statistics Authority. "2015 Census of Population." psa.gov.ph/statistics/census/2015-census-of-population.
Pleins, J. David. *The Social Visions of the Hebrew Bible: A Theological Introduction*. Louisville: Westminster John Knox, 2001.
Plummer, A. Introduction to *The Pulpit Commentary*. Edited by H. D. Spence and Joseph S. Exell. Vol. 7. Westchester, IL: Wilcox & Follett, n.d.

Polzin, Robert. *Deuteronomy, Joshua, Judges*. Part 1 of *Moses and the Deuteronomist: A Literary Study of the Deuteronomic History*. New York: Seabury, 1980.

Porter, J. Roy. "The Succession of Joshua." Pages 139-62 in *Reconsidering Israel and Judah: Recent Studies on the Deuteronomistic History*. Edited by Gary N. Knoppers and J. Gordon McConville. Winona Lake: Eisenbrauns, 2000.

Portier-Young, Anathea E. *Apocalypse against Empire: Theologies of Resistance in Early Judaism*. Cambridge: Eerdmans, 2011.

Postgate, J. N. "Royal Ideology and State Administration in Summer and Akkad." Page 395 in vol. 1 of *Civilizations of the Ancient Near East*. Edited by Jack M. Sasson. New York: Scribner's, 1995.

Powers, E., S. J. *A Catholic Commentary on Holy Scripture*. New York: Nelson, 1953.

Pressler, Carolyn. *Joshua, Judges, and Ruth*. London: Westminster John Knox, 2002.

Pritchard, James B., ed. *Ancient Near East Text Relating to the Old Testament*, Princeton: Princeton University Press, 1955.

———, ed. *The Ancient Near East: An Anthology of Texts and Pictures*. Princeton: Princeton University Press, 1958.

———, ed. *A New Anthology of Texts and Pictures by James Pritchard*. Vol. 2 of *The Ancient Near East*. Translated by Robert D. Biggs. Princeton: Princeton University Press, 1975.

Quirino, Carlos. *Filipinos at War*. Philippines: Vera-Reyes, 1981.

Rafael, Vicente. *Contracting Colonialism*. Quezon City: Ateneo de Manila University Press, 1988.

Rappaport, Roy. *Ritual and Religion in the Making of Humanity*. London: Cambridge University Press, 1999.

Reade, Julian. "Ideology and Propaganda in Assyrian Art." Pages 329-43 in *Mesopotamia: Power and Propaganda; A Symposium on Ancient Empires*. Edited by Mogens Trolle Larsen. Copenhagen Studies in Assyriology 7. Copenhagen: Akademik Forlag, 1979.

Rea, John. "Joshua." Pages 205-32 in *The Wycliffe Bible Commentary*. Edited by Charles F. Pfeiffer and Everett Harrison. London: Lowe & Brydone, 1963.

Revira, Temario C. *Landlords and Capitalists*. Quezon City: University of the Philippines Press, 1994.

Rhodes, Arnold B. *The Mighty Acts of God*. Louisville: Geneva Press, 2000.

Richardson, Jim. *The Light of Liberty Documents and Studies on the Katipunan, 1892-1897*. Quezon City: Ateneo de Manila University Press, 2013.

Ricouer, Paul. *Lectures on Ideology and Utopia.* New York: Columbia University Press, 1986.
Roberts, J. J. M. *The Bible and the Ancient Near East.* Winona Lake: Eisenbrauns, 2002.
Robinson, Charles Alexander, Jr. *Ancient History: From Prehistoric to the Death of Justinian.* 2nd ed. New York: MacMillan, 1951.
Rodgers, Perry M., ed. *Aspects of Western Civilization Problems and Sources in History.* Vol. 2. 3rd ed. New Jersey: Prentice Hall, 1997.
Rodriguez, Junius P. "Pyramid Construction." Pages 399-401 in *O-Z and Primary Documents.* Vol. 2 of *Encyclopedia of Slave Resistance and Rebellion.* Edited by Junius P. Rodriguez. Westport, CT: Greenwood, 2007.
Rollston, Christopher A. *Writing and Literacy in the World of Ancient Israel: Epigraphic Evidence from the Iron Age.* Atlanta: Society of Biblical Literature, 2010.
Römer, Thomas C. *The So-Called Deuteronomistic History: A Sociological, Historical and Literary Introduction.* New York: T&T Clark, 2007.
Rose, Martin. "Deuteronomistic Ideology and Theology of the Old Testament." Pages 425-55 in *Israel Constructs Its History: Deuteronomistic Historiography in Recent Research.* Edited by Albert de Pury, Thomas Römer, and Jean-Daniel Macchi. Sheffield: JSOT, 2000.
Rostovtzeff, M. *A History of the Ancient World.* Translated by J. D. Duff. Vol. 1. Oxford: Clarendon, 1930.
Rowlett, Lori. "Inclusion, Exclusion, and Marginality in the Book of Joshua." *JSOT* 55 (1992): 14-23.
Ruether, Rosemary Radford. *Goddesses and the Divine Feminine: A Western Religious History.* Berkley: San Francisco University Press, 2005.
Rusling, James. "Interview with President William McKinley." Pages 22-23 in *The Philippines Reader.* Edited by Daniel Schirmer and Stephen Rosskamm Shalom. Boston: South End Press, 1987.
Sabino A. Vengco "Another Look at Inculturation." *Philippine Studies* 32 (1984): 181-96.
Saggs, H. W. F. "The Divine in History." Pages 17-48 in *Essential Papers on Israel and the Ancient Near East.* Edited by Frederick E. Greenspan. New York: New York University Press, 1991.
Said, Edward W. *Culture and Imperialism.* New York: Alfred Knauf, 1993.
———. *Orientalism: Western Conceptions of the Orient.* 3rd ed. London: Penguin, 1991.
———. *The World, the Text, and the Critic.* Cambridge: Harvard University: 1983.
Salgado, Perdo V. *Ang Kristiano ay Rebolusyonaryo.* Manila: Lucky, 1995.
Sanders, James A. "Adaptable for Life: The Nature and Function of Canon." Pages 531-60 in *Magnalia Dei: The Mighty Acts of God; Essays on the Bi-*

ble and Archeology in Memory of G. Ernest Wright*. Edited by F. M. Cross, W. E. Lemke, and P. D. Miller. Garden City, NY: Doubleday, 1976.

———. *From Sacred Story to Sacred Text*. Philadelphia: Fortress, 1987.

Sanders, Paul. "Missing Link in the Hebrew Bible Formation." *BAR* 41.6 (2015): 46–52.

San Juan, E., Jr. *After Postcolonialism: Remapping Philippines-Unites States Confrontations*. Maryland: Rowman & Littlefield, 2000.

———. *Beyond Postcolonial Theory*. New York: St. Martin's, 1999.

Sarna, Nahum M. "Naboth's Garden Revisited (1 Kings 21)." Pages 119–26 in *Tehillah le-Moshe: Biblical and Judaic Studies in Honor of Moshe Greenberg*. Edited by Mordechai Cogan, Barry L. Eichler, and Jeffrey H. Tigay. Winona Lake: Eisenbrauns, 1997.

Schermerhorn, R. *Comparative Ethnic Relations*. New York: Random House, 1970.

Schiffman, H. *Texts and Traditions: A Source Reader for the Study of Second Temple Judaism*. Hoboken, NJ: Ktav, 1998.

Schniedewind, William M. *A Social History of Hebrew: Its Origins through the Rabbinic Period*. London: Yale University Press, 2013.

———. "Orality and Literacy in Ancient Israel." *RSR* 26 (2000): 327–32.

———. "Aramaic, the Death of Written Hebrew, and Language Shift in the Persian Period." Pages 141–52 in *Margins of Writing, Origin of Cultures*. Edited by Seth L. Sanders, Leslie Schramer, and Thomas Urban. University of Chicago Oriental Institute Seminars 2. Chicago: University of Chicago Press, 2006.

Schoenhals, G. Roger, ed. *John Wesley's Commentary on the Bible*. Grand Rapids: Zondervan, 1990.

Schultz, Carl. "The Political Tensions Reflected in Ezra Nehemiah." Pages 221–44 in *Scripture in Context Essays on Comparative Method*. Edited by Carl Evans, William B. Halo, and John B. White. Pittsburgh: Pickwick, 1980.

Schumacher, John N., S.J.. *Revolutionary Clergy: The Filipino Clergy and the Nationalist Movement 1850–1903*. Quezon City: Ateneo De Manila University Press, 1981.

Scott, Henry William. *Slavery in the Philippines*. Manila: De La Salle University Press, 1991.

Scott, James C. *Domination and the Arts of Resistance: Hidden Transcripts*. New Haven: Yale University Press, 1990.

Seckhar, Raja G. "Colonialism and Imperialism and Its Impact on English Language." *Asia Journal of Multidimensional Research* 1.4 (2012): 111–20.

Segundo, Juan Luis. *The Liberation of Theology*. Maryknoll, NY: Orbis, 1976.

The Sermon Bible: Genesis to Samuel. Vol. 1. New York: Funk & Wagnalls, 1909.

Sevilla, Fred. *Poet of the People Francisco Balatas and the Roots of Filipino Nationalism: Life and Times of the Great Filipino Poet and His Legacy of Literary Excellence and Political Activism.* Manila: Trademark, 1997.

Shah, Anup. "Consumption and Consumerism." Global Issues. 05 January 2014. http://www.globalissues.org/issue/235/consumption-and-consumerism.

———. "Effects of Consumerism in Global Issues." Global Issues. http://www.globalissues.org/article/238/effects-of-consumerism.

Shea, William H. "Sennacherib's Second Palestinian Campaign." *JBL* 104 (1985): 401–18.

Sherwood, Yvonne. "Francisco de Vitoria's More Excellent Way: How the Bible of Empire Discovered the Tricks of [the Argument from] Trade." *BibInt* 21 (2013): 215–75.

Sicat, Ma. Teresa. "The Philippine Nation in Literary Discourse." Pages 420–33 in *Nationalist Literature: A Centennial Forum.* Edited by Elemer A. Ordoñez. Quezon City: University of the Philippines and PANULAT, Philippine Writers Academy, 1996.

Silva, Moisés. *God, Language and Scripture.* Grand Rapids: Zondervan, 1990.

Sizoo, Joseph R. "The Book of Joshua." Pages 631–32 in *The Interpreter's Bible: Leviticus, Numbers, Deuteronomy, Joshua, Joshua, Ruth, Samuel.* Edited by George Arthur Buttrick. New York: Cokesbury, 1953.

Smend, Rudolf. "Das Gesetz und die Völker: Ein Beitrg zur deuteronomistischen Redakti-onsgeschichte." Pages 494–509 in *Probleme biblischer Theologie: Gerhard von Rad zum 70. Geburtstag.* Edited by Hans Walter Wolff. Munich: Kaiser, 1971.

———. "The Law and the Nations: A Contribution to Deuteronomistic Tradition History." Pages 95–111 in *Reconsidering Israel and Judah: Recent Studies on the Deuteronomistic History.* Edited by Gary N. Knoppers and J. Gordon McConville. Winona Lake: Eisenbrauns, 2000.

Smith-Christopher, Daniel L. *A Biblical Theology of Exile.* Overtures to Biblical Theology. Minneapolis: Fortress, 2002.

———. "The Politics of Ezra: Sociological Indicators of Postexilic Judean Society." Pages 545–47 in *Community, Identity, and Ideology: Social Science Approaches to the Hebrew Bible.* Edited by Charles E. Carter and Carol L. Meyers. Winona Lake: Eisenbrauns, 1996.

———. *The Religion of the Landless: The Social Context of the Babylonian Exile.* Bloomington: Meyer Stone Books, 1989.

Smith, Anthony. *The Ethnic Origins of Nations.* Basil: Blackwell, 1986.

Smith, Morton. *Palestinian Parties and Politics That Shaped the Old Testament.* New York: Columbia University Press, 1971.

Smith, Robert Houston. "The Book of Joshua." Pages 123–24 in *Interpreter's One-Volume Commentary*. Nashville: Abingdon, 1971.

Snyman, G.F. "Texts Are Fundamentally Facts of Power, Not of Democratic Exchange." Pages 133–48 in *Past, Present, Future: The Deuteronomistic History and the Prophets*. Edited by Johannes C. De Moor and Harry F. Van Rooy. Leiden: Brill, 2000.

Sparks, Kenton L. *Ethnicity and Identity in Ancient Israel*. Winona Lake: Eisenbrauns, 1998.

Sternberg, Meir. *The Poetics of Biblical Narrative: Ideological Literature and the Drama of Reading*. Bloomington: Indiana University Press, 1987.

Stern, Ephraim. "The Babylonian Gap: The Archeological Reality." *JSOT* 28 (2004): 273–77.

Stone, Elizabeth C. "The Development of Cities in Ancient Mesopotamia." Pages 235–48 in vol. 1 of *Civilizations of the Ancient Near East*. Edited by Jack M. Sasson. New York: Scribner's, 1995.

Sugirtharajah, R. S. *Postcolonial Criticism and Biblical Interpretation*. Oxford: Oxford University Press, 2002.

Sweeney, Marvin. "The Portrayal of Assyria in the Book of Kings." Pages 274–84 in *The Bible as a Human Witness to Divine Revelation: Hearing the Word of God through Historically Dissimilar Traditions*. Edited by Randall Heskett and Biran Irwin. London: T&T Clark, 2010.

Taitz, Emily. *Introduction to the World's Major Religions Judaism*. Connecticut: Greenwood, 2006.

Talmon, Shemaryahu. "The 'Comparative Method.'" Pages 320–56 in *Biblical Interpretation—Principles and Problems: Congress Volume: Göttingen 1977*. VTSup 29. Leiden: Brill, 1978.

Tano, Rodrigo D. *Theology in the Philippine Setting: A Case of Contextualization of Theology*. Quezon City: New Day, 1985.

The World Bank. "The Philippines: A Strategy to Fight Poverty." http://web.worldbank.org/WBSITE/EXTERNAL/TOPICS/EXTPOVERTY/EXTPA/0,,contentMDK:20204974~menuPK:435735~pagePK:148956~piPK:216618~theSitePK:430367,00.html.

———. "The Critical Asian Principle." https://web.archive.org/web/20070222131109/http://www.atesea.org:80/CAPrev.htm.

Thiong'O', Ngugi Wa. *Decolonizing the Mind: The Politics of Language in African Literature*. Portsmouth, NH: Heieneman: 1986.

Thomas, Levy E., ed. *The Archeology of Society in the Holy Land*. London: Leicester University Press: 1998.

Thomas, Oral. "A Resistant Biblical Hermeneutics within the Carribean." *BT* 6 (2008): 330–42.

Thompson, Thomas L. "The Exile in History and Myth: A Response to Hans Barstad." Pages 101–19 in *Leading Captivity Captive*. Edited by L. L. Grabbe. JSOTSup 278. Sheffield: Sheffield Academic, 1998.

Thornton, A. P. *Doctrines of Imperialism*. London: Wiley, 1965.

Tillich, Paul. *Systematic Theology*. Vol. 1. Chicago: University of Chicago Press, 1951.

Torres-Yu, Rosario. "The State of Philippine Literature." Pages 317–44 in *Nationalist Literature: A Centennial Forum*. Edited by Elemer A. Ordoñez. Translated by Cheree Quizon. Quezon City: University of the Philippines Press and PANULAT, Philippine Writers Academy, 1996.

Tov, Emanuel. *Textual Criticism of the Hebrew Bible*. Minneapolis: Fortress, 1992.

Turner, Ralph. *The Great Cultural Traditions*. Vol. 1. New York: McGraw-Hill Book, 1941.

Van Seters, John. *In Search of History: Historiography in the Ancient World and the Origins of Biblical History*. Winona Lake: Eisenbrauns, 1997.

Velunta, Revelation E. "Onesimus and Today's OFW's: Reading Philemon Inside a Jeepney." *The Union Seminary Bulletin* 4 (2007): 109–31.

Vengco, Sabino A. "Another Look at Inculturation." *Philippine Studies* 32 (1984): 181–96.

Vernon McGee, J. *Joshua–Psalms*. Vol. 2 of *Thru the Bible with J. Vernon McGee*. Nashville: Nelson, 1982.

Villarroel, Fidel. *The Dominicans and the Philippine Revolution 1896–1903*. Manila: University of Santo Thomas, 1999.

Villa-Vicencio, Charles. *A Theology of Reconstruction: Nation Building and Human Rights*. Cambridge: Cambridge University Press, 1992.

Vogt, Peter T. *Deuteronomic Theology and the Significance of Torah: A Reappraisal*. Winona Lake: Eisenbrauns, 2006.

———. "Social Justice and the Vision of Deuteronomy." *JETS* 51 (2008): 35–44.

Von Rad, Gerhard. *Old Testament Theology*. Vols. 1 and 2. New York: Harper & Row, 1965.

Vriezen, Th. C. *The Religion of Ancient Israel*. Philadelphia: Westminster, 1963.

Walvaren, Klaas, and Jon Abbink, eds. "Rethinking Resistance in African History." Pages 1–40 in *Rethinking Resistance: Revolt and Violence in African History*. Leiden: Brill, 2003.

Warrior, Robert. "Canaanites, Cowboys, and Indians: Deliverance, Conquest, and Liberation Theology Today." *Christianity and Crisis* 49 (1989): 261–65.

Weber, Max. *Ancient Judaism*. New York: Free Press, 1952.

Wee, John Zhu-En. "Assyria." Pages 33–35 in vol. 1 of *Encyclopedia of World History*. Edited by Marsha E. Ackermann, Michael J. Schroeder, Janice J.

Terry, Jiu-Hwa Lo Upshur, and Mark F. Whitters. New York: Facts on File, 2008.

Weinberg, Saul S. "Post-exilic Palestine: An Archeological Report." *Proceeding of Israel Academy of Sciences and Humanities* 4.5 (1971): 78–97.

Weinfeld, Moshe. *Deuteronomy and the Deuteronomic School*. Winona Lake: Eisenbrauns, 1992.

———. *Normative and Sectarian Judaism in the Second Temple Period*. London: T&T Clark, 2005.

Wenham, Gordon J. "The Deuteronomic Theology of the Book of Joshua." Pages 194–203 in *Reconsidering Israel and Judah: Recent Studies on the Deuteronomistic History*. Edited by Gary N. Knoppers and J. Gordon McConville. Winona Lake: Eisenbrauns, 2000.

Whelchel, James R. *The Path to Liberation: The Theology of Struggle in the Philippines*. Quezon City: New Day, 1995.

White, Manchip Jon. *Everyday Life in Ancient Egypt*. New York: Peter Bedrick, 1991.

Whitelam, Keith W. *The Invention of Ancient Israel: The Silencing of Palestinian History*. London: Routledge, 1996.

Widengren, Geo. "The Persian Period," Pages 489–538 in *Israelite and Judean History Israelite and Judean History*. Edited by John H. Hayes and J. Maxwell Miller. Philadelphia: Westminster, 1977.

Wilson, Charles R. *Joshua–Esther*. Vol. 1.2 of *The Wesleyan Bible Commentary*. Grand Rapids: Eerdmans, 1967.

Wilson. H. S. "A Tryst with Theology: Self Theologizing as a Perennial Discipleship Mandate." A lecture delivered at the ATESEA Theological Union Methodology Seminar in Adventist Institute for Advanced Studies (AIAS) Silang Cavite. Philippines, June 13, 2013.

Wilson, Robert R. "Deuteronomy, Ethnicity, and Reform." Pages 107–124 in *Constituting the Community: Studies on the Polity of Ancient Israel in Honor of S. Dean McBride Jr.* Edited by John T. Strong and Steven S. Tuell. Winona Lake: Eisenbrauns, 2005.

———. *Prophecy and Society in Ancient Israel*. Philadelphia: Fortress, 1980.

Wimbush, Vincent L. Introduction to *Interpreting Resistance, Resisting Interpretations of Resistance: A Colloquy on Early Christianity as Rhetorical Formation. Semeia* 79 (1997).

Woods, Robert G. "Origin of the Colorum." *Philippine Magazine* 16 (1929): 428–29.

Worley, Demetrice A., and Jesse Perry Jr., eds. *African American Literature: An Anthology of Nonfiction, Fiction, Poetry, and Drama*. Lincolnwood, IL: National Textbook Company, 1993.

Wright, Jacob L. "Introduction." Pages 1–13 in *Warfare, Ritual, and Symbol in Biblical and Modern Context*. Edited by Brad E. Kelle, Frank Ritchel Ames, and Jacob L. Wright. Atlanta: Society of Biblical Literature, 2014.
Yadin, Yigael. *The Art of Warfare in Biblical Lands in the Light of Archeological Study*. Vol. 2. New York: McGraw-Hill, 1963.
Yamauchi, Edwin. "The Eastern Jewish Diaspora under the Babylonians." Pages 356–77 in *Mesopotamia and the Bible: Comparative Explorations*. Edited by Mark W. Chavalas and K. Lawson Younger Jr. Grand Rapids Michigan: Baker, 2002.
Yoffee, Norman. *Myths of the Archaic State: Evolution of the Earliest Cities, States and Civilization*. New York: Cambridge University Press, 2004.
Younger, K. Lawson, Jr. *Ancient Conquest Accounts: A Study in Ancient Near Eastern and Biblical History Writing*. Sheffield: JSOT, 1990.
———. "The Deportation of the Israelites." *JBL* 117 (1998): 210–27.
———. "Recent Study on Sargon II, King of Assyria: Implications for Biblical Studies." Pages 288–329 in *Mesopotamia and the Bible*. Edited by Mark W. Chavalas and K. Lawson Younger Jr. Grand Rapids: Baker Academic, 2002.
Zaide, Gregorio F., ed. *Documentary Sources of Philippine History*. Vol. 9. Manila: National Bookstore, 1990.
Zimmerli, Walther. *Old Testament Theology in Outline*. Translated by David E. Green. Atlanta: John Knox, 1978.

Index of Biblical Passages

Genesis		18:6–18	71
11:1–10	96	26:5–8	57
12:1–2	109	27:18–19	125
12:7	109	28:1–14	125
25	36	29:1–30:20	125
32:1–21	36	29:9–12	71
		31:17	120
Exodus		31:23	109, 124
3:8	109	32:1–52	87, 100
15:1–18	120	34:9	109
31:1–15	122		
		Joshua	
Deuteronomy		1:1	122
1:6	124	1:2	122
1:7	124	1:3	113, 122, 135
1:9	124	1:4	32
1:18	124	1:6	122
1:28	120	1:1–5	118, 120, 122–24
3:14	66	1:1–6	118, 120
5:25–27	71	1:6	127
6:23	109	1:6a	119
6:7–9	23, 85	1:6b	119
7:1	81	1:6–7	137
7:7	81	1:6–9	6, 120
8:17	81	1:7–9a	120
9:1–2	81	1:7–9	123–25
10:8	66	1:9b	119
11:5	66	1:1–9	5, 7–10, 18, 21–22, 109, 114, 115, 117–20, 124–26, 133, 137–38, 161, 163–66, 173
12:18–27	65		
14:22–29	65		
15:4	127	1:1–18	137, 165
16:1	73	1:11	120
16:1–17	65	1:11–15	122
16:18–20	72–73	1:12	122
17:14–20	73	1:12–15	122
17:16	51	1:15	120
17:18–20	73, 119	1:18	122
17:18–27	73, 127	2:1–24	75, 111–12

5:9	66	Judges	
5:14–18	113	1:21	66
6:13–15	110	1:26	66
6:25	112	2:18–19	65
6:30–35	109	9:1–57	114
7:26	66	13:1–16:31	114
8:1	113	17:1–18:31	114
8:28	66	19:1–21	114
9:27	66, 111	19:25	114
10:5	112		
10:17–18	113	1 Samuel	
10:28	111	12:6–12	57
10:30	111		
10:32	111	2 Samuel	
10:33	111	8:1–11	43
10:34	111	11:1–27	80
10:38	111		
10:40	111	1 Kings	
11:5	112	8:3–51	57
11:11	111	8:46–53	87
11:12	111	11:29–31	74
12:1	120	11:29–33	78
13:1	20, 120	12:16–17	78
13:2–6	20, 123	14:25–26	30
13:13	20, 66, 111	15:17–19	43
14:3	113	15:29	43
14:14	66	21:21–22	127
15:15	111		
15:63	20, 66	2 Kings	
16:10	20, 66	9:6–9	74
19:18–20	113	9:25–26	74
19:30	113	10:1–6	74
20:21	113	10:27	66
22:3	66	11:29–31	74
22:9	66	16:6	66
22:10–12	123	17:2	81, 96
22:22–27	123	17:5–6	33
23:4	123	17:12–18	77, 81
23:5	111, 120	17:12–31	78
24:1–27	109	17:21	66
24:1–33	75, 112	17:24	44
24:5–12	57	17:27–33	45
24:15	66	18:1–37	78
24:25	66	18:13–16	46
		18:13–37	45
		18:17–19:37	81

18:26	84	42:22	55
19:5–7	49	51:23	55
19:33–37	78	65:1–7	59
20:17	66		
21:1–29	80	Jeremiah	
21:2	48	7:9	59
21:3	74	7:18	59
21:2–15	46	7:31	59
21:9–10	49	27	53
22:13	87	29	53
23	49	40:7–12	55
23:4	49	41:3–5	52
23:5	49	44:3	59
23:5–20	50	44:17–19	59
23:6	49		
23:7–14	49	Lamentations	
23:24	49	5:2	55
23:25	30	5:4	55
23:34–35	52	5:5	55
24:1–2	53	5:11	55
24:2	36	5:12	55
25:21	67		
		Ezekiel	
2 Chronicles		1:3	55
30:11	52	3:15	55
33:1	46		
33:11–13	46	Joel	
34:9		4:4	47
Ezra		Micah	
2:59	55	1:8–15	45
		6:8	74
Psalms			
18	120	Nahum	
24	120	3:1	35
137	57		
		Zephaniah	
Nehemiah		1:1–5	50
9:16–19	2	1:8–12	46
Isaiah		1:12	56
8:1–17	49	2:4	50
8:23–9:6	50	2:8–9	36
30:8–11	49		

Index of Subjects

Aguinaldo, 140
Ahaz, 43, 81
Ahikkam, 54
Ahmose I, 30
Akhenaton, 39
Akkadian, 30
Amalekites, 36
Ammon, 36
Anak ng Bayan, 10
ancient cities, growth of, 38
ancient Near East nations
    elites in, 27
    estates in, 27
    farmers in, 26–27
    peasants in, 27
    revolts in, 29
Andres Bonifacio, 9, 10, 11, 148, 149
anti-empire studies, 21
    sentiments, 59
Apolinario Mabini, 148
Aramaic, 47, 84–85
Arameans, 30
Ashur, 44, 119
Ashurbanipal, 34
Assyrian/s, 32
    anti-Assyrians, 46
    army, 33
    connection of EP, 68
    gods, worship of, 47
    peak of power, 47
    polemics against Jerusalem, 78
    pro-Assyrians, 46
    rule of Judah, 96
    treaties, 66
    unmasked, 106–7
ATSSEA/ATESEA, 157
autocratic rule, 38
Bathala, 10–11, 141

Babylon/Babylonian/s, 35, 96
    exile, 54–55
    pro-Babylonian party, 54
    religious policies of, 52
Bernardo Carpio, 146
bureaucratic structure, 100
Bible
    colonial captivity of, 21
    imperial context of, 23, 25–26
biblical resources, 7
Cambyses, 58
Canaan/Canaanites, 42
    extermination of, 111
canonical interpretation, 104–7
capitalist system, 3
Catholic Biblical Association of the
    Philippines, 158
Cebu, 140
Cebuano, 9
city walls, 52
class interest, 100
    in literature, 101
colonial
    language, 84
    victimization, 48, 78, 90
colonization, 14
context of interpreters, 12
    of EP, 68
    of Joshua, 163
contextual meaning/interpretation/
    reading, 4, 12, 22
    meaning construction, 155
    translation, 13, 155
covenant ceremony, 6–7, 111
    central in Israel's identity, 163
    with Yahweh, 113
Critical Asian Principle, 157
Cyrus, 36, 58

damay, 144, 168
Darius, 58
David, 96, 126
Deuteronomy, 67, 69, 72
    as critique of ruling establishment, 72
    as national polity, 72
    as resistance literature, 93
    polemics against foreigners in, 77–78
deuteronomic law, 77
deuteronomist's ideology, 81
development of centralized organization, 38
Diaryong Tagalog, 144
divide and conquer, 141
divine warrior concept, 163
Diwa, 158
domination, 3, 92
Don Juan Teñoso, 145
early prophets (EP), 48, 49
    and Torah, 71
    anti-imperialism, 48, 52
    as canonical text, 103
    as class ideology, 101–2
    as critique, 82, 86
    as historiography, 82, 86–87
    as national ideology, 83, 86
    as propaganda, 82
    as resistance literature, 86, 94, 97, 98, 106
    as social construction, 73
    as subversion, 82
    Assyrian connection of, 68, 82
    central themes, 71–72, 98–99
    class interest in, 100
    composite work, 70
    context of, 60, 62, 66, 70, 96, 104
    Deuteronomy connection, 70
    land in, 83, 97
    liberation in, 98
    national program/narrative, 74, 98
    openness of, 82–83
    redaction, 67–68
    reform movements and EP, 97
    royal theology in, 82
    self-critical, 88
    social construction of, 99–100
    theories of authorship, 6
    worship in, 73
Edom, 36
Egypt
    power of, 47
    pyramids, 28
    skilled workers in, 28
Egyptian
    empire, 29
    literature, 39
    lore, 39
    religion, 39
Elephantine community, 55
Elijah-Elisha stories, 74
Eloquent peasant, 39
Emilio, Jacinto, 148
empire, 3
encomienda, 141, 149
English language, 12
    as part of Western culture, 12
    as culture carrier, 13
    as medium of instruction, 170
Ethnic
    consciousness, 75–76
    elements, 78
    formation, 79
exile group, 59
faith in Yahweh/God, 76
    as source of identity, 107
family gatherings, 56
family-centered rituals, 56
feminine, 118
    aspects of resistance, 126
Filipino/s, 39
    American pacification of, 149
    aspiration for land, 149
    Bible interpretation, 157–58
    colonial education of, 170
    colonized people, 5
    coopted Filipino elites, 148–49
    cultural resistance, 146
    cultural resources, 151
    cultural values, 144

Index of Subjects | 213

folk Christianity, 143
identity, 147
illustrados, 140, 144
law, 148
national narrative, 170
peasant organizations, 149–50
popular literature, 143–46
present situation, 152–53
religiosity, 149
resistance against dominant culture, 15
resistance against Spain, 140, 143
resistance bible reading, 160
resistance movements against government, 152
supreme God, 141
victims of imperialism, 3
worldview, 9, 148
Filipino revolution against Spain, 150
social and economic causes, 149
Florante at Laura, 145
Folk-Christianity, 168
Gedaliah, 55
Gibeonites, 77
Hebrew language, 85
Hebrew Bible
and ancient Near East, 25
as authoritative text, 163
as resistance literature, 2, 85–86, 93, 94
context of production, 2, 25–26, 60, 65, 107
main impetus in production, 58
resistance function of, 161
scripture of the weak, 15
traditional interpretation, 2
hegemonic worldview, 40
construction, 92
culture, 161
hegemony, 3
imperial, 21
masculine, 21
hermeneutics, 2
liberation of, 22
of privatism, 13
as engagement with reality, 15

hermeneutical community
at the service of peripheral societies, 22
Hezekiah, 45, 47, 96
historiography, 100
Hittites, 32
Hiya, 144
holy war, 8, 113, 118–19
Hosea, 50
Hurrians, 32
HUKBALAHAP, 150
Hyksos, 30
historical-critical studies, 8, 14, 15
identity
based on kinship/brotherhood, 75
religious, 77–78
in EP, 99
ideology
analysis of, 101
as propaganda, 29
of warrior kings, 38
Ilocano, 9
Ilonggo, 9
Imperial
Bible reading, 14
expansion of, 26
ideology, 92
military built-up, 26
origins of conquest stories, 107
power center, 26
propaganda, 85
reading of Joshua, 107
slavery, 29
system, 23
violence, 112
wealth, 26
imperialism, 61
doctrines of, 89
ideology of, 62
Inang Bayan, 10, 153, 168, 169
installation formula, 119, 120
internal politics in Israel, 25
interpreters
bias of, 15
location of, 15
Isaiah, 76

Israel (ancient)
    affinity with Canaanites, 113
    cultural values, 113
    ethnic composition of, 6
    identity, 77, 164
    kinship and religious ties, 75–76
    national ideology, 76, 164
    powerlessness of, 81
    religion, 6, 23
    religious symbols, 23
Israel (northern kingdom), 43, 48
    affinity with Judah, 51–52
    and Josiah's reform, 51
    deportation/resettlement of, 45
    in EP, 69, 104
    population of, 44
Israelites, 42
Jehoiachin, 53
Jehoiakim, 35, 53
Jeremiah, 50
Jerusalem
    Babylonian siege of, 53
    fall of, 46, 53, 54
    location of, 43
    traditions, 56
Jew/Jewish
    exiles, 56
    identity, 41
    political parties, 58
Josiah, 6, 30, 48
    death of, 52, 67
    his reforms, 48–49
    resistance against colonial powers, 51
Joshua (book of) 71, 77
    as literature, 110
    as resistance text, 8, 95
    authorship, 6
    Canaanites in, 111
    military image, 120
    royal image, 119
    violence, 112
Joshua, 6, 10, 71
    military image of, 118
    Moses, assistant of, 12a
    Moses, successor of, 109, 123
    prophetic leader, 109–10
    obedience of, 122
    royal image of, 109
Judah, 43
    affinity with Israel, 81
    alliance with Egypt, 53
    as ally of Assyria, 45
    deportation of population, 54
    foreign policy of, 47
    middle of imperial battles, 47, 53
    revolts of, 96
    under empires, 96
Judaism, 59
Judges (book of), 95, 113–14
kagandahang-loob, 10, 148
kalayaan, 10, 144, 147
Katipunan, 9–10, 80, 147–48, 169
    primer of, 148
kingship, 80
    rise of, 38
kinship conceptualization, 75
knowledge
    hegemonic, 15
    mediated, 12
laborers
    daily rations of, 45
Lamentations, book of, 53, 55
land (Canaan)
    allotments, 112
    borders of, 123
    inseparable with people/nationhood, 164
    Israel's claim of, 8
    possession of, 123
Landas, 158
Language
    as part of culture, 12
    as part of identity, 84
    as resistance, 173
law (Old Testament), 10
    as resistance, 164
    emphasis on, 120
    preserves culture, 163
    protects the poor and the marginalized, 163

liberation, 92
    activity of God, 107
lineage, 56
lingap, 144
literature production, 38
    as means of subverting hegemonic knowledge, 93
liwanag, 144
Luzon, 9
makabayan, 10
makadiyos, 10
makatao, 10
Manasseh, 46–47, 96
masculine strength, 118
Merodach-Baladan, 45
Mesopotamia, 30–31
    influence on Judah, 52
Midianites, 36
Miguel Lopez de Legaspi, 140
military imperialism, 30
Moab, 36
monarchs
    legitimacy of, 163
    limit to power, 163
moro-moros, 143
Moses, 17, 71
    ideal leader, 123
    revolutionary leader, 123, 125
Mycenaean cities, 36
Naboth, 74, 80
Nahum, 35
National Council of Churches in the Philippines, 158
national identity, 49
national ideology, 69
nationalist
    education, 78
    policy, 67
Nebuchadrezzar, 35, 53
Necho II, 30
Neo-Babylonian Empire, 35
Non-temple piety, 54, See also Yahweh worshippers
objectivity, 14
    preoccupation with, 23
pagbabagong loob, 148
palaces, 38

Palestinians, 1, 140
Pasyons, 143, 168
peace treaties, 111–12
peasants, 80
    in ancient Near East, 27
    revolts, 40
Pekah, 43, 44
peoplehood, 165
people of the land, 48
Persia/Persians, 57–58
    base in Palestine, 58
    imperial policy, 59
    tolerance policy, 58
Pharaohs
    Amenemhet I, 39
    Necho, 52
Philippine/s, 3
    American occupation of, 5, 149–51
    Biblical interpretation in, 154–55
    Christianization of, 22, 140–42
    colonization of, 140
    context of the, 7, 139
    faith-based resistance, 155–57
    neocolonial, 150–51
    poverty threshold, 150
    pre-Spanish, 139–140
    Spanish occupation of, 5, 139–43
Pilipino (language), 9
    Joshua 1:1–9 translation to, 10–11
political expediency, 57
postcolonial identity, 79
postexilic, 57
postmodern interpretation, 5
power
    and knowledge, 106
    exercise of, 90–91
    operation of, 106
prehistoric religion, 37
propaganda, 40
    Persian, 57
Prophecy of King Merykare, 39
Prophecy of Neferti, 39

prophetic
  view of history, 110
prophets, 47
  peripheral location of, 71–72
  true/false, 50–51
Protestant churches in the Philippines, 157–58
Psammatichus I, 30
pyramids, 39
Rahab, 77, 110–11, 125–26
Ramses II, 30
Ramses III, 30
reformation
  Josiah's, 49–50
refugees, 46, 62
personal religion, 129
religious imperialism, 7
religious instruction, 142
religious literature, 143
remedy of colonial captivity, 21
resistance
  against Assyria, 81
  against colonialism, 68, 78
  armed struggle as, 90
  civil, 78–79
  culture as, 90, 92, 171
  feminine aspects of, 126
  forms of, 90–91
  hermeneutics, 4
  literature as way of, 89, 170, 173–74
  text/literature, 8
  through education, 78
  to dominant culture, 75, 155
  to imperialism, 63
rituals, 37
  family centered, 56
returnees
  conflicts among, 58
revolution
  against oppression, 74
  against Spain, 140
  development of, 144
  economic and social causes, 150
Rizal, 9

Roman Catholic faith
  colonial imposition of, 141
  correspondences with folk religion, 141
  religious instruction, 142
royal theology
  critique of, 95
salvation
  spiritual, 4
Samaria, 43–44
  defeat of, 46
Samuel, book of, 113
Sargon I of Akkad, 28
Sargon II, 44, 121
Saul, 96
scribal schools, 38–39
Sedition Law, 170
Sennacherib, 34, 40, 45, 121
Shalmanezer III, 84
Shamaneser V, 44
siege, 46
  trauma of, 56
slaves, 40
  in ancient Near East, 27
social change, 93
social classes, 26–27, 38
social groups
  earliest, 37
  leadership, 38
Solomon, 74, 80, 127
Spain/Spanish
  colonial ideology, 144
  colonial ideology, 144
  educational policy, 142
  ideology, 144
  language, 142
state mechanism, 69
statist system, 42
status-quo
  critique of, 91
strangers, 62
Sumerian, 30
survival strategy, 59
syncretism/syncretistic, 47, 54, 55
Syria-Palestine, 36

Tagalog/s, 9, 146
temples
    in the ancient Near East, 37
theocratic imperialism, 57
thoughts/ideas
    effects of material environment 24–25
Tiglath-pileser I, 35, 43
trade, internationalization of, 43
tribute, 43, 46
triumphalist
    faith, 24
    ideology, 24
translation, 8–9
    as interpretation, 12
tinubuang lupa, 10
utang na loob, 144, 168
Vatican II, 157
vernacular language, 83, 155
victory feasts, 65
violence
    justification of, 16, 61
    in Joshua, 112
war
    experiences, 23, 61
warfare, 61
warrior god, 120, 125
    against colonialism, 163
warrior kings, 38, 119
    divine encouragement of, 121
Western
    bias, 15
    dominance, 15
    interpretation, 8, 129
    worldview, 13
Western hegemony
    dismantling of, 22
    liberation from, 22
White-Afrikaneer speaking people, 79
workers
    in ancient Near East, 27–28
Yahweh alone movement, 98
Yahweh worshippers, 54

Yahweh's people
    claim of, 14
    distinctiveness of, 72
    superior power, 76, 78
Zionism, 1

Index of Modern Authors

Alter, Robert	93	Düttmann, Alexander García	99, 102
Altieri, Charles	93, 101, 103	Fernandez, Ely	159
Amit, Yaira	95	Fewell, Dana Nolan	19
Anderson, Bernhard W.	18	Flanders, Henry Jackson	18
Aoanan, Melanio L.	158	Fleming, James	17
Apilado, Mariano, C.	158	Fohrer, Georg	7
Arias, Evaristo	147	Gangel, Kenneth O.	136
Auld, Graeme C.	35	Geertz, Cliffors	23
Bahktin, Mikhail	99	Gelacio, Guillermo	174
Baltazar, Francisco	145	Gillmayr-Bucher, Susanne	95
Bewer, Julius	16	Gorringe, Tim	3–14
Blair, Hugh, J.	133	Gottwald, Norman	20–21
Blanton, Richard, E.	79	Hamlin, John	19
Block, Daniel	49	Harlow, Barbara	89–90
Bolin, Thomas O.	95	Harris, Gordon	136
Boling, Robert, G.	17	Henry, Matthew	133
Brett, Mark	100	Hobbs, T. R.	79, 92
Brueggemann, Walter	20, 93, 104	Hobsbawn, E.	79
Butler, Trent, C.	137	Holmes, Samuel	131–32
Callahann, Dwight	99	Horseley, Richard	91
Capulong, Noriel C.	18, 159	Huffman, John	135
Castro, Jovita	143	Ileto, Reynaldo, Clemeña	146–47
Chapman, Stephen	93, 101–5	Joyce, E. J.	133
Childs, Brevard	17	Kaiser, Otto	18
Cone, James	14	Keil, C. F.	17, 129
Constantino, Renato	150	Keller, Phillip	18
Coogan, Michael David	16	Knafani, Ghassan	89
Coote, Robert	18, 19	Knauf E. Axel	95
Mary Coote	19	Larkin, William	167
Corpus, Onofre D.	169	Levinson, Bernard M.	105
Davies, Phillip	102	Lias, J. J.	131
Davis, John J.	135	Longcare, Lindsay, B.	17
Davis, Ralp Dale	135	Madvig, Donald H.	135–36
De Vaux, Roland	17	Malina, Bruce	167
Deist, Ferdinand	79	Marchant, F. G.	130
Delitzsch, F.	17, 129	Mbuwayesango, Dora	20
Driver, S.R.	16	McConville, J. G.	21
Dummelow, J. R.	131	McGee, Vernon	135

McNutt, Paula	167
Mendoza, Everett	158, 160
Mendoza, Lily S.	171–72
Mercado, Leonardo	9
Miller, Maxwell	17
Mulder, Chester O.	134
Oginde, David	136
Pernia, Antonio, M.	158
Plummer, A.	130
Porter, Roy G.	119
Portier-Young, Anathea E.	94
Powers, E.	134
Pressler, Carolyn	18
Prolov, Steve	95
Rafael, Vicente	146
Raleigh, A.	131
Ranger, T.	79
Rea, John	134
Recouer, Paul	101
Rees, William	175
Rhodes, Arnold	19
Ruther, Rosemary Radford	169
Said, Edward	92, 103–4
Salgado, Pedro V.	158
San Juan Jr. E.	172
Sanders, James A.	105
Scniedewind, William M.	49
Scott, James	91–92
Segundo, Juan Luis	14
Sizoo, Joseph R.	17
Smend, Rodulf	118
Smith, Morton	19
Smith, Robert Houston	19
Smith-Christopher, Daniel L.	70–71
Snyman, G. F.	103–4
Spurgeon, Charles, H.	129
Stalker, J.	131
Stone, Elizabeth	38
Tano, Rodrigo D.	159
Tillich, Paul	14–15
Velunta, Revelation E.	159
Vriezen, Th. C.	16
Wehelchel, James R.	158
Wesley, John	129
Whitcomb, John	135
Wilson, Charles R.	134